FATHER,
FORGIVE

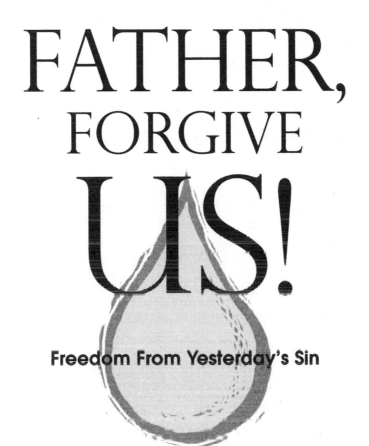

US!

Freedom From Yesterday's Sin

Other Books and Materials by Jim W. and Michal Ann Goll

The Lost Art of Intercession

Encounters With a Supernatural God

Kneeling on the Promises

Fire on the Altar

Women on the Frontlines: A Call to Courage

There are 12 complete Study Guides on subjects such as Prayer and Intercession, Prophetic Ministry, and Empowered Ministry Training.

Hundreds of audio teaching tapes and numerous videotapes are available.

For more information, contact Ministry to the Nations:

www.ministrytothenations.org
E-mail: info@ministrytothenations.org
Phone: 615-365-4401
FAX: 615-365-4408
Address: MTTN
           P.O. Box 338
           Antioch, TN 37011-0338

FATHER, FORGIVE US!

Freedom From Yesterday's Sin

JIM W. GOLL

Destiny Image₍ᵣ₎ Publishers, Inc.
P.O. Box 310
Shippensburg, PA 17257-0310

"Speaking to the Purposes of God for This Generation
and for the Generations to Come"

ISBN 0-7684-2025-3
Library of Congress Catalog Card Number: 99-76298

For Worldwide Distribution
Printed in the U.S.A.

This book and all other Destiny Image, Revival Press, Mercy Place, Fresh Bread, and Treasure House books are available at Christian bookstores and distributors worldwide.

For a U.S. bookstore nearest you, call **1-800-722-6774**.
For more information on foreign distributors, call **717-532-3040**.
Or reach us on the Internet: **http://www.reapernet.com**

Acknowledgments and Dedication

The production of this book has truly been a major team effort. I am extremely grateful to the Lord for my family, who sacrifices so that I can fulfill this ache in my heart; our staff at Ministry to the Nations for their work and patience; and our many personal intercessors and supporters, who have helped in the birthing of this dream: *Father, Forgive Us!* Once again the Lord was so faithful as He gave me a dream showing me a book cover with this title on it and commissioned me to compose this needed additional tool for the prayer chest.

Thanks go to Don Nori and Don Milam of Destiny Image Publishers for believing in me and in the "dream" the Lord gave to me. You have gone out on the limb with me again, and I am grateful. Bless you for all your time, commitment to me personally, and your many efforts to spread this needed message.

Also, from the bottom of my heart, I want to express heartfelt appreciation and gratitude to the many other team members at Destiny Image Publishers. Thanks, Steve, for your research, writing skills, and many hours; Elizabeth, for your kindness, communication skills, and coordination; Tony, for his sensitive artistic work on the cover design; and all the others too numerous to mention. Blessings to each of you!

Lastly, I wish to dedicate this book to the "oppressed." That might seem too vague to you right now, but after reading the book you will know who and what I mean. *Father, Forgive Us!* is more than just another book about intercession. It deals with the heart of God for His justice to rule on earth; for righting wrongs that we have committed generationally; for seeing His Kingdom come and His will be done on earth as it in Heaven. Therefore, with contrition and compassion, I dedicate this book to the oppressed in this life. *Father, forgive us, for we have sinned.*

Identifying in Intercession,
Jim W. Goll

Endorsements

"*Father, Forgive Us!* is a crucial book for our times. God has given Jim Goll strategic new insights that will take the Body of Christ to a new level of effectiveness in advancing the Kingdom of God here on earth. I highly recommend it!"

—C. Peter Wagner
Chancellor, Wagner Leadership Institute

"I read this book with shouts of joy and an overwhelming sense of relief. After a long travail, a birth of great importance has taken place We now have a readable adventure that captures the heart of what is going on in today's prayer movements, a renewed understanding of priestly mediation. This is clear, bold teaching that cuts through confusion and equips the emerging generation for ministry to the nations."

—John Dawson
Founder, International Reconciliation Coalition

"John the Baptist declared that with the appearance of Christ, 'the ax is laid to the root of the trees.' The Church's effective expression of the redeeming virtue and ministry of Christ has often been defiled, confused, and constricted by many historic 'root' transgressions. This new study of generational sin in the

Church and of our need for genuine repentance is long overdue. Who likes to be hit with an ax? No one. But you will be spiritually cut free from inherited prejudice if you dare to read this passionate presentation with an open heart."

—Gary Bergel
President, Intercessors for America

"Father, Forgive Us! is at once a powerful insight into the many facets of intercession and a passionate plea for God's people to set aside religious and cultural notions that block its potentials."

—Jack Taylor
Dimensions Ministries

"Jim Goll's *Father, Forgive Us!* is an intriguing, masterfully written work. He has done the Body of Christ a great service by distilling the numerous teachings on corporate repentance. This book is destined to help release the destiny of nations. It's a must-read!"

—Dr. Cindy Jacobs
Co-founder, Generals of Intercession

"Jim Goll is a well-known prophetic leader and intercessor who gives us a practical theology and manual of praying the kind of prayers of identificational repentance that we see throughout God's Word in the lives of the prophets, leaders, and ordinary people of God—people such as Moses, the prophets, the psalmists, Daniel, Ezra, Nehemiah, and others. This is a well-documented prayer pattern in the Word of God that is largely unpracticed by North American Christians, to our detriment. I agree with Jim that identificational repentance is a key factor in removing the obstacles that delay a worldwide awakening and revival. First Peter 2:9 says that we are a royal priesthood. Confessing the sins of our families, cities, and nations is one way that we can step into our God-ordained role of praying the lost into God's Kingdom."

—Dr. Gary S. Greig
Professor of Biblical Languages and Old Testament
The King's Seminary, Van Nuys, California
Wagner Leadership Institute, Colorado Springs, Colorado

"Jim Goll has written a fine book that is part of the growing corpus of writings that show us the way to revival. It is not the way of psychological hype and 'feel good' phrases. Rather, it comes from squarely facing the issues of individual and corporate sins in the individual, the Church, the nation, and among various groupings in society. The book is timely because, if the words being spoken concerning revival will come to pass, the lessons of this book must certainly be first applied."

—Dr. Daniel C. Juster
Director, Tikkun International

"This is a richly anointed book that clearly and beautifully expresses the Father's heart. It calls us to let go of our self-centered focus on attaining the glorious promises of God and to obediently lay down our lives, giving ourselves wholly to follow Him in the line of His priorities, which lead to an eventual glory that covers the earth and affects all people. We say amen to Jim's recognition of the necessity for daily confession and repentance to cleanse our own hearts. We applaud his insistence that we then go beyond ourselves to sensitively identify with others as we confess and repent of corporate sins and intercede for the world, that our sin not block our Father God's promises. We appreciate Jim's understanding of the importance of acknowledging and confessing generational sin as a key part of the process of cleansing and reconciliation. With accurate scholarship and historical review, this is a book that specifically convicts, challenges, and encourages the Church at the same time. It is a 'must' for this generation!"

—Paula and John Sandford
Authors, Teachers, and Co-founders of Elijah House, Inc.

"Blending together biblical teaching, responsible research, and passion for prayer, Jim W. Goll has made a significant contribution in his latest book, *Father, Forgive Us!* Blockades to revival are identified and the way to remove them powerfully explained in practical and easy steps. Intercessors committed to revival will be benefited by reading this book."

—Mike Bickle
Author and Founder of Friends of the Bridegroom
Director of International House of Prayer
Grandview, Missouri

"Jim Goll listens to the Lord. He listens when he reads Scripture. He receives fresh insights and is able to pass them along. This book on 'corporate confession' of sins is biblically sound and profoundly relevant for our day. Listen for the Lord while reading. If we will listen to what the Lord is saying through Jim and participate, we will experience a greater outpouring of the Lord's grace and fullness for our day."

Dr. Don Finto
Director of Caleb Company
Nashville, Tennessee

"Using words like bullets and phrases as spears, Jim Goll writes a classic textbook on sanctification. Sanctification is learning to walk in the purity and passion of the Father's forgiveness. Foregiveness is one of the forgotten ordinances of the Church and a significant part of her foundation. This book is a road map to restoring the power and passion of forgiveness. How could we have neglected it so long? *Father, forgive us!*"

Tommy Tenney
Author of *The God Chasers*

Contents

Foreword

The modern prayer movement began around 1970. Since then the spread of the movement has been exponential. In October of this year (1999) an estimated 50 million Christians around the world prayed daily for the evangelism of the same nations. Incredible! The bowls of Revelation 5 and 8 are filling more rapidly than we ever could have imagined, and the corresponding fruit is expectedly glorious.

The fact that a restorative prayer "movement" is underway is both a grievous indictment (what we are seeing happening as a renewal should have been the norm in the Church) and an incredible joy to those of us who have had a voice in it. My prayer is that, at some point, prayer will cease to be a movement and become a lifestyle to the Christian world. If that happens, one of the reasons for it will be people like Jim Goll.

I first heard of Jim in the late 1980s. Only in the past two or three years, however, has God allowed us the privilege of developing a relationship. One of my first contacts with him was in 1995 when he said to me, "God says, 'There's a book in you and it's time to get it out.' " The book *Intercessory Prayer* was "born" in 1996. Thanks, Jim!

Since then, I've had the privilege of teaching, prophesying, praying, laughing, and crying with Jim Goll. Actually, during some of our times together, *weeping* would be a more accurate term than *crying*. Those who know Jim recognize that he is like Jeremiah of old, a weeping prophet who carries the heart of God to the nations of the earth. He is also a true intercessor and a great teacher. This wonderful combination of anointings is probably why the Holy Spirit chose him to give the Body of Christ this valuable tool that you hold in your hand.

Scholarly, well researched, easily understood, and reader friendly are all accurate descriptions of *Father, Forgive Us!* I realize that some of those descriptions seem contradictory, but believe me, in this case they are not. You will grow in your understanding, you will be challenged in your heart (not condemned), you will know the ways of God more thoroughly, and you will be more effective in your "lifestyle" of prayer after you read this book. And pastors, you will preach from it!

I'm sure some in America are beginning to ask the question, "Do we really need more books on prayer?" Some might even ask, "Why this one?" It is extremely important for you to know how much I believe what I'm about to propose as the answer to that question. This book is urgently needed because there is no more important issue facing the Church than the one Jim Goll deals with in *Father, Forgive Us!*—identificational confession and intercession. No issue will have greater impact on the coming harvest than this one. I urge you to delve into this excellent book and let it change your life—and then the world as together we embrace these truths.

Thank you, Jim, for doing it with scholastic integrity and yet making it so easily grasped. Thank you for modeling what you teach and for teaching it with such humility. Thank you for being a leader who leads. Thank you for your contribution to the world-wide harvest!

There was an incredibly important book in you, Jim. Thanks for getting it out.

Pastor Dutch Sheets
Author of *Intercessory Prayer*
Colorado Springs, Colorado

Introduction

These are exciting times to be living in if you are a member of the Church of Jesus Christ of Nazareth. Even though we are shifting and shaking and very clumsily finding our way into the next historical season, I believe that the Spirit of the Lord is giving us tools to assist us as we transition. *Father, Forgive Us!* is one of those key tools that will encourage and instruct us as how to enter into our future with new confidence and boldness.

The Body is going toward the next spiritual position of authority that will cause it to overcome powers that have withstood the release of the greatest spiritual harvest the world has seen. We are moving from one portion of strength to a new portion of strength (see Ps. 84). We are coming from one measure of faith to a new measure of faith (see Rom. 1). We have seen and experienced one level of glory and now we are on the verge of experiencing the next release of visitation that will result in our seeing His glory in another level—one that will cause all of us in His temple to cry "Glory!" (see 2 Cor. 3:17-18) As you read this book you will shout, "Yes! That is what the next move of God looks like. Yes! This is what is in my heart!"

One of the greatest transitions in the Bible can be found in John 20. The Lord had been crucified. He had faced hell in such a confrontational, humble, sacrificing way, that death and the tomb were overcome. He revealed Himself to Mary first. He then found the disillusioned, broken, and fearful disciples who had walked with Him for three years and said, "Peace be with you." In other words, He said, "Be whole; I have a future and a hope for you." He then commissioned them apostolically by releasing the two key elements that would cause them to be victorious in the assignments that lay before them. He said, "Receive the Holy Spirit," then breathed on them the breath of Life and resurrection power that was in Him. This was the same breath that brought order out of chaos in the beginning. Jesus then said, "Go in forgiveness! Here is your message—you are sent forth with *salvation* and you bring its meaning into reality through *forgiveness!*" There is not a document anywhere in modern times that better depicts this commission. There is not a book anywhere that better documents the authority of these words and their historical transference from generation to generation.

Jim Goll captures the heart of God and the apostolic history of the Church, then prepares us for future victory and transformation—all in this one book. Not only does *Father, Forgive Us!* bring us revelation personally, but it also brings key insights on how we have a responsibility to acknowledge and eradicate sin corporately and territorially. As I was reading Jim's way of logically communicating forgiveness, I found myself understanding the power of sin in a new, simple, logical way. When you read this book, you will see sin's corporate magnitude and effect on the land in which you live. However, Jim builds within your belief systems the faith and authority you need to deal with the issues confronting you. I believe that this was the Lord's attempt and method of communication. *Father, Forgive Us!* captures the heart and Spirit of our Savior's commissioning.

I am an avid reader and have many opportunities to read the "latest" book that attempts to motivate the Body to move forward.

I have not found one that communicates the call to intercession, reconciliation, and reformation as well as this one. Jim Goll could not have written this book if these were not a reality in his life. May *Father, Forgive Us!* cause the latter day glory recorded in the Book of Haggai to become a reality in your life. Read, release forgiveness, and watch transformation begin!

Chuck D. Pierce
Executive Director, World Prayer Center
Vice President, Global Harvest Ministries
Colorado Springs, Colorado

Section I

We Have Sinned!

Chapter 1

The Promise and the Problem

A prophetic and intercessory cry is arising: "Open the way for the beginning of a great visitation!" What an exciting and challenging time to be alive! Today God is moving mightily across the earth. Renewal and revival are coming to the nations! Great change is on the way! Many are declaring that a new "great awakening"—the greatest in history—still lies before us. Could this really be true? I believe so. Let's look at some facts that could substantiate this belief.

Since 1977 the number of evangelical Christians worldwide has nearly *quadrupled*, from 150 million to a current total of 560 million, with as many as 150,000 people coming to Christ each day. This means that evangelical Christians now comprise ten percent of the world population of 5.6 billion people, with the number increasing daily! Currently, evangelical Christians are growing at a rate *three times* that of the rest of the world.[1] Clearly, something *major* is happening!

As the Waters Cover the Sea

These statistics really shouldn't surprise us. After all, God clearly portrayed in His Word His desire and intention to bring revival to His people and spiritual awakening to the earth. His promise is straightforward:

> *For the earth shall be filled with the knowledge of the glory of the Lord, as the waters cover the sea* (Habakkuk 2:14 KJV).

A day is coming when the knowledge of the glory of the Lord will *fill the earth*. In that end-time season all people will see Him and, willingly or not, acknowledge His presence and His glory. Some good ole turning and squeezing of our arms behind our back by Papa God might be used to help speed up the process a bit—but whatever means He uses, it is all for His glory! Christ will be magnified and glorified in His Church and His name exalted above every other name so that every knee will bow and every tongue confess that He is Lord, to the glory of God the Father (see Phil. 2:9-11). All things will be put in subjection under Christ's feet, who then will subject Himself to the Father, in order that "God may be all in all" (see 1 Cor. 15:27-28).

The Scriptures are full of similar promises from God of an end-time revival of global proportions. Consider these verses:

> *You shall make an altar of earth for Me, and you shall sacrifice on it your burnt offerings and your peace offerings, your sheep and your oxen; **in every place where I cause My name to be remembered, I will come to you and bless you*** (Exodus 20:24).

Where will God's name be "remembered"? Everywhere. Where is the place that we are building our altar of worship, praise, prayer, and intercession? The whole earth is to be offered up as an altar where the fire shall be kept burning and never go out! (See Leviticus 6:9-13.)[2] His glory will fill the earth.

> *Do not fear, for I am with you; **I will bring your offspring** from the east, and gather you from the west. I will say to the north, "Give them up!" And to the south, "Do not hold them back." Bring My sons from afar, and My daughters from the ends of the earth, **everyone who is called by My name, and***

whom I have created for My glory, whom I have formed, even whom I have made (Isaiah 43:5-7).

"Sing for joy and be glad, O daughter of Zion; for behold I am coming and I will dwell in your midst," declares the Lord. **"And many nations will join themselves to the Lord in that day and will become My people.** *Then I will dwell in your midst, and you will know that the Lord of hosts has sent Me to you"* (Zechariah 2:10-11).

And it will come about in that day that living waters will flow out of Jerusalem, half of them toward the eastern sea and the other half toward the western sea; it will be in summer as well as in winter. And **the Lord will be king over all the earth; in that day the Lord will be the only one, and His name the only one** (Zechariah 14:8-9).

The dramatic rise in the number of evangelical Christians in the world over the past 20 years is encouraging evidence that we may be witnessing the beginning fulfillment of these scriptural promises; however, there is still a long way to go. But it is important also to realize that 82 percent of all evangelical Christians in the world today live outside the West.[3] This phenomenal growth is occurring primarily in Central and South America, Africa, and Asia, not in North America or western Europe. Certainly there are many places in the West where God is moving and where many people are being touched, but not yet to the same degree as that which is found in other parts of the world. "What's up, doc?" might be an appropriate question to ask!

Why is this? Why isn't the West experiencing the same level of revival and awakening as other parts of the world? Where is the fullness of the glory of the Lord in the earth as promised in Scripture? What is causing the delay? Could there be human hindrances—man-made obstacles—that must be removed in order for the fullness of God's promise to come forth?

A People of Unclean Lips

Sin is an obstacle that stands in the way of the fulfillment of God's promise. The psalmist said, "If I regard iniquity in my heart, the Lord will not hear me" (Ps. 66:18 KJV), and Proverbs 28:9 warns that "he who turns away his ear from listening to the law, even his prayer is an abomination." Remember, the greater the light a nation or a people has, the greater is their accountability before God. Confession and repentance are the keys that remove the obstacle of sin and open the way for the blessings of God to pour forth. "If we confess our sins, He is faithful and righteous to forgive us our sins and to cleanse us from all unrighteousness" (1 Jn. 1:9). Peter told the crowd that gathered after the healing of a lame man, "Repent therefore and return, that your sins may be wiped away, *in order that* times of refreshing may come from the presence of the Lord" (Acts 3:19). Repentance *precedes* revival. It always has, and it always will!

When the prophet Isaiah saw a vision of "the Lord sitting on a throne, lofty and exalted" (Is. 6:1) and surrounded by worshiping seraphim, he was overcome by the majesty of God. The glory of the Divine presence brought Isaiah to the place of confession, which resulted in his cleansing.

> *Then I said, "Woe is me, for I am ruined! Because I am a man of unclean lips, and I live among a people of unclean lips; for my eyes have seen the King, the Lord of hosts." Then one of the seraphim flew to me, with a burning coal in his hand which he had taken from the altar with tongs. And he touched my mouth with it and said, "Behold, this has touched your lips; and your iniquity is taken away, and your sin is forgiven"* (Isaiah 6:5-7).

It wasn't a list of "do's and don'ts" that affected Isaiah so strongly. There was no "checklist" of sins that brought him under such deep conviction. So what happened? How did he get this "revelation" anyhow? The Presence came. God in all His holiness appeared on the scene and invaded Isaiah's unholy comfort zones. Instead of a list, the God of the list showed up. Isaiah was caught up into a new realm in the spirit where he saw the brilliance of God's glory as never before. He felt so lost and so dirty that all he could do was cry out, "Woe is me, for I am ruined! Because I am a man of unclean lips...."

Greater Light; More Darkness

One of the authentic proofs that God has appeared on the scene is this: The brighter His light shines, the more darkness it exposes in us. I have discovered in my own experience that the closer I get to God, the more darkness I see in me and the farther away from Him I feel initially. New levels of light reveal new levels of sin. Does that mean that all of a sudden I become worse than I am? No. It simply means that I can see myself more clearly the way I really am—the way *God* sees me. The sin is already there; the light of God merely brings it into view. Psalm 36:9 says it this way: "In Thy light we see light."

In August of 1998 this understanding was driven home to me. While attending a conference in another city, I encountered a visionary experience that enlightened me all the more. In this vision, I saw a staircase leading up into Heaven that was covered with white clouds and a mist of the Lord's presence. I was invited to climb this stairway into His increased presence.

Each step I took up the stairs, I encountered greater degrees of His brilliant, white, piercing light. Eventually I came to the top of the stairs and stood on what seemed to be a platform. Nothing but loving yet convicting light shone on this platform. It seemed to go right through me—both from head to foot and from side to side at the same time. It was beautiful; it appeared to me to be a sampling of the "transcendent majesty" of Christ. I wept. I sobbed. I cried out loudly, "You're beautiful! You're beautiful!" I was overcome by the loveliness of the presence of Jesus.

When the electrifying experience was over, two things remained with me: 1) a greater knowledge of His love and presence; and 2) a greater awareness of how darkness keeps us separated

7

from Him! You see, the greater the light is, the more darkness you see!

Yet God's purpose is redemptive! He loves us in spite of our sin and He loves us too much to leave us in our sin. Therefore God reveals sin in our lives because He wants to deal with it. He wants us to confess it so that He can forgive and cleanse us. This was Isaiah's experience. Once he confessed his sin of unclean lips, one of the attending seraphim touched his lips with a coal from the altar and said, "Behold, this has touched your lips; and your iniquity is taken away, and your sin is forgiven" (Is. 6:7b).

Confession of personal sin is *fundamental* if we want to realize the purpose and power of God in our lives and see His glory fill our temple. There is, however, a deeper element. Notice that Isaiah's confession had two parts. First, there was a *personal* dimension: "I am a man of unclean lips"; and second, there was a *corporate* dimension: "I live among a *people* of unclean lips." Confessing his own sins was not enough; Isaiah was moved upon to confess the sins of his people. We each have the responsibility to continually confess our personal sins to God in our devotional prayer times with Him, but He wants to take us further. God wants to release us into a new and higher realm of *identificational* confession and intercession that reaches beyond ourselves and our families to embrace our churches, our cities, our states, our nation, and our world. I am personally convinced that "confessing the sins of our people"—identificational repentance—is a key factor in removing the obstacles that are delaying a worldwide awakening.

How Big Is Your Heart?

John Wesley once said, "The world is my parish." Nothing less than a global vision could have contained the Divine call on his life or the spiritual fire in his bones. How big is your heart? How much room is there for God and for a priestly burden for others? When you go before God, whom do you represent? On whose behalf do you stand when you go before the King of creation? The apostle Peter said that we, the Body of Christ, are "a chosen race, a royal priesthood, a holy nation, a people for God's own possession" (1 Pet. 2:9a). We are priests of God—every one of us—and one thing that a priest does is represent others before God.

When the priests of the Old Testament performed their priestly functions and duties they represented not themselves alone, but *all* their people. As they administered the daily sacrifices and other rites they were standing in the place of confession and intercession for all the people. The high priest's garments included an ephod and a breastpiece, both of which had mounted on them precious stones representing the 12 tribes of Israel (see Ex. 28:9-29). Whenever the high priest entered the presence of the Lord he carried over his heart and on his shoulders reminders that he was coming before God for the entire nation.

Intercession is more than just another word for prayer. "Intercession is coming to God on behalf of another. All intercession is prayer, but not all prayer is intercession."[4] Expressed another way, intercession is "the act of pleading by one who in God's sight has a right to do so in order to obtain mercy for one in need."[5] I think a little word study will help us better understand this concept.

Five Distinct Pictures

The basic Hebrew word for intercession is *paga*, which is found 44 times in the Old Testament. Although it is translated as "intercession" only a handful of times, *paga*, when we consider all its variations and shades of meaning, gives us a wonderful understanding of what it means to intercede.

1. *Paga* means "to meet," as in meeting with God for the purpose of reconciliation. "Thou dost *meet* him who rejoices in doing righteousness..." (Is. 64:5).

2. *Paga* means "to light upon." "And he [Jacob] *lighted upon* a certain place, and tarried there all night..." (Gen. 28:11 KJV). That night that place became one of Divine visitation for Jacob. By God's working of grace, our Divine "Helper" stands by, ready to aid us

in our intercession, moving us from the natural to the supernatural and from finite ability to infinite ability, taking hold of situations with us to accomplish the will of God.

3. *Paga* means "to fall upon, attack, strike down, cut down." "And David called one of the young men, and said, Go near, and *fall upon* him. And he smote him that he died" (2 Sam. 1:15 KJV). Intercession is the readiness of a soldier to fall upon or attack the enemy at the command of his lord, striking and cutting him down!

4. *Paga* means "to strike the mark." "He covers His hands with the lightning, and commands it to *strike the mark*" (Job 36:32). Intercession releases the glory of God to flash forth to a desired situation and "strike the mark" like lightning.

5. *Paga* means "to lay upon." Intercession reached its fullest and most profound expression when our sins were "laid upon" Jesus: "...the Lord hath *laid on* Him the iniquity of us all" (Is. 53:6 KJV); "...and He bare the sin of many, and *made intercession* for the transgressors" (Is. 53:12 KJV). Jesus fully identified with us when the totality of our sins were placed upon Him. Then, as the scapegoat, He carried them far away (see Lev. 16:8-10,20-22). There is an aspect of this form of intercession into which we can enter as we "share on behalf of His body (which is the church) in filling up that which is lacking in Christ's afflictions" (Col. 1:24b).

The Book of Revelation tells us that the throne of Heaven will be surrounded by a multitude of people from every tribe, every kindred, every tongue, every race, every ethnic group, and every nation. As believers, we are called as priests to stand in the place of confession and intercession for the nations. Jesus said that the fields are "white for harvest" (Jn. 4:35) and commanded us to "beseech the Lord of the harvest to send out workers into His harvest" (Mt. 9:38). When you go before His presence, what stones are you carrying on your heart? For whom do you stand before the Lord?

A New Testament Model of Priestly Prayer

At this point some of you may be protesting, "Wait a minute, Jim. All that about the corporate confession of sin and identifying with our people and our nation and standing like priests in the place of confession and intercession—that's just Old Testament stuff! There's no pattern for that in the New Testament."

Wait—hold on to your hat for a moment—I'm going to take you on a revolutionary prayer ride! Haven't you ever recited in church at some time in your life what we call the "Lord's Prayer" or the "model" prayer of Jesus? How does it go? "*My* Father who art in heaven, hallowed be Thy name. Thy kingdom come. Thy will be done, on earth as it is in heaven. Give *me* this day *my* daily bread. And forgive *me* *my* debts, as *I* also have forgiven *my* debtors. And do not lead *me* into temptation, but deliver *me* from evil."

What's that? That's not the way *you* pray it? Are you sure? I think that if we are honest, most of us would have to admit that even though this isn't how we *say* it, it *is* how we *mean* it. We say "*Our* Father" but interpret it as "*My* Father"; we say "forgive *us* our debts" but understand it as "forgive *me* my debts." We may *pray* it corporately, but we *apply* it most all the time individually.

While lining up in your personal devotional prayer with each of the petitions of the Lord's Prayer is important, Jesus did not *teach* it that way. The Lord's Prayer is, first of all, a model of *corporate* prayer. He taught us to say *our* Father; give *us* this day *our* daily bread; forgive *us* our debts as *we* forgive *our* debtors; lead *us* not into temptation, but deliver *us* from evil.

This is really a *priestly* prayer. In reality, when we pray the Lord's Prayer (or model prayer) we are to enter into the place of confession, petition, and intercession not just for ourselves alone, but for every member of whatever people group we are carrying in our hearts. The petition "give *us* this day our daily bread," is first of all a request for *spiritual* food and secondarily a request for natural provision. It is a prayer for the *revival* of a congregation, a city, a region, a state, or a nation. When we pray "forgive *us* our debts" we should be asking for forgiveness not for our personal sins alone, but for those of our family, our neighbors, the people in our cities, and any others with whom we identify—for those whom we care for and carry like "living stones" upon our hearts just as the priests of old did.

Forgive Us Our Debts

The most pertinent part of the Lord's Prayer, as far as this book is concerned, is the phrase "forgive *us* our debts, as *we* also have forgiven *our* debtors." From a corporate, intercessory standpoint, this means that we identify with our own sinfulness and need for forgiveness as well as with the sinfulness of others. Identifying with sin—that of others as well as our own—involves our agreeing with God regarding sin. That's what it means to confess our sins. Confession is *agreeing* with God concerning our sin. God says, "You have sinned," and we reply, "Yes, Lord, we *have* sinned. Father, forgive us!" Like soldiers at attention, we salute our Master Sergeant and say, "Whatever You say, Sir!"

It's important to understand that we are not talking here about forgiveness of sin for our initial salvation experience. The Lord's Prayer is for *believers* and is in the context of the new covenant. What we are concerned with is the daily sins that we fall into—the sins which, if left unconfessed and unforgiven, hinder our fellowship with God.

The Greek words for "debts" and "debtors" come from the same root. *Opheilema* (debts) carries the sense of "that which is legally due"; *opheiletes* (debtors) means "one that has not yet made amends to one whom he has injured."[6] Debt refers to the consequences of sin—the obligations we owe to God or others because of our sin. God has set a standard for us, and when we fail to meet it we sin. Likewise, we set standards in our minds of how others should treat us. When they fail to meet it we feel that they have an outstanding "debt" toward us.[7] God's forgiveness of our debts is conditional upon our forgiveness of the debts owed us by others. Author Jeff Day explains it this way: "If we don't forgive those who have offended (are indebted to) us, we still have sin in our heart, because the Lord has not forgiven us. If we have sin in our heart there is no cleansing and no righteousness."[8]

Sin is an obstacle that must be removed if we are to see the glory of God fill the earth. We must begin by confessing our own sins *daily*; this should be a part of our regular devotional life with God. There is a great sense of immediacy in the Lord's Prayer: "Give us *this day*...." The same phrase is implied in the rest of the prayer: "And forgive us our debts [*this day*], as we also have forgiven our debtors [*this day*]...." It's important that we confess our sins every day, every time we sin, as soon as we are aware of it. Just cry, "Help!" and He will hear your cry.

Confession of personal sin is the starting point, but we should not stop there. In this intercessory posture we are dealing with the sins of others: family, friends, neighbors, or perhaps an entire city, nation, or even the world. Again, the key is *daily confession*. Sin occurs all the time—day and night—wherever there are people. As intercessors, we must confess sin daily—as it happens—in a persistent, ongoing manner until the sins continue no more; until light has penetrated darkness.

Paul wrote to the Romans, "Owe nothing to anyone except to love one another; for he who loves his neighbor has fulfilled the law" (Rom. 13:8). "Owe" in Greek is *opheilo*, which is the root for the Greek words for "debt" and "debtor." Jesus said, "Greater love has no one than this, that one lay down his life for his friends" (Jn. 15:13). In the greatest possible expression of intercession, Jesus laid down His life for us. As followers of Christ, the debt of love we owe to our neighbors is to lay down our lives for them—in *intercession.* This means identifying with their sins and circumstances the way Jesus identified with ours. Just as He who was without sin became sin for us said, "Father, forgive *them*," we in turn pray, "Father, forgive *us!*"

Coming Into Agreement

This is why corporate intercession is so critical. The effectiveness of the Church's ministry in the world centers around believers coming into *agreement* together concerning God's will and purpose in the earth. Jesus told Peter, "I will give you the keys of the kingdom of heaven; and whatever you shall bind on earth shall be bound in heaven, and whatever you shall loose on earth shall be loosed in heaven" (Mt. 16:19). At another time He said to His disciples,

> *Truly I say to you, whatever you shall bind on earth shall be bound in heaven; and whatever you loose on earth shall be loosed in heaven. Again I say to you, that if two of you agree on earth about anything that they may ask, it shall be done for them by My Father who is in heaven. For where two or three have gathered together in My name, there I am in their midst* (Matthew 18:18-20).

These references to the "keys of the kingdom" and binding and loosing appear in the context of the only three occurrences in the Gospels of the word *church* (see Mt. 16:18; 18:17). As such, they reveal much about the nature of the primary calling of the Church. We have been given the keys to lock and unlock (bind and loose, forbid and permit) truths of the Kingdom of Heaven. Noted healer and author, the late John Wimber, wrote that "binding and loosing means that the Church is doing what the Father has already ratified."[9]

So what is the prayer of agreement? It is more than simply clasping hands and saying, "Brother, let's agree on this together." The prayer of agreement is the "orchestra of God," finely tuned and playing in perfect harmony. It is the by-product of building relationships—of lives forged together under God's Kingdom of righteousness, peace, and joy. Again, John Wimber said, "We have authority given to us by Jesus to work out the plan and purpose of God in the world today. Because authority is placed on us, whatever we agree with is likely to happen."[10] The thing that ties all of this together with corporate confession and intercession is the fact that Jesus' words about agreeing and binding and loosing in Matthew 18:18-20 occur in the context of some of His teachings on *forgiveness* (see Mt. 18:15-35). Now watch this—don't miss this point—one of the great "keys of the kingdom" that unlocks prison doors is an act of humble, agreeing, confession of sin! *O God, give us these keys!*

When the Ladder Comes Down

When believers on earth come into agreement together in harmony with the plan and purpose of God, earth and Heaven come into agreement and a "ladder" can come down from Heaven to release God's glory on the earth.

Genesis chapter 28 tells how Jacob, fleeing from the wrath of his brother Esau, "lighted upon [Heb. *paga*] a certain place, and tarried there all night" (Gen. 28:11a KJV), using a stone for a pillow. (Have you ever felt like you were in a desert and were "between a rock and a hard place"? That is how Jacob felt!) In that very place, however, Jacob received a dream in which he saw a ladder between earth and Heaven with the angels of God ascending and descending on it. Above the ladder stood the Lord. He spoke to Jacob and renewed the promise that He had made to Abraham and Isaac to give to their descendants the very land on which Jacob lay. Then the Lord said, "And behold, I am with you, and will keep you wherever you go, and will bring you back to this land; for I will not leave you until I have done what I have promised you" (Gen. 28:15).

> *Then Jacob awoke from his sleep and said, "Surely the Lord is in this place, and I did not know it." And he was afraid and said, "How awesome is this place! This is none other than the house of God, and this is the gate of heaven"* (Genesis 28:16-17).

15

Jacob took the stone he had used as a pillow, set it up as a pillar, and anointed it with oil as a monument to God. He then named the place "Bethel" (house of God).

When Jacob had arrived the night before, he had not seen anything special about the spot. He was scared, tired, and perhaps hungry. He probably lost no time trying to sleep. During the night, however, God changed Jacob's resting spot from a desert place to a place of Divine visitation. When Jacob awoke in the morning, he had an entirely different perspective on his surroundings. What he had first seen as a desolate place he now saw as the "house of God." What changed Jacob's outlook? His vision of the ladder from Heaven brought his earthly perspective into agreement with Heaven's reality, and God's glory came down. Earth came into agreement with Heaven. When earth comes into agreement with God's perspective and aligns with His laws and His principles, a ladder can come down and the supernatural presence of God can come tumbling forth!

Twenty years later Jacob returned to the land of Canaan, where he had another Divine visitation. "Now as Jacob went on his way, the angels of God met him. And Jacob said when he saw them, 'This is God's camp.' So he named that place Mahanaim" (Gen. 32:1-2). After living with his uncle Laban for 20 years, marrying Laban's daughters Leah and Rachel, and accumulating great flocks of sheep, Jacob fled because of Laban's ongoing mistreatment of him. The two men had been in conflict for years. Immediately prior to his second Divine encounter, however, Jacob and Laban had *reconciled* with one another and then separated in peace (see Gen. 31). Out of the ministry of reconciliation, cleansing had come. As a result, an open Heaven occurred and the next thing Jacob knew, he had stumbled into an entire encampment of angels. Reconciliation between men preceded Divine visitation. It always has, and it always will!

Getting Rid of the Rubble

What does all this mean for us? We all want revival; we all want an awakening to come, the heavens to open, and the ladder of God to come down. We all want our "deserts" to become an awesome place—the place of the "house of God" and the "gate of Heaven." These are principles of reality. If we want to come into the place of God's presence and see His glory fill the earth, we simply cannot ignore the corporate place of identifying with the sin of the people in our cities.

First there must be cleansing of sin and reconciliation of one brother to another, one tribe to another. There are many "tribes" in the Body of Christ, and much misunderstanding and suspicion exist between us. We need to drop our prideful, prejudicial thinking and our spirits of offense. We must learn to appreciate diversity and embrace our brothers, washing each other's feet and coming into agreement together that we all have "clay feet" and stand in need of the love and forgiveness of our Father. *Father, forgive us!* Forgive us *this day* for the sin of pride. Forgive us *this day* for the sin of prejudice.

Second, we must understand that there is much hostility, hurt, anger, and division between the Church and much of the rest of the world because of past sins that go back generations and, in some cases, centuries. Here, too, there must be cleansing of sin and reconciliation.

We've got to get rid of the rubble blocking the path of God's glory in the earth. The prophet Isaiah wrote:

And it shall be said, "Build up, build up, prepare the way, remove every obstacle out of the way of My people." For thus says the high and exalted One who lives forever, whose name is Holy, "I dwell on a high and holy place, and also with the contrite and lowly of spirit in order to revive the spirit of the lowly and to revive the heart of the contrite" (Isaiah 57:14-15).

Let's compare those verses to another passage in Isaiah.

Go through, go through the gates; **clear the way for the people**; *build up, build up the highway;* **remove the stones**, *lift up a standard over the peoples. Behold, the Lord has proclaimed to the end of the earth, say to the daughter of Zion, "Lo, your salvation comes; behold His reward is with Him, and His recompense before Him." And they will call them, "The holy people, the redeemed of the Lord"; and you will be called, "Sought out, a city not forsaken"* (Isaiah 62:10-12).

Getting Desperate

Who is going to seek us out? God. But how do we catch the glimmer of His eye to stay when He glances across our family, our life, our congregation, our tribe, our denomination, our city? By the desperate prayer of the heart, that's how!

We have sinned. Father, forgive us. This act of desperation and humility released through the power of confession is a little key that opens a big door. It unlocks the "gate of Heaven" and releases the grace of God for fulfilling the prophetic destiny for our generation.

We've got to get rid of the rubble. We've got to get real, identify our trash piles, and start pushing for God's sake! Yes, let's come together and find our agreement in Him so the revelation of His transcendent majesty can show up on the scene. As we lay down our lives in identificational intercession for the sins of ourselves and our people, the ladder of Heaven will descend and God's glory will fill the earth. Then we will see for ourselves the fulfillment of Isaiah's vision:

A voice is calling, "Clear the way for the Lord in the wilderness; make smooth in the desert a highway for our God. Let every valley be lifted up, and every mountain and hill be made low; and let the rough ground become a plain, and the rugged terrain a broad valley; then the glory of the Lord will be revealed, and all flesh will see it together; for the mouth of the Lord has spoken" (Isaiah 40:3-5).

We each want God's glory to come; we each want to see an unprecedented revival—a new "great awakening"—come to our cities and nations. But let me drive this point home. Before that will happen we must first come to the place where we cry out in desperation, *"We have sinned! Father, forgive us!"*

Reflection Questions

1. What are some of the Scriptures that you know that foretell of a great last days outpouring of the Holy Spirit?

2. What are the promises in God's Word that need to be met for "revival" to come to our nation?

3. What are some of the obstacles in today's society that hinder revival from coming?

Recommended Reading

The Lost Art of Intercession by Jim W. Goll (Revival Press, 1997)

Intercessory Prayer by Dutch Sheets (Regal Books, 1996)

Why Revival Tarries by Leonard Ravenhill (Bethany House Publishers, 1982)

Endnotes

1. Gregg Caruso, "Startling Statistics." 12 July 1999 <http://members. aol.com/_ht_a/carusohsc/myhomepage/index.html>. These facts were drawn from information developed by the U.S. Center for World Mission, Pasadena, California; AD-2000 Research; David Barrett; Lance Lambert/Dr. Jonathan Chao; DAWN Research.

2. For more discussion on this topic, read the author's first book, *The Lost Art of Intercession* (Shippensburg, Pennsylvania: Revival Press, 1997).

3. Caruso, "Startling Statistics."

4. C. Peter Wagner, *Prayer Shield* (Ventura, California: Regal Books, 1992), 26.

5. P.J. Mahoney, "Intercession," *The New Catholic Encyclopedia* (New York: McGraw-Hill Book Company, 1967), 566, as quoted in Wagner, *Prayer Shield*, 27.

6. Jeff Day, *Forgive: Release and Be Free!* (Tonbridge, Kent, England: Sovereign World Ltd., 1997), 15.

7. Day, *Forgive*, 16.

8. Day, *Forgive*, 16.

9. John Wimber, *Teach Us to Pray* (Anaheim, California: Mercy Publishing, 1986), 39.

10. Wimber, *Teach Us to Pray*, 40.

Chapter 2

Identification in Intercession

In September 1991 my wife and I were ministering in Queens, New York City, when early one morning in our bedroom I felt the presence of the Holy Spirit come and rest on me. His voice spoke clearly to me these words: *"I will release new understandings of identification in intercession whereby the legal basis of the rights of the demonic powers of the air to remain will be removed."* This statement opened volumes of understanding to me that morning.

Identification in intercession is perhaps one of the highest yet most overlooked aspects of true intercession. It truly has been a "lost art," but it is being restored to the Church's arsenal of prayer in this hour. What is identification in intercession? Let me take a moment to give definition to this terminology.

Defining Our Terms

Identification in intercession means identifying with the needs of other people to such an extent that we become one in heart with them. Through the Holy Spirit we learn to feel their pain, to dream their dreams, to laugh with their joys, and to cry

21

with their sorrows. Our hearts ache out of compassion, contrition, and desperation, and they pound with others' sufferings as if they were our own. As we receive the Father's heart by the Spirit of revelation, in a very real sense those hurts *become* our own. We identify with God's righteous judgments but burn with His desire for mercy. We feel the crushing weight of their sin and the terrifying alienation from God that it causes. Then, by choosing to identify with them and laying aside our own position, our hearts are burdened by the Spirit of God and a wrenching cry of confession of sin, disgrace, failure, and humiliation bursts forth from our hearts to the Lord. Such prayer has gone past merely changing linguistic terminology—*their* burden, desires, heart, and need—it has become *ours*!

This form of intercession is a lost art in our modern-day, materialistic, success-oriented society. I am convinced, however, that the Lord wants to restore it. God's heart for the nations is mercy, not judgment. He is looking for intercessors who will "stand in the gap before [Him] for the land" (Ezek. 22:30). Let's pray for His deeper workings in our lives so that we may stand in partnership with God in our day as vessels through which He can pour out over all the nations His compassion, mercy, forgiveness, and reconciliation.

Another way to understand identification in intercession is to think of it as a wedding of the spirit of revelation (see Eph. 1:17-18) and the spirit of conviction (see Jn. 16:7-8). The spirit of revelation imparts "wisdom and insight" (Eph. 1:8) regarding the nature, degree, and depth of national and even generational sin, while the spirit of conviction awakens within us a deep identificational burden for those sins before God and a desperate desire for confession, repentance, and forgiveness. This wedding of revelation and conviction gives birth to a heart cry for the removal of the sin obstacles that hinder the fullness of spiritual awakening in the earth.

When the Lord finds a people interceding before Him out of brokenness, humility and identification through the confession of sin, the obstacles can be removed. Then that company of intercessors can be trusted with the investment of His authority and, out of that special place, a gift of faith can be given and a Divine word spoken. The legal basis for the demonic powers of the air to remain may be stripped away, the heavens opened, and the glory and blessings of God can begin to flood the earth.

Pause right now and lift this initial prayer with me:

Father, through the grace of Jesus Christ, enlarge my heart and expand my understanding. Reveal to me the lessons and applications You desire to show me concerning identification in intercession.

Five Essentials

There are five essential requirements for this type of identificational intercession.

1. *People who are willing to look with their eyes open.*
   We must see the sinful condition of others without justifying their actions. Jesus said, "Lift up your eyes, and look on the fields, that they are white for harvest" (Jn. 4:35b). When we truly lift up our eyes to look, they will be filled with the horrifying condition of the people's present situation. The "harvest," when we first look, is not a pretty sight. But when Christ's compassion is imparted into our own hearts and we know what it is to see and to feel with His heart, then the scene begins to change. It will drive us outside the four walls of the church to see things we don't like to see: the poor and the destitute, the single mom trying to raise three kids alone, the AIDS patients, and the drug addicts. It will awaken us to our own helplessness and powerlessness, and from that place of broken dependency we will look up to Jesus, who alone can heal and help.

2. *People who are willing to give up their lives.*

   Jesus said, "Greater love has no one than this, that one lay down his life for his friends" (Jn. 15:13). Then He showed us what He meant by laying down His life on the cross for His friends—for us. Christ identified with our sinful condition to the point of death, and now He ever intercedes for us at the right hand of the Father (see Rom. 8:34). Likewise, we must be willing to lay down our lives in intercession for the sinful condition of others: our families, our people group, our nation, and our world. This can't be done with two minutes here and two minutes there; it requires a real sacrifice of time, effort, and energy.

3. *A broken heart.*

   King David the psalmist wrote, "The sacrifices of God are a broken spirit; a broken and a contrite heart, O God, Thou wilt not despise" (Ps. 51:17). The key to forgiveness is confession and repentance from a heart broken over sin. When we enter into identification in intercession, our hearts are broken over the sins of those whom we carry in our hearts. God responds to broken and contrite hearts; then the rubble of sin is cleared away and the pathway is opened for healing and restoration.

4. *Grace to carry the burdens of others.*

   The apostle Paul instructed the Galatians to "bear one another's burdens, and thus fulfill the law of Christ" (Gal. 6:2). "Burden bearing" is a normal part of Christian living, and it is only by the grace of God that we can do it. Hebrews 4:16 says that we can approach God's throne with confidence to receive the mercy and the grace we need. This verse appears in the context of a discussion of the intercessory role of high priests in general and of Jesus, the great High Priest, in particular. Whenever we enter into intercession we can do so confident in the knowledge that the grace of God is present to give us the strength to bear the burdens of those for whom we are interceding.

5. *Desperate people willing to be the answer to prayers.*

When the prophet Isaiah had his vision of God in the temple, he responded with confession of both his own sins and those of his people. After he received cleansing Isaiah heard the call of God: " 'Whom shall I send, and who will go for Us?' Then I said, 'Here am I. Send me!' " (Is. 6:8) Isaiah had prayed for his people and now he was ready to be God's instrument in answering those prayers. As we intercede for others and become more acutely aware of the desperateness of their condition, we may feel the burden to be part of God's answer to the problem. There is a certain quality about prophetic intercession and identification in intercession that causes us to go out and walk out what we're praying. God gets hold of our hearts and we reach back into His heart for the grace necessary to rewrite history.

Confession in Intercession

One of the most important elements in the process of identification in intercession is *confession*. Sin is a blockage that must be removed and confession is the first step. Remember, in this type of prayer we are not dealing with our own individual sins; those should be taken care of during our private devotional times. Here we are focusing on the sinful condition of others—a city, a race, or perhaps even an entire nation.

John Dawson, in his powerful book *Healing America's Wounds*, explains the importance of identificational confession and intercession.

"If we have broken our covenants with God and violated our relationships with one another, the path to reconciliation must begin with the act of confession. The greatest wounds in human history, the greatest injustices, have not happened through the acts of some individual perpetrator, rather through the institutions, systems, philosophies, cultures, religions and governments of mankind. Because of this, we, as individuals, are tempted to absolve ourselves of all individual responsibility.

"Unless somebody identifies themselves with corporate entities, such as the nation of our citizenship, or the subculture of our ancestors, the act of honest confession will never take place. This leaves us in a world of injury and offense in which no corporate sin is ever acknowledged, reconciliation never begins and old hatreds deepen.

"The followers of Jesus are to step into this impasse as agents of healing. Within our ranks are representatives of every category of humanity. Trembling in our heavenly Father's presence, we see clearly the sins of humankind and have no inclination to cover them up. Thus, we are called to live out the biblical practice of identificational repentance, a neglected truth that opens the floodgates of revival and brings healing to the nations."[1]

Author and co-founder of Generals of Intercession, Cindy Jacobs, brings us additional understanding of this neglected area of teaching. Cindy Jacobs states, "Remitting of sins is not something that has been widely taught nor understood in the past but which we are now coming to understand as a vital part of spiritual warfare. Jesus modeled this principle on the cross when He said, 'Father forgive them, for they do not know what they do' (Luke 23:34)."[2]

Dr. Gary Greig, Associate Professor of Hebrew and Old Testament at Regent School of Divinity, has done extensive study in this area of prayer for revival and of identificational repentance. Dr. Greig states, "The deepest scheme is the enemy's attempt to keep hidden the defilement of the land through historic sins and the enemy's attempt to keep the Church from its priestly role of asking God to forgive these sins and of leading the way in repenting of these sins that have defiled the land, grieved God's heart, and empowered the enemy here."[3] I simply add a loud and confirming "Amen!" to this brilliant theological statement.

The Learning Curve

Over 20 years ago I, along with thousands of others, began praying about the abortion situation in the United States. My prayer went something like this: "Lord, forgive us for our immorality. Forgive us of our abortions." The first time I did this some people came up to me frightened and shocked by the way I was praying. They said, "We had no idea that you were like that!" You see, I was never personally involved in sexual immorality or abortion situations. These folks simply didn't understand that I was trying to identify with the sins of my college, city, state, and nation concerning abortion. I probably could have done it a little better, but at least I was stepping out into what were uncharted waters for me at that time.

Certainly we need wisdom to know how to walk in this kind of intercession. There's more to identification than simply changing the pronouns from "them" to "us." Something much deeper is involved. Identification is a deliberate act of the will to join ourselves heart and soul with the plight of other people. John Dawson defines identification as "the act of consciously including oneself within an identifiable category of human beings."[4] It is a matter of the heart, not just of the mind and of the words in our mouths.

I believe in process prayer. For example, God gives us a burden concerning a particular situation—let's say it's abortion—and as we begin to pray He leads us into deeper levels of understanding and personal identification. We begin to ask such questions as, "Father, what led to this sin? What led to the horrifying condition of its being multiplied so much across our land?" As we continue to pray and wait on the Lord, the spirit of conviction wedded to the spirit of revelation leads us to deal personally with related issues such as greed, immorality, rape, pride, and lust. Before confession can be turned outward, it must be turned inward as we let the finger of the Holy Spirit touch us wherever there may be a trace of any of those sins in us.

Through confession comes cleansing. After we are cleansed through the blood of Jesus Christ we become sanctified vessels, humbled through brokenness over our own sin and able through personal experience to identify in compassion with others who are caught in sin. It is only after we are broken ourselves that God can come and invest His authority into us.

When the Lord Changed His Mind

One of the most amazing truths in the Bible is that our prayers can change God's mind. As priestly intercessors, we have the privilege of writing and rewriting history before the throne of God. I want to illustrate this by looking at a prayer uttered by one of the greatest intercessors of them all—Moses. In this prayer Moses' holy arguments with God prevailed, permitting God to act in mercy instead of judgment.

And the Lord said to Moses, "I have seen this people, and behold, they are an obstinate people. Now then let Me alone, that My anger may burn against them, and that I may destroy them; and I will make of you a great nation." Then Moses entreated the Lord his God, and said, "O Lord, why doth Thine anger burn against Thy people whom Thou hast brought out from the land of Egypt with great power and with a mighty hand? Why should the Egyptians speak, saying, 'With evil intent He brought them out to kill them in the mountains and to destroy them from the face of the earth'? Turn from Thy burning anger and change Thy mind about doing harm to Thy people. Remember Abraham, Isaac, and Israel, Thy servants to whom Thou didst swear by Thyself, and didst say to them, 'I will multiply your descendants as the stars of the heavens, and all this land of which I have spoken I will give to your descendants, and they shall inherit it forever.' " So the Lord changed

His mind about the harm which He said He would do to His people (Exodus 32:9-14).

At the time of this conversation, Moses was still on the mountain where he received the Ten Commandments. The Israelites down in the valley had just committed their great sin with the golden calf. God informed Moses of His intention to destroy the sinful people and to start over with Moses to build a nation. Let's examine Moses' prayer to see how he changed God's mind.

1. *Moses argued from the history of God's redeeming acts.*
   He told God that it would be out of character with His great acts of mercy (verse 11) if, after leading the Israelites in triumph and glory out of Egypt, He destroyed them now. Moses interceded for God's redeeming acts, that they would align with His character.

2. *Moses argued for the glory of God's name.*
   In effect, Moses said to God, "Don't give the Egyptians a reason to slander You because You failed to provide for Your people." Moses was concerned about vindicating the holiness of God's great name in the earth (verse 12).

3. *Moses argued from God's faithfulness to His servants.*
   He reminded God of the lives of Abraham, Isaac, and Israel (Jacob) and of the promises that He had previously given to them (verse 13). Moses boldly quoted back to God the promise God had made and held God accountable to His own Word!

As a result of Moses' bold intercession, *God changed His mind!* That is truly awesome! God listened to the voice of a man and changed His mind!

Why would God allow His mind to be changed by the voice of men? For one thing, God chose from the beginning to use people as His instruments for accomplishing His purpose in the earth. He has invited us to be history-changers. As priests unto God through Jesus Christ we have the right and the privilege to "stand in the gap" between God's righteous judgments that are due and mankind's need for mercy. We stand before God on the people's behalf, pleading on the basis of God's reputation in the earth, His faithfulness to His covenant Word that He has previously stated, and for the sake of His glory being revealed and established.

The Presence Factor

A second intercessory prayer by Moses reveals the importance of the presence of God among His people. In Exodus 33:1-3 God tells Moses to take the people to Canaan, but says that He will not go with them because they are an obstinate people and He might destroy them on the way. This is still during the aftermath of the golden calf incident.

> *Then Moses said to the Lord, "See, Thou dost say to me, 'Bring up this people!' But Thou Thyself hast not let me know whom Thou wilt send with me. Moreover, Thou hast said, 'I have known you by name, and you have also found favor in My sight.' Now therefore, I pray Thee, if I have found favor in Thy sight, let me know Thy ways, that I may know Thee, so that I may find favor in Thy sight. Consider too, that this nation is Thy people." And He said, "My presence shall go with you, and I will give you rest." Then he said to Him, "If Thy presence does not go with us, do not lead us up from here"* (Exodus 33:12-15).

Look at the progressive nature of Moses' prayer. He begins by reminding God of His own Word that Moses had found favor in His eyes (verse 12). Moses builds on this in verse 13 when he says, "If I have found favor in Thy sight, *let me know Thy ways, that I may know Thee.*" This is an important key for us to grasp. Moses wanted more than just the favor of God; he wanted to know God's *ways.* In learning the ways of God, he would learn the character of God and, ultimately, be drawn into the intimate knowledge of God Himself. Awesome! *Teach us these ways, Lord!*

In the latter part of verse 13 Moses turns from personal appeal to corporate intercession. Starting from the place of his personal favor before God, his prayer expands to take in his whole nation: "Consider too, that this nation is Thy people."

Once again, God changes His mind because of Moses' intercession. "And He said, 'My presence shall go with you, and I will give you rest' " (verse 14).

Intercessory prayer involves praying for the release of several things. One is for the release of the gifts of the Spirit, which deal with the empowering of the Church to do the works of Jesus Christ. Another is for the release of the fruit of the Spirit, which deals with the character of Christ. A third element, and one that is too often neglected, is for the release of the wisdom ways of God. Many movements of the Spirit have been birthed with power but were cut short because those involved did not understand or seek the wisdom ways of God. That has been one of the hidden strands lost in the Church. The wisdom of God has a lot to do with the fear of the Lord because "the fear of the Lord is the beginning of wisdom, and the knowledge of the Holy One is understanding" (Prov. 9:10).

Then Moses said, "If Thy presence does not go with us, do not lead us up from here" (verse 15). The single outstanding, distinctive characteristic of the people of God is not how we dress or what songs we sing, but the *presence factor*. The highest weapon of spiritual warfare is God Himself present with His people in power and glory. Moses stood in the gap for the presence of God among his people, and that is what we need to be doing on behalf of our congregations, the full Body of Christ, our cities, and our nation. We need to pray for the opening of the heavens and for God's presence factor to be released on the earth.

Pardoned According to Your Word

There's a third intercessory prayer of Moses that I want to look at briefly. In many ways it is similar to the first one in Exodus chapter 32. In Numbers 14:1-10 the Israelites have rebelled against

God by heeding the bad report of ten of the spies sent to check out the land of Canaan and despising the good report given by the other two spies, Joshua and Caleb. God declares in verses 11 and 12 that He will destroy the people and begin again with Moses. Once again Moses steps in to intercede for the people. In verses 13-18 Moses appeals to God on the basis of His great reputation in the earth, reminds God of His covenant promises, and speaks back to God His own words regarding His loving-kindness and forgiveness. Finally, in verse 19 Moses reaches the focal point of his prayer.

> *"Pardon, I pray, the iniquity of this people according to the greatness of Thy lovingkindness, just as Thou also hast forgiven this people, from Egypt even until now."* So the Lord said, *"I have pardoned them according to your word; but indeed, as I live, all the earth will be filled with the glory of the Lord"* (Numbers 14:19-21).

Moses asks God to pardon the people based on His reputation, His promises, and His merciful, loving, and forgiving nature. Look at the Lord's incredible statement in verse 20. *"I have pardoned them according to your word."* God pardoned the people *according to the word of Moses!* It was the intercessory prayer of Moses that moved God's heart and changed God's mind.

Verse 21 is phenomenal also: "As I live, all the earth will be filled with the glory of the Lord." Many times we quote this verse without considering its context. This prophetic promise of God that all the earth will be filled with His glory comes on the heels of righteous intercession, of Moses' getting in God's face and reminding God of His holy reputation in the earth, His faithfulness, His covenant nature, His mercy and loving-kindness, and His promises. A bold intercessor stood in the gap before God for his people, and God listened to the voice of a man.

God has established a basis for all of us as believers and intercessors to come boldly and *"get in His face."* Have you ever wanted to give God a word? Don't be bashful. Remember that the Lord is *looking* for people who will "stand in the gap" (Ezek. 22:30) before Him for the land. Let us rise up out of passivity, lay hold of our right and heritage as children of God, and with humble tenaciousness, *"get in God's face."*

Christ, Our Priestly Model

The fullest and most profound expression of intercession came in the life and ministry of Jesus Christ. He fully identified with us as our sinful condition was placed upon Him, and as the "scapegoat" (see Lev. 16:10), He carried our transgressions away from us "as far as the east is from the west" (Ps. 103:12a). How did Jesus accomplish this?

1. *He humbled Himself through extreme means.*

    Jesus "emptied Himself, taking the form of a bond-servant, and being made in the likeness of men. And being found in appearance as a man, He humbled Himself by becoming obedient to the point of death, even death on a cross" (Phil. 2:7-8).

2. *He took on the sins of mankind.*

    "He made Him who knew no sin to be sin on our behalf, that we might become the righteousness of God in Him" (2 Cor. 5:21).

3. *He lifted and carried away our transgressions.*

    "Surely our griefs He Himself bore, and our sorrows He carried....He poured out Himself to death, and was numbered with the transgressors; yet He Himself bore the sin of many, and interceded for the transgressors" (Is. 53:4a,12b).

As believers we are part of a "royal priesthood" and a "holy nation" (1 Pet. 2:9). Jesus, our great High Priest, has given us a model to follow. Just as Jesus bore our sins and sorrows, so we are to bear the burdens of others as priests before God. "Now we who are strong ought to bear the weaknesses of those without strength and not just please ourselves" (Rom. 15:1). "Bear one another's burdens, and thus fulfill the law of Christ" (Gal. 6:2). The Greek word translated "bear" in both of these verses is *bastazo*, which means "to lift up" or "carry" with the idea of carrying off or removing. It is the same word used in reference to Christ in Matthew 8:17: "In order that what was spoken through Isaiah the prophet might be fulfilled, saying, 'He Himself took our infirmities, and *carried away* [*bastazo*] our diseases.' "

Rees Howells, a mighty British intercessor of an earlier generation, discovered three critical components of intercession that were exemplified in Christ's life and ministry.

1. *Identification.*

    Howells said that this was law number one for every intercessor and that Christ was the supreme example. He was numbered with the transgressors (see Is. 53:12) and became our High Priest, interceding on our behalf (see Heb. 2:17). Born in a manger, God's Son pitched His tent in our camp, making Himself a brother to all men. He suffered with the suffering and walked the rocky roads that we mortals walk. Jesus was the epitome of lasting love, and His life defined the intercessor as one who identifies with others.

2. *Agony.*

    "If we are to be an intercessor," Howells said, "we must be fully like the Master." Jesus "offered up both prayers and supplications with loud crying and tears" (Heb. 5:7). Gethsemane was the deepest depth in Christ's ocean of agony. There His heart was broken as none have known. Christ's example teaches that a critical function of an intercessor is to agonize for souls.

3. *Authority.*

    Howells stated, "If the intercessor is to know identification and agony, he also knows authority. He moves God, this intercessor. He even causes Him to change His mind." Rees Howells claimed that when he gained a place of intercession for a need, and believed it God's will, he always had a victory.[5]

Taking Up the Burden

Not long ago the Lord gave me a taste of what it really means to agonize. I have agonized before during times of travail in prayer, but on this occasion the burden of the Lord that descended on me was especially heavy. All of a sudden everything around me seemed to be darkness, and I began to cry because of the darkness. Although the entire experience lasted only a few moments, the Lord opened up to me the agony of the uncovered. For those few excruciating seconds I felt what it was like not to have God's umbrella of protection around me and not to have the name and the blood of Jesus over me or the community of believers surrounding me. God allowed me to tap into the feelings of the sufferings of others, and all I could do was sob vehemently. For those precious few moments, He ushered me into that place of agony that Rees Howells talked about.

In my book *Kneeling on the Promises: Birthing God's Purposes Through Prophetic Intercession*, I briefly rehearsed a life-changing encounter I had while having a divine appointment with Rees Howells' son Samuel Howells. Let me bring a portion of this before you.

"In October 1998 I was honored to visit the Bible school that Rees Howells founded in Swansea, Wales. I visited with his elderly son, Samuel Howells, still active at age 86 in his priestly role of intercession before the throne. What a joy it was to be in the very room where crisis intercession arose on behalf of the Jewish people!

"At the close of my appointment with Samuel Howells, I asked how his father, Rees Howells, had received revelation from God on what to pray. Did it come by dreams, visions, the burden of God—or just how? Mr. Howells' remark to me was short and piercing. 'Oh, you must understand, the Lord's servant was possessed by God.'

"That answered it all! New levels of authority with God and over the enemy come from new levels of possession by God."[6]

That might seem so far out of reach, so far from any of our grasp today. But in spite of what seems impossible to our minds, God's grace is sufficient for every need. In fact, an invitation into Divine participation is being extended.

An Invitation Extended

There is no way we can add anything to what Christ has done, but we can model what He did. We can take upon ourselves the burdens and weaknesses of others for intercessory purposes and carry them to God's throne of grace. There the Holy Spirit can then appropriate the benefits of the cross and we can acknowledge and receive as completely sufficient the grace of our Lord and the power of His shed blood. *We have sinned! Father, forgive us!*

An invitation is being extended right now. It is as though you are Queen Esther and have come into the Kingdom of God for such a time as this. The King has personally lowered His scepter toward you, and the right to approach His throne has been extended. You ask, "What shall I say before this King of the universe?" Perhaps this closing prayer will help you express your desire before His Majesty the King.

Holy Father, grant us Your heart and Your grace for this deepening work of identification in intercession. Open our eyes to see the needs and grant us Your broken heart. Help us to lay down our lives, grace us to agree with the sin and condition of Your people and help us to carry their burdens. Make us true intercessors, willing to be the answer to our prayers. Help us, Jesus, to model Your life. For the sake of Your Kingdom and Your glory, amen.

Reflection Questions

1. What does the phrase "identification in intercession" mean to you?

2. Have you ever experienced the "burden of the Lord" for a people different from yourself?

3. Ask the Father now to give you His heart of compassion and the Spirit of prayer to be a change maker in your generation.

Recommended Reading

Rees Howells Intercessor by Norman Grubb (Christian Literature Crusade, 1987)

John Hyde by Francis McGaw (Bethany House Publishers, 1970)

Cure of All Evils by Mary Steward Relfe (League of Prayer, 1998)

Endnotes

1. John Dawson, *Healing America's Wounds* (Ventura, California: Regal Books, 1994), 30.
2. Cindy Jacobs, "Identificational Repentance Through Biblical Remitting of Sins," in Stephen Mansfield, *Releasing Destiny* (Nashville, Tennessee: Daniel 1 School of Leadership, 1993), 51.
3. Dr. Gary Greig, from the teaching outline *Praying for Revival: Focusing Our Intercession, Spiritual Warfare & Protecting Ourselves in the Battle* (Virginia Beach, Virginia: Regent University, 1996), 2.
4. Dawson, *Healing America's Wounds*, 31.
5. Dick Eastman, *No Easy Road* (Grand Rapids, Michigan: Baker Book House, 1971).
6. Jim Goll, *Kneeling on the Promises* (Grand Rapids, Michigan: Baker Book House, 1999), 210-211.

Chapter 3

Confessing Generational Sin

ack in 1991 some friends and I were in Prague, the beautiful capital city of what was then Czechoslovakia. I was the main speaker at a conference that was held in what once had been the largest Communist party hall in the city. There I was, a little country boy from Cowgill, Missouri, population 259, standing before a crowd of around 2,000 Czechs and Slovaks and trying to exhort them about the prophetic and the necessity of identification in intercession.

Czechoslovakia had a checkered history of conquest and oppression by the Russians and the Germans and many other groups that had left a legacy of crimes and atrocities, heartache, anguish, sorrow, bitterness, and hatred. As I looked out over that throng of people the Lord suddenly woke me up inside and reminded me of my own German heritage. I stepped to the microphone and said to this gathering of Czechs and Slovaks, "You need to understand something. Goll is a German name. I am German by ancestry. I am the first Goll to return to my homeland as well as stand in your midst today. I am asking you to forgive us, the Germans, for what we did to your beautiful country in World War II."

A trickle of tears began. Then the dam broke. All over the room people started to weep in brokenness, and cleansing began to occur. Then it dawned on me that one of the friends with me was Jewish. I asked David Dreiling, my traveling partner, to come up and explain to the crowd who he was. Then I turned to David and, as a German, confessed to him the sins of the German people against the Jews and asked his forgiveness.

At that point the meeting took on a life of its own and wonderful things began to happen. A strong spirit of forgiveness and reconciliation filled the room. All over the hall people came up and confessed their ethnic rivalry and hatred toward one another. Slovaks confessed to Czechs and Czechs confessed to Slovaks.

I was praising God because I had come to this conference with only one mission. The Lord had placed on my heart a burden unlike any I had ever felt before; it was a burden for two peoples in one country. Communism had fallen and Czechoslovakia was on the verge of splitting in two. The people had to choose whether they would stay together as one nation or divide into two. If they divided, they had to choose whether to do it peacefully or hatefully. My burden from God was that these two different groups would be reconciled to each other.

As it turned out, the country did divide into the Czech Republic and the Slovak Republic, but the separation occurred in a very peaceful manner.

Remove, Repair, and Restore

The meeting that day in Prague is a good illustration of both the practice and the power of confessing generational sins. Although I personally was never involved in the sins of the German people against the Czechs, the Slovaks, or the Jews, I was under a godly burden to identify with my German heritage and acknowledge the sins of previous generations of Germans. The Lord used a humble attempt at identification and open confession to clear the path for reconciliation and healing to begin. Under the leadership of the Spirit, sincere confession and a simple, heartfelt plea for forgiveness can literally work wonders in the hearts of people who are estranged from each other by hostility, bitterness, resentment, and historical, national, racial, or religious hatred.

This concept is nothing new; on the contrary, it is older than the Scriptures and was birthed in the heart of God Himself. That's why I call it "following the ancient paths." Confessing generational sin, although a neglected practice among many Christians, is a key part of the process of removing the obstacle of sin, repairing the breaches caused by sin, and restoring the relationships disrupted by sin. Isaiah 57:14b says, *"Remove every obstacle out of the way of My people."* In the very next chapter we read, "And those from among you will rebuild the ancient ruins; you will raise up the age-old foundations; and you will be called the *repairer of the breach*, the *restorer of the streets* in which to dwell" (Is. 58:12).

In 1989 picks, jackhammers, and bulldozers brought down the Berlin Wall, that hated symbol of separation between eastern and western Germans. The social and ideological walls between them, however, were not torn down as easily. In the same way, the obstacles of individual and corporate sin cannot be removed by the devices of men. God has ordained only one way—confession—to clear away the sins that stand between us individually and corporately and between Him and the families, cities, and nations of the earth. If we want to witness a worldwide awakening in our day, there are individual, corporate, generational, and even national sins that must be removed. The only way to remove them is to honestly confess them.

Convinced, Convicted, and Confessing

What exactly does it mean to "confess"? The New Testament contains two Greek words that are translated as "confess": *homologeō* and *exomologeō*. An example of the former is First John 1:9: "If we confess [*homologeō*] our sins...." According to *Vine's Complete Expository Dictionary of Old and New Testament Words*, the word *homologeō* means "to speak the same thing, to assent, accord, agree with, to confess, declare, admit." In the context of First John 1:9 it means, "to confess by way of admitting oneself guilty of what one is accused of, the result of inward conviction."[1] An example of the latter is James 5:16, "Therefore, confess [*exomologeō*] your sins to one another…," where in context it means "to confess forth, freely, openly," in the sense of "a public acknowledgment or confession of sins."[2] Both words carry the sense of "agreement." Confession of sin means "agreeing" with God regarding sin, our own as well as others'.

True confession arises from a heart under conviction. Conviction is "the state of being convinced of error or compelled to admit the truth; a strong persuasion or belief; the state of being convinced." The verb *convict* means "to find or prove to be guilty; to convince of error or sinfulness."[3] So confession goes far beyond mere verbalizing or admitting wrong; it is a deep acknowledgment of guilt, a profession of responsibility from a convicted heart, which is a heart absolutely convinced of the reality and horror of sin. I believe that this is a revelatory act that comes only through the working of the Holy Spirit.

Confession Begins at Home

Before any of us can enter into an effective ministry of intercession or even of confessing generational sin, we must make sure that our own hands are clean. Each of us must first find the place of personal cleansing. First Peter 4:17 says that judgment begins with the household of God. Confession always begins at home as we each get alone with God and acknowledge our guilt and our sin before Him. We have to unload our own sin burdens before we can take up those of others. This should be a consistent practice, one done daily or as often as necessary. It is only with clean hands and a pure heart that we can properly intercede for others at any level.

Beyond our personal cleansing, we need to realize as members of the Body of Christ that collectively our hands are not clean. In our sinfulness and rebellion we have allowed doctrinal walls, theological barriers, and sectarian suspicion and misunderstanding to divide us as Christians, in clear violation of the word and spirit of Scripture. The apostle Paul wrote, "There is neither Jew nor Greek, there is neither slave nor free man, there is neither male nor female; for you are all one in Christ Jesus" (Gal. 3:28), and "For there is no distinction between Jew and Greek; for the same Lord is Lord of all, abounding in riches for all who call upon Him" (Rom. 10:12). Jesus said, "A new commandment I give to you, that you love one another, even as I have loved you, that you also love one another. By this all men will know that you are My disciples, if you have love for one another" (Jn. 13:34-35). Jesus also prayed that we would be one as He and the Father are one (see Jn. 17:22). Divisions within the Body of Christ hinder our witness to the world and our ability to fulfill our call as intercessors.

Author and pastor Joseph Garlington in his book *Right or Reconciled?* named 12 distinctions that often divide the Church today. These distinctions are racial, cultural, national, gender oriented, economic, class (or social), religious, "singleness" related, divorce related, AIDS oriented, political, and educational.[4] Furthermore, he adds,

> "Paul told us under divine authority that there are *no distinctions* between us in God's eyes. The only reason we can stand before Him is because His Son, Jesus Christ, personally paid the price for our freedom and washed us in His blood. Period. Everything beyond that is stuff that belongs in God's 'damned trash can,' where you will find Paul's impeccable racial bloodline and fancy theological schooling as well as Peter's temper and racial prejudice."[5]

International Bible teacher Derek Prince has identified seven areas or points of confession and intercession that we need to raise on behalf of the Western Church. These points clarify where we as the Body of Christ have sinned.

1. We have not given Jesus His due headship and pre-eminence (see Eph. 1:22-23; Col. 1:18).

2. We have slighted and grieved the Holy Spirit (see 2 Cor. 3:17).

3. We have not loved one another (see Jn. 13:34-35).

4. We have not fulfilled the Great Commission (see Mt. 28:18-20; Mk. 16:15-16).

5. We have not cared for the weak and the helpless (see Rom. 15:1; Jas. 1:27).

6. We have despised and mistreated the Jewish people (see Rom. 11:15-31).

7. We have compromised with, and been defiled by, the spirit of this world (see Jas. 4:4; 1 Jn. 2:15-17).[6]

This is convicting stuff! Today the Western Church labors under the pressing weight of past sins that have multiplied over decades, generations, and in some cases, even centuries of disobedience and neglect. Church, our hands are not clean! *We have sinned! Father, forgive us!*

A Painful Privilege

One of the most awesome privileges we can have as children of God is the opportunity to come before God with a broken and a contrite heart over the sins of others, and then to walk in that brokenness, allowing God's broken heart to be expressed through us. While such a walk may be painful, it is still a glorious privilege. It is also a sobering responsibility. Because this kind of confession and prayer is a "lost art" in much of the Church today, I believe there is much we can learn from the examples of Daniel, Nehemiah, and Ezra, three men who were drawn into spiritual brokenness and confession of the generational sins of their nation. Let's take a quick glance at the prayer lives of these three gatekeepers.

Daniel: "O Lord, Hear! O Lord, Forgive!"

In the first year of [Darius'] reign I, Daniel, observed in the books the number of the years which was revealed as the word of the Lord to Jeremiah the prophet for the completion of the desolations of Jerusalem, namely, seventy years. So I gave my attention to the Lord God to seek Him by prayer and supplications, with fasting, sackcloth, and ashes. And I prayed to the Lord my God and confessed and said, "Alas, O Lord, the great and awesome God, who keeps His covenant and lovingkindness for those who love Him and keep His commandments, we have sinned, committed iniquity, acted wickedly, and rebelled, even turning aside from Thy commandments and ordinances" (Daniel 9:2-5).

One day Daniel was meditating on the writings of the prophet Jeremiah, specifically Jeremiah 29:10-14, which prophesied that the children of Israel would go into captivity in Babylon for 70 years and then be restored to their land. The word of God enlightened Daniel's understanding and brought his heart under deep conviction. He began seeking the Lord earnestly in order to know what blockades of sin existed that might hinder or prevent the fulfillment of the promise. Daniel did not just simply assume that all was well. He understood that the fulfillment of these promises was contingent upon the obedience of the people. He wanted to make sure nothing stood in the way.

As Daniel sought the Lord he began to confess the generational sins of his people that had led to the captivity, even though they had happened before he was born. (See Daniel 9:4-19 for Daniel's complete prayer.) Daniel did not respond presumptuously; rather, he sought the Spirit's remedy so that the promise could be fulfilled. Laying aside any sense of self-justification, in humility and brokenness Daniel confessed his nation's sins as his own. More than simply changing a few pronouns in his prayer, Daniel entered into deep identification with his people and the horrifying condition of their sin. Through the spirit of revelation wedded to the spirit of conviction, he understood God's promise as well as the conditions that had to be met in order for the promise to be fulfilled. Becoming truly one with his people in intercession, Daniel pleaded for God's mercy and for the fulfillment of the prophetic promise.

> *O Lord, in accordance with all Thy righteous acts, let now Thine anger and Thy wrath turn away from Thy city Jerusalem, Thy holy mountain; for because of our sins and the iniquities of our fathers, Jerusalem and Thy people have become a reproach to all those around us....O Lord, hear! O Lord, forgive! O Lord, listen and take action! For Thine own sake, O my God, do not delay, because Thy city and Thy people are called by Thy name"* (Daniel 9:16,19).

God heard Daniel's plea and God's promise was fulfilled!

Nehemiah: "I and My Father's House Have Sinned"

> *And they said to me, "The remnant there in the province who survived the captivity are in great distress and reproach, and the wall of Jerusalem is broken down and its gates are burned with fire." Now it came about when I heard these words, I sat down and wept and mourned for days; and I was fasting and praying before the God of heaven. And I said, "I beseech Thee, O Lord God of heaven, the great and awesome God, who preserves the covenant and lovingkindness for those who love Him and keep His commandments, let Thine ear now be attentive and Thine eyes open to hear the prayer of Thy servant which I am praying before Thee now, day and night, on behalf of the sons of Israel Thy servants, confessing the sins of the sons of Israel which we have sinned against Thee; I and my father's house have sinned. We have acted very corruptly against Thee and have not kept the commandments, nor the statutes, nor the ordinances which Thou didst command Thy servant Moses"* (Nehemiah 1:3-7).

Like Daniel, Nehemiah had lived his entire life in captivity. He was serving as the king's cupbearer when he received the news of the shameful and desolate condition of Jerusalem. Nehemiah understood that the fall of the city and the exile of the Jews were God's judgment on them because of their sins. Under the burden of this distressing news Nehemiah wept and mourned for days. Then he began to pray and confess his and his people's sins. (See Nehemiah 1:5-11 for the complete prayer.) In verses 8 and 9, Nehemiah reminded God of His prophetic promises to Moses, and in verse 10 he appealed to God on the basis of His redemptive work. Finally, in verse 11 he implored God for favor with the king and asked for success.

Nehemiah desired and felt a Divine call to go to Jerusalem and rebuild the walls of the city. The entire Book of Nehemiah is devoted to the story of how he accomplished this. Nehemiah carried a deep love and burden for his nation and his people that motivated him to identify and intercede fervently before God. In addition, Nehemiah was willing to be the answer to his own prayer, which he proved when he sought the king's favor for his mission to Jerusalem (see Neh. 2:1-5). Once again, not only did an earthly king hear, but the heavenly King also heard and Nehemiah was released with a blessing to accomplish his heart's desire.

Ezra: "Our Guilt Has Grown Even to the Heavens"

Ezra was a priest who led a group of Jewish exiles back to Jerusalem and took charge of the project of rebuilding the temple. Upon his arrival in the city some of the leaders informed Ezra that many of the people, including priests, Levites, and civic leaders, had intermarried with the pagan people in the surrounding region in direct violation of the commandments of God. The Mosaic Law required the Israelites to remain separate from other tribes or nations in order to preserve their spiritual purity and integrity. Ezra's gut-wrenching reaction is recorded in chapter 9 of the Book of Ezra.

> *And when I heard about this matter, I tore my garment and my robe, and pulled some of the hair from my head and my beard, and sat down appalled. Then everyone who trembled at the words of the God of Israel on account of the unfaithfulness of the exiles gathered to me, and I sat appalled until the evening offering. But at the evening offering I arose from my*

humiliation, even with my garment and my robe torn, and I fell on my knees and stretched out my hands to the Lord my God; and I said, "O my God, I am ashamed and embarrassed to lift up my face to Thee, my God, for our iniquities have risen above our heads, and our guilt has grown even to the heavens. Since the days of our fathers to this day we have been in great guilt, and on account of our iniquities we, our kings and our priests have been given into the hand of the kings of the lands, to the sword, to captivity, and to plunder and to open shame, as it is this day" (Ezra 9:3-7).

Ezra was in great distress and agony over the sins of his people. His actions express deep remorse for their offenses against God. The reference in verse 5 to Ezra's "humiliation" indicates that he was probably fasting as part of his humbling of himself before God in mourning and repentance. Ezra's thorough identification with his people moved him to the place of intercession and confession of their corporate, generational sins. In verses 6 and 7 he named the sins as though they were his own. Notice the complete absence of any self-righteousness on Ezra's part. Although he himself was not guilty of these sins, he felt a deep sense of responsibility because the people who were guilty were his people; he was one with them.

In verses 8 and 9 Ezra recalled God's grace, mercy, faithfulness, and loving-kindness in raising up and restoring a remnant to the land to rebuild the city of Jerusalem and the temple. Verses 10-12 state the case against Israel and speak back to God the specific law that the people had broken. In verse 13 Ezra acknowledged that even the punishment and judgment that had befallen the people was less than they deserved, and in verses 14 and 15 he prayed concerning the importance of maintaining the remnant in the land. Verse 1 of chapter 10 describes Ezra as "praying and making confession, weeping and prostrating himself before the house of God."

Ezra's public display of weeping, confession, and repentance galvanized the rest of the people. Deeply convicted of their sin, they committed themselves anew to God, renounced their sins, and pledged to follow Ezra's example in the path of righteousness and restoration. The rest of the chapter describes the dramatic, specific actions the people took to set things right and to demonstrate the sincerity and depth of their repentance. Oh, that this kind of "revival" would happen in our day!

Dare to Be a Daniel

Daniel, Nehemiah, and Ezra were all effective burden bearers for their people. In each instance God heard and answered, restoration came, and the people experienced renewal. Their examples clearly demonstrate the scriptural truth that "the effective prayer of a righteous man can accomplish much" (Jas. 5:16b).

We need to pray that today the Father will raise up more Daniels, more Nehemiahs, and more Ezras—people who will stand in the gap for their cities and nations. Let us pray at the same time that we might be given the opportunity to be the answer to our own prayers. Let revelation and contrition find each other and, out of their union, a new generation of authentic, apostolic believers in Christ Jesus come forth!

Most of us understand as Christians the need to confess individually our personal faults, failures, and sins to God and to ask for forgiveness and cleansing by the blood of Jesus Christ. As priests, however, our responsibility goes further than that. We are called not just to confess our individual sins, but also to stand in the gap and lift up an intercessory plea for our corporate faults, failures, and sins. Besides admitting our personal shortcomings, we must include the larger boundaries of our family, city, and nation, both of the secular community of which we are a part and the Body of Christ. The same is true for the prayers of blessing. As New Testament believers in Jesus, we are to identify with our many spheres of responsibility and authority and stand before God for the removal of the blockage of sin and various curses as well as for the release of hope, provision, and promise. It's time for the slumbering Bride to awaken from sleep and take her place in the throne room of God.

The Legal Basis of Demonic Activity

As I mentioned in Chapter 2, the Lord gave me a word in New York in 1991 in which He said, "I will release new understandings of identification in intercession whereby *the legal basis of the rights of the demonic powers of the air to remain will be removed.*" We need to take a closer look at the second part of that statement: the legal basis for demonic activity.

Conditions exist all over our world that give the demonic powers of the air "legal authority" to remain and operate against God's purpose and the good of humanity. I am convinced that a full global awakening cannot occur until this legal authority is removed. The only way to remove it is by the confession of the corporate and generational sins that established the authority in the first place, and their forgiveness through faith in Christ and the cleansing power of His blood.

Demonic spirits have no true authority to influence an area without permission. Certain conditions give them access points, or authority, to set up a base of operations from whence they exercise their oppression. What are some of these conditions?

1. *Idolatry.*

   Stated simply, idolatry is the worship of anything or anyone other than God. The key word here is *worship*. "I am the Lord your God....You shall have no other gods before Me. You shall not make for yourself an idol....You shall not worship them or serve them..." (Ex. 20:2-5). Our Lord is a jealous God, and He wants to eradicate and bring cleansing from anything that receives worship other than Him. You see, we become slaves to whomever or whatever we worship. Idols represent evil spirits (see 1 Cor. 10:19-20), and where idols exist, there also exists the legal right for the demonic spirits they represent to exercise influence. (More will be brought forth on this issue in Chapter 10 of this book.)

2. *Temples to pagan religions.*

This deals not only with the construction of "high places" of demonic and occultic worship (see 2 Kings 17:11; Ps. 78:58; Jer. 19:5; 32:35), but also with more subtle, destructive forms such as Masonic lodges and other things of this nature that are of the Luciferian foundation. During President Eisenhower's time a decision was reached between the governments of the United States and Afghanistan to erect a Christian church building in Kabul for the use of U.S. government officials. In return, a Muslim mosque would be constructed in Washington, D.C. A rioting mob destroyed the church three years after its completion, but the mosque still stands. I am convinced that this unwise decision and the construction of this mosque in the seat of our government established a legal basis for the demonic spirit of Islam to enter the United States. *Have mercy, dear God! Remove the high places in this generation.*

3. *Murder and the shedding of innocent blood.*

"You shall not murder" (Ex. 20:13). "For the life of the flesh is in the blood, and I have given it to you on the altar to make atonement for your souls; for it is the blood by reason of the life that makes atonement" (Lev. 17:11). "'So you shall not pollute the land in which you are; for blood pollutes the land and no expiation can be made for the land for the blood that is shed on it, except by the blood of him who shed it" (Num. 35:33). Today, of course, we deal not only with external wars accompanied by great shedding of blood, but also with internal wars in the shedding of the blood of infants legally killed while hidden in the supposedly safe sanctuary of their mother's womb. "God have mercy," is all we can say!

4. *Witchcraft.*

   "There shall not be found among you anyone who makes his son or his daughter pass through the fire, one who uses divination, one who practices witchcraft, or one who interprets omens, or a sorcerer, or one who casts a spell, or a medium, or a spiritist, or one who calls up the dead. For whoever does these things is detestable to the Lord" (Deut. 18:10-12a). At first satan only requires the blood of animals, but the more control in society he gains, the more he demands. So then comes human sacrifice. How prevalent is this today? Great Britain alone has an estimated 40,000 people actively involved in witchcraft and magic. In the United States all you have to do is turn on almost any television set and you can be exposed to witchcraft practitioners under the guise of giving you "your word for the day" and be blasted by satan's deception. "Deliver us," must be our cry!

5. *The removal of prayer and Bible reading from our schools.*

   The beginning of the current moral and spiritual deterioration of American society coincides with the day prayer and Bible reading were declared unlawful in the United States' public education system. "And it shall come about if you ever forget the Lord your God, and go after other gods and serve them and worship them, I testify against you today that you shall surely perish" (Deut. 8:19). When God was "kicked out," the god of secular humanism filled the void. Whenever we assume God's position and take it upon ourselves to solve problems that only Deity can handle, we make ourselves out to be gods. The worship of self is dangerously evil. If we continue in this way, we will destroy ourselves. This deterioration of our society has been shockingly driven home by recent shootings and murders at our various public school institutions. *O Father, forgive us! For we have sinned!*

6.   *Adultery, sodomy, perversion, and all other sexual sins.*
     Scripture speaks plainly numerous times regarding these sins. They all represent the twisting and distorting of a God-given drive in order to satisfy man's sinful desires and lustful imaginations. Historically, much idol worship has been linked with immoral and perverted sexual practices. Chapters 18 and 20 of the Book of Leviticus give clear guidelines, especially 18:22-23 and 20:10,13. (See also Deuteronomy 23:17 and Romans 1:24-28.) This one category alone is enough to keep you weeping before God for the rest of the day. How we have fallen from our first love! This is not just the sin of the world; it is the sin of a modern-day, worldly Church! *Forgive us!*

7.   *Substance abuse—alcohol, drugs, etc.*
     This is nothing more than witchcraft under a deceptively "fun" disguise, and as such it gives entrance for demonic powers to have a legal basis to rule. Revelation 21:8 mentions the word *sorcerers*, which in Greek is *pharmakeus*. It is derived from *pharmakon*, which means a drug or spell-giving potion. Revelation 22:15 uses a related word for sorcerer, *pharmakos*. So the use of drugs (including alcohol) is related to witchcraft, or the "magic arts." Let us repent of our acts of sorcery and witchcraft and close this legal access point of the devil's blatant schemes.

8. *Fighting, anger, hatred, cursing, and unforgiveness.*
Just about everyone can identify with these. They are all dangerous attitudes and mind-sets that can open the door for demonic activity. "He who returns evil for good, evil will not depart from his house" (Prov. 17:13). Romans 12:14 tells us to bless those who persecute us and not to curse them. First Peter 3:9 says that we are not to return evil for evil or insult for insult, but to give a blessing instead. Tied in with all this is the importance of forgiveness (see Mt. 18:21-35), of having clean hearts as we approach the Lord's table (see 1 Cor. 11:27-30), and being in proper relationship with those in authority (see Ex. 20:12; Rom. 13:1-2).

These are just eight categories that give the enemy a legal basis of operation. I'm sure there are more. But don't get depressed now; look up! There is a promise for every problem.

Rising to the Challenge

In his book *Warfare Prayer*, C. Peter Wagner writes,

"Suppose demonic strongholds actually exist in a nation or a city, affecting society in general and resistance to the gospel in particular. What can be done about it?

"Just as in the case of demonized individuals, if sin is present, repentance is called for, if curses are in effect they need to be broken, and if emotional scars are causing pain, inner healing is needed.

"We know from the Old Testament that nations can be guilty of corporate sins. This was not only true of Gentile nations, but of Israel as well. Both Nehemiah and Daniel give us examples of godly persons who felt the burden for sins of their nations.

"It is important to note that both Nehemiah and Daniel, while they were standing before God on behalf of their entire nation, confessed not only the corporate sins of their people, but also their individual sins. Those who remit the sins of nations must not fail to identify personally with the sins that were or are being committed even though they might not personally be as guilty of them as some other sins."[7]

God is looking for people who are ready and willing to stand in the gap for their families, cities, and nations. He is searching for people who, through intercession, will take on the burdens of corporate and generational sin and not simply carry them and be weighed down, but carry them *away* like the scapegoat in the wilderness. Then, it is my conviction, that the legal basis for the powers of the air to remain will be removed and the blessing, healing, and restoration of the Lord can potentially come down.

Will you rise to the challenge? Will you enter into that place of identification and confession and cry out to God with me, "*We have sinned! Father, forgive us!*"?

Reflection Questions

1. What are the generational sins in your region that you believe need to be seriously addressed?

2. What are the generational sins in the Church that you believe need to be seriously confronted?

3. According to Scripture, how far does the love of God extend? What can separate us from the love of God in Christ Jesus?

Recommended Reading

Daniel by Dr. Paul Yonggi Cho (Creation House, 1990)

When a Pope Asks Forgiveness by Luigi Accattoli (Pauline Books & Media, 1998)

Sins of the Fathers by Brian Mills and Roger Mitchell (Sovereign World, 1999)

Endnotes

1. W.E. Vine, Merrill F. Unger, and William White, Jr., *Vine's Complete Expository Dictionary of Old and New Testament Words* (Nashville, Tennessee: Thomas Nelson Publishers, 1985), 120.
2. Vine, Unger, and White, *Vine's Expository Dictionary*, 120.
3. *Merriam-Webster's Collegiate Dictionary*, 10th edition (Springfield, Massachusetts: Merriam-Webster, Inc., 1996), 254.
4. Joseph Garlington, *Right or Reconciled?* (Shippensburg, Pennsylvania: Destiny Image Publishers, 1998), 126.
5. Garlington, *Right or Reconciled?*, 126.
6. Derek Prince, taken from the audiotape "Intercession and Confession," preached at Fort Lauderdale, Florida.
7. C. Peter Wagner, *Warfare Prayer* (Ventura, California: Regal Books, 1992), 130-131.

Chapter 4

No Common Ground Allowed!

As children of God we were born in the *midst* of a war and we were born *for* war.

From the beginning of time the satanic powers of darkness have fought savagely against God and against everything He stands for. Now, realize that all true spiritual warfare centers around the placement of the Son of God. The collision of Heaven and earth is the battlefield; at stake is the eternal spiritual destiny of humanity. It is a conflict of cosmic proportions; it is an all-out war to the death, winner-take-all with no quarter given to the loser.

Each of us who has been born again by the Spirit of God through the death and resurrection of Jesus Christ was born into a Kingdom that is geared for war. As citizens of that Kingdom and as members of the royal family we have been groomed for battle since day one. Our Father, the King, has provided every resource we need—training, clothing, and weapons—and expects us to take to the field to fight in His name, under His authority, and with His power. Victory is assured; the enemy, in fact, has already been defeated. Christ won the victory on the cross. The day is coming when Christ will return in glory and all His enemies will be put under His feet (see Mt. 16:27; 22:44). Until that day, however, the war rages on and we are called to do our part. (Please see the Appendix at the back of this book for additional material to complement the teaching in this chapter.)

Our Lord Is a Man of War

If we as children of God are born and called to war, then there must be a part of our Father's nature and character in which He Himself is a warrior. The Scriptures support this view of God. After the Israelites witnessed the destruction of the Egyptian army at the Red Sea, they danced and celebrated and sang a song of praise to God that included these words: "The Lord is a warrior; the Lord is His name" (Ex. 15:3). The King James Version renders it as, "The Lord is a *man of war.*" When Moses was preparing Joshua to lead the nation of Israel into the Promised Land, he said to Joshua concerning the nations they would meet across the Jordan River, "Do not fear them, for the Lord your God is the one fighting for you" (Deut. 3:22). When Isaiah prophesied judgment against Babylon, he spoke of "a sound of tumult on the mountains, like that of many people! A sound of the uproar of kingdoms, of nations gathered together! The Lord of hosts is mustering the army for battle" (Is. 13:4).

Our Lord is a warrior, and He is mustering His army for battle against the forces of darkness. We need not fear marching under His banner because He will not be defeated. "But thanks be to God, who always leads us in His triumph in Christ" (2 Cor. 2:14a). Part of this triumph is the historic act of the perfect and complete work on the cross that Christ has already accomplished on our behalf. Other triumphs come as we faithfully follow His leadership. The key here is following where God *leads*. Wherever God leads, if we follow we experience triumph. Victory is not guaranteed if we go off on our own; in that case, defeat is all but certain. Our part in the victory is to trust God and to follow Him with humility and without presumption.

Humility is the first requirement for God's warriors.

Now it came about when Joshua was by Jericho, that he lifted up his eyes and looked, and behold, a man was standing opposite him with his sword drawn in his hand, and Joshua went to him and said to him, "Are you for us or for our adversaries?" And he said, "No, rather I indeed come now as captain of the host of the Lord." And Joshua fell on his face to the earth, and bowed down, and said to him, "What has my lord to say to his servant?" And the captain of the Lord's host said to Joshua, "Remove your sandals from your feet, for the place where you are standing is holy." And Joshua did so (Joshua 5:13-15).

In the presence of the Lord Joshua fell prostrate and asked, in effect, "What do You require of me?" The Lord's answer was, "Humble yourself; bow before Me; take your sandals off, for you are on holy ground." I am convinced that such a posture of humility on our part is absolutely necessary if we are to be victorious as warriors.

Crushing the Serpent's Head

The battle lines for this war were drawn way back in the Garden of Eden when God said to the serpent, "And I will put enmity between you and the woman, and between your seed and her seed; he shall bruise you on the head, and you shall bruise him on the heel" (Gen. 3:15). This verse is the first Messianic prophecy in the Bible; the seed of the woman refers to Christ. Paul makes this clear in Galatians: "Now the promises were spoken to Abraham and to his seed. He does not say, 'And to seeds,' as referring to many, but rather to one, 'And to your seed,' that is, Christ" (Gal. 3:16). Abraham, of course, was a descendant of Eve (one of her "seed"). He was also the one with whom God made a covenant to make of him a great nation, out of which would come One who would bless all the nations of the earth.

According to this prophecy the serpent (satan) would strike or bruise the heel of the Messiah; it would be a painful and annoying wound, but not life-threatening. When Jesus died on the cross it seemed as though, from outward appearances at least, that satan had won. In God's eternal scheme, however, satan's best efforts were no worse than a bite on the heel. Christ, on the other hand, would inflict on satan a severe and eventually fatal head wound. Some translations use the word *strike* or *crush* to describe what the woman's seed would do to the serpent's head.

The head is a symbol of authority; it is the seat of government, so to speak. When the Messiah came He crushed the serpent's head, destroying satan's right to rule over us. By His death and resurrection Christ crushed satan's nerve center—his strategies and power. Do you know what happens when you crush or cut off the head of a snake? The body thrashes about wildly for a little bit. When Christ crushed the serpent's head, satan, realizing that his time was short, went on a wild fling, thrashing violently about trying to spill blood, bite, and spread venom wherever, however, and to whomever he could.

Although satan's power and authority over us have been destroyed, his final destruction lies in the future. "And the God of peace will *soon* crush Satan under your feet" (Rom. 16:20a). The coming day of the final crushing of satan is described in the Book of Revelation: "And the devil who deceived them was thrown into the lake of fire and brimstone, where the beast and the false prophet are also; and they will be tormented day and night forever and ever" (Rev. 20:10).

According to Exodus 15:3, *the Lord is a warrior*; Romans 16:20 says he is "*the God of peace.*" He is both. Peace comes through war. On the world stage, treaties result from the resolution of conflicts, and the parties involved have the responsibility of observing and enforcing the terms of the treaty. In the spiritual realm, Christ overcame and defeated satan and established victory for the Kingdom of Heaven. The enforcement of Christ's victory in the earth is

60

enacted through us as we follow in obedience and walk in the character of Christ. This is one of the reasons why I believe that we have a part to play in determining how long satan's "final fling" lasts. At any rate, we are soldiers in God's army and are called to the fray. The God of peace will crush satan under *our* feet, and the only place that can happen is on the field of battle.

We Are Called to Battle

There has always been enmity between the children of light and those who willfully remain in the darkness. Those who are in the darkness hate the light because it exposes their evil deeds (see Jn. 3:20). Jesus said, "If the world hates you, you know that it has hated Me before it hated you. If you were of the world, the world would love its own; but because you are not of the world, but I chose you out of the world, therefore the world hates you" (Jn. 15:18-19). James wrote, "You adulteresses, do you not know that friendship with the world is hostility toward God? Therefore whoever wishes to be a friend of the world makes himself an enemy of God" (Jas. 4:4).

As children of God we are agents of light behind enemy lines in a world trapped in darkness. We cannot avoid the conflict. The issue is not *whether* we battle, but *how* we battle. Strategy is of critical importance. We need Divine wisdom to keep us from fighting the wrong battle at the wrong time, to minimize casualties, and to guard us from the presumption of assuming that we can simply sit back and expect God to fight all the battles for us. Wisdom also will help us avoid both a "religious" or self-righteous spirit and a "woe is me" victim mentality.

Part of developing strategy is understanding the nature of the conflict. All-out war calls for all-out commitment from the warriors. Only through total allegiance to Christ and absolute surrender to His Lordship will we experience victory in spiritual warfare. Jesus could not have made it any plainer:

> *He who loves father or mother more than Me is not worthy of Me; and he who loves son or daughter more than Me is not*

61

worthy of Me. And he who does not take his cross and follow after Me is not worthy of Me. He who has found his life shall lose it, and he who has lost his life for My sake shall find it (Matthew 10:37-39).

The Nature of the Enemy

It is also important to understand the nature of the enemy. Paul wrote in Ephesians, "For our struggle is not against flesh and blood, but against the rulers, against the powers, against the world forces of this darkness, against the spiritual forces of wickedness in the heavenly places" (Eph. 6:12). Satan does not fight the way we do. We have been called for a wrestling match—for closed-in, hand-to-hand combat. Of all the "armor of God" that Paul describes in Ephesians 6:13-17—the belt of truth, the breastplate of righteousness, the shoes of the gospel of peace, the shield of faith, the helmet of salvation, and the sword of the Spirit—all except the sword are primarily defensive in nature. They are designed to protect from attack near at hand. The sword is for attacking the enemy, but only when he is within arm's reach.

Satan, on the other hand, prefers to fight from a distance. Ephesians 6:16 says that we can use the shield of faith "to extinguish all the flaming missiles of the evil one." Instead of coming in close, satan would rather shoot fiery arrows at us from the shadows. I believe that this is because he fears us. Satan knows that he is defeated and that we have an invincible ally. He knows he can't win, so he tries instead to produce in us an inordinate fear of *him*. Now, certainly we need to have a healthy respect for satan's limited ability. He is still powerful—too powerful for any of us to take on in our own strength. However, it seems that satan understands the power available to us better than we do. He doesn't want us to get close enough to wrestle with him because he knows that if we do, we just might lay hold of him and in the power of God knock him down for the count.

Strongholds of the Mind

The first battle we must win is the battle of the mind. Our minds are satan's primary target. He constantly bombards us with fiery barbs designed to stir up feelings of fear, discouragement, depression, inferiority, insecurity, failure, jealousy, resentment, anger, bitterness, and any number of other negative thoughts that tear down our spirits. If these thoughts take hold and are allowed to fester, they will grow into destructive mental strongholds that resist even the will and Word of God.

Edgardo Silvoso of Harvest Evangelism in Argentina says, "A stronghold is a mind-set impregnated with hopelessness that causes the believer to accept as unchangeable something that he or she knows is contrary to the will of God."[1] It is often extremely difficult to dislodge and tear down a stronghold, but it is not impossible. Listen to the words of the apostle Paul:

> For though we walk (live) in the flesh, we are not carrying on our warfare according to the flesh and using mere human weapons. For the weapons of our warfare are not physical [weapons of flesh and blood], but they are mighty before God for the overthrow and destruction of strongholds, [inasmuch as we] refute arguments and theories and reasonings and every proud and lofty thing that sets itself up against the [true] knowledge of God; and we lead every thought and purpose away captive into the obedience of Christ, (the Messiah, the Anointed One), being in readiness to punish every [insubordinate for his] disobedience, when your own submission and obedience [as a church] are fully secured and complete (2 Corinthians 10:3-6 AMP).

This is a very popular Scripture passage in circles that are always addressing the issue of pulling down demonic strongholds in the heavenlies, but that is not primarily what Paul is talking about here. Let's read the Scripture in its proper context. Paul is referring to strongholds of the mind; to philosophies and ways of thinking—"paradigms," to use a popular term of recent years. The

Greek word for "strongholds" is *ochuroma*, which means "to forti-
fy, through the idea of holding safely." Used in a figurative sense,
it means "argument."[2] Paul is speaking figuratively here. In verse
5, words such as *arguments*, *theories*, and *reasonings*, as well as
imaginations (KJV) and *speculations* (NAS), make it clear that the
realm of the mind is in view.

The words of author Dean Sherman are insightful in this
passage.

"I have heard people use the term 'strongholds' to refer
to humanism, Islam, communism, and other religions
and institutions. However, in Second Corinthians,
'strongholds' does not refer to massive, complex systems,
human or demonic. Here it refers to the strongholds of
the mind. These strongholds are castles in the air built up
in our minds through wrong thinking—through unbe-
lieving, depressed, fearful, and negative thinking.

"Two mental strongholds are extremely common today
among Christians and non-Christians alike: thoughts of
inferiority, and thoughts of condemnation.

"Inferior thoughts constantly tell us, 'You're not big
enough. You're not smart enough. You don't look good.
You're not really making it in life. You're worthless.'
These barbs keep us competing with and envying others.

"Satan also accuses, 'You're not pleasing God. You are
not spiritual enough. You do not read your Bible enough.
You're not close to God.' These thoughts make us feel as
if we can never break through into the fresh air and sun-
shine of God's approval. Some Christians live every day
of their lives in dreary condemnation. These two strongholds must be cast down through spiritual warfare, as
we refuse them and instead accept what God says about
us in the Bible."[3]

Possessing the Land Within

How do we tear down the strongholds of negative thinking that have gained a place in our minds? How do we guard ourselves against future satanic attacks in the mental realm? How do we keep our minds and hearts free? One key weapon of our warfare is walking in obedience—which requires discipline and commitment. As we yield ourselves to the Lord in obedience we develop mental discipline and learn to "lead every thought and purpose away captive into the obedience of Christ" (2 Cor. 10:5 AMP). Obedience to Christ is absolutely essential to successful warfare.

Another key to victorious warfare is the principle of allowing no common ground with the enemy. No successful army shares common ground with its enemy; it seizes territory, dispossesses the enemy, and then occupies the land. This is the principle God wanted the Israelites to follow when they entered the Promised Land. They were to destroy or drive out completely the pagan inhabitants of the land. Nothing was to remain that might open the door for moral and spiritual contamination. Israel's failure to follow this principle caused continual problems for them and was one of the reasons for their eventual downfall.

Likewise, if we want to be successful and victorious warriors and intercessors, we must allow no common ground with the devil in our minds and hearts. Anything we have in common with satan gives him a foothold, a point of entrance, or an access point from which to attack us. It may be an issue of personal sin or disobedience; or it may simply be negative strongholds of the mind where our thoughts and attitudes are influenced by the words and nature of the devil. The battles of the heart and the mind must be won *first*, before any other warfare can be undertaken. Minister and author Terry Crist expressed it this way: "If you are going to gather people for battle, you must free them from their captivity...You can't possess the land *without*, until you possess the land *within*."[4]

Possessing the land within means eliminating any mental common ground with satan. We need to have clean minds and pure hearts. Consider these Scriptures:

Who may ascend into the hill of the Lord? And who may stand in His holy place? He who has clean hands and a pure heart, who has not lifted up his soul to falsehood, and has not sworn deceitfully (Psalm 24:3-4).

Create in me a clean heart, O God, and renew a steadfast spirit within me (Psalm 51:10).

Now flee from youthful lusts, and pursue righteousness, faith, love and peace, with those who call on the Lord from a pure heart (2 Timothy 2:22).

Finally, brethren, whatever is true, whatever is honorable, whatever is right, whatever is pure, whatever is lovely, whatever is of good repute, if there is any excellence and if anything worthy of praise, let your mind dwell on these things (Philippians 4:8).

Keeping our hearts and minds clean and pure removes the common ground that we may have once had with the enemy. Dr. David Yonggi Cho explains it this way:

"The devil is just like a fly. He hates clean places. Just as we remove a dirty garbage can to keep flies from gathering around it in our homes, we should treat sins as if they were garbage cans, removing them from our hearts. If we fail to do this, we have no reason to complain of being tempted by the devil."[5]

The Law of Purification

Another critical key to successful warfare is understanding and observing the "Law of Purification."

Then Eleazar the priest said to the men of war who had gone to battle, "This is the statute of the law which the Lord has commanded Moses: only the gold and the silver, the bronze, the iron, the tin and the lead, everything that can stand the fire, you shall pass through the fire, and it shall be clean, but it shall be purified with water for impurity. But whatever cannot stand the fire you shall pass through the water. And you shall wash your clothes on the seventh day and be clean, and afterward you may enter the camp" (Numbers 31:21-24).

This is also sometimes called the "Law of Battle." Every weapon, every garment, every piece of armor or other equipment for battle must go through the fire and water of purification, both *before* battle, for preparation, and *after* battle, for cleansing. The same is true for us. As Terry Crist writes, "If you and I are going to be spiritual warriors, we must pay the price to separate ourselves through purification."[6] We need to be purified in the fire of the Holy Spirit and then washed with the water of the Word—the Bible and the truth within its pages.

As with every other area of our lives, Jesus Christ Himself is our greatest example of purification and of allowing no common ground with the enemy. On the night before He died, Jesus told His disciples, "I will not speak much more with you, for the ruler of the world is coming, and he has nothing in Me" (Jn. 14:30). What did He mean by the phrase, "he has nothing in Me"? I think the Amplified Bible makes it a little clearer.

I will not talk with you much more, for the prince (evil genius, ruler) of the world is coming. And he has no claim on Me. [He has nothing in common with Me; there is nothing in Me that belongs to him, and he has no power over Me] (John 14:30 AMP).

Satan had no power over Jesus because they shared no common ground. There was nothing in Jesus to give the devil a foothold or any kind of claim over Him. The sinless Son of God was totally separate from the author of sin and the father of lies. Again Terry Crist aptly explains it this way:

"The reason Jesus could stand in such power and authority and deal so effectively with the wicked oppressor of the nations was because no common ground existed between Him and His

adversary. When the devil struck at Jesus, there was nothing whatsoever in Him to receive the 'hit.' When satan examined Him, there was nothing for him to find. Jesus and satan had no relationship one to another, no common ground. There was nothing in Jesus that bore witness with the works of darkness! One reason so many ministers and intercessors have been spiritually 'hit' by the fiery darts of the enemy is because they have not responded to the law of purification."[7]

What about you? Are you prepared for battle? Are you walking in obedience to the Lord? Are you keeping your heart and mind clean and pure? Have you been through the purifying fire of the Spirit and the cleansing water of the Word of God? Are you ready?

Our Hands Are Not Clean

Millions of people in our world stumble along in spiritual blindness and the bondage of sin. In many regions spiritual darkness has shrouded the eyes of the masses for generations, centuries, and even millennia. There are many strongholds of demonic activity and authority that hold sway over entire people groups because curses, idolatry, immorality, greed, perversion, hatred, and many other sins established a legal basis for those demons to remain and operate. These legal rights must be removed if we are ever to see true worldwide evangelization take place.

What's more, the sad and shameful truth is that throughout the centuries the Christian Church in general, and the Western Church in particular, has done much to contribute to the current state of spiritual darkness in the world. What I mean is that across the past 2,000 years many sinful and shameful things were perpetrated against different people groups by those who supposedly were acting in the name of Christ and for the advancement of His Kingdom. The second section of this book, "Guilty Hands and Unclean Hearts," focuses in detail on some of these issues.

Consider, for example, the treatment that Jews and Muslims have received at the hands of "Christians"; how the Church has treated women, not only socially and domestically, but also regarding ministry roles in particular; how the vast majority of believers have been marginalized by the supposed "separation" between clergy and laity; how the Church in America condoned and in many cases participated in the displacement of Native Americans and the enslavement of African-Americans; and how the Church has in many ways compromised and made peace with a world characterized by greed, immorality, and idolatry. *Clearly, our hands are not clean!*

These sins of the Church have left legacies—sometimes centuries-old—of hatred, fear, suspicion, anger, bitterness, and estrangement, and these sins helped establish the legal right for demonic spirits to enter and exercise influence. Again, these legal rights must be removed if we hope to see global awakening. We must be willing, through identificational intercession, to accept responsibility for these generational sins, confess them before God, and seek His forgiveness as well as the forgiveness of those persons and groups who were wronged by the sinful attitudes and actions of our ancestors. This can remove the legal basis for the demonic powers to remain and open the way for cleansing, healing, and the outpouring of God's Spirit.

Overpowering the Strong Man

These strongholds *can* be broken. Once, when the Pharisees accused Jesus of casting out demons by demonic power, He responded by saying that a house divided against itself would fall, then asked how satan's kingdom could stand if he was divided against himself (see Lk. 11:15-19). The absurdity of their argument was plain. Then Jesus continued:

> But if I cast out demons by the finger of God, then the kingdom of God has come upon you. When a strong man, fully armed, guards his own homestead, his possessions are undisturbed;

69

but when someone stronger than he attacks him and overpowers him, he takes away from him all his armor on which he had relied, and distributes his plunder (Luke 11:20-22).

C. Peter Wagner identifies the "strong man" as referring specifically to Beelzebub, a high-ranking demonic principality and probably a territorial spirit. The term can also apply to any demonic principality. The strong man's "possessions" are unsaved people whom he strives to keep in that condition. As long as the strong man is "fully armed," his "possessions" are "undisturbed."[8] If he is overpowered, however, his "possessions" can be set free. When the demonic authority is removed, those held in bondage by him can be released into the freedom of Christ.

Who, then, is the "someone stronger" who overpowers the strong man? Most people would immediately answer, "Jesus." Jesus is certainly stronger than any demonic principality, but C. Peter Wagner says that Jesus was not referring specifically to Himself, but rather to the Holy Spirit. The key to understanding this is in the phrase "the finger of God" in verse 20. In Matthew's parallel account, Jesus says, "But if I cast out demons by the Spirit of God..." (Mt. 12:28). "The 'finger of God' is therefore a synonym for the Holy Spirit."[9] It was through the power of the Holy Spirit that Jesus cast out demons.

Where does that leave us? How are we to see removed the demonic authority that binds our cities, our nations, and our world? How are we to tear down the walls of estrangement that centuries of generational sin have erected? We are to do it the same way Jesus did—in the power of the Holy Spirit. Again, here is C. Peter Wagner:

"Only the Holy Spirit can overcome the territorial spirits, destroy their armor and release the captives under their wicked control. Where is the Holy Spirit today? He is in us who have been born again and have asked God to fill us with the Holy Spirit. Jesus' last words ever spoken directly to His disciples were, 'But you shall receive power when the Holy Spirit has come upon you; and you shall be witnesses to Me' (Acts 1:8). Here we find spiritual power tied in directly with evangelism. Jesus assured His disciples that the same power He used while on earth would be fully available to them. And it was up to them to move out and do the work of evangelism."[10]

The *same power* that Jesus used is available to us! That is truly an awesome thought! The irresistible, probing "finger of God" can uproot and cast out all demonic powers and principalities—no matter how strong they are—and bring healing to the nations. That "finger" is in each of us as believers, and through the power of the Spirit we can see territorial demonic authority over our cities and nations removed. There is much to confess and forgive, and there is much restitution to be made.

The finger of God is at work in our world as never before, and I say, "Let it come!" I make this appeal, however: Let us pray that the finger of God will come first to us inwardly and bring cleansing. Then we can arise in the strength of the Lord and, "having done everything, to stand firm" (Eph. 6:13) against the powers of darkness in the great name of Jesus! *Just point out the sin, Lord, and we will wage war through personal and identificational repentance.* We can remove the legal basis that allows the demonic forces of the air to remain by letting the finger of the Holy Spirit point into and pierce our hearts and remove the common ground we have held with the enemy personally and generationally.

We have sinned! Father, forgive us! Let the finger of God come! Remove the common ground!

Reflection Questions

1. What areas do you have in common with the enemy that you want cleansed in the blood of Jesus?

2. What are some of the wisdom issues that all intercessors need to learn and apply?

3. What personally spoke to you (touched or convicted your heart) through this chapter, "No Common Ground Allowed!"?

Recommended Reading

Engaging the Enemy by C. Peter Wagner (Regal Books, 1991)

Ridding Your Home of Spiritual Darkness by Chuck Pierce and Rebecca Wagner Systema (Wagner Institute for Practical Learning, 1999)

Endnotes

1. Cindy Jacobs, *Possessing the Gates of the Enemy: A Training Manual for Militant Intercession* (Grand Rapids, Michigan: Chosen Books, 1991), 102.
2. James Strong, *Strong's Exhaustive Concordance of the Bible* (Peabody, Massachusetts: Hendrickson Publishers, n.d.), **ochuroma**, #G3749.
3. Dean Sherman, *Spiritual Warfare for Every Christian: How to Live in Victory and Retake the Land* (Seattle, Washington: YWAM Publishing, 1990), 44-45.
4. Terry Crist, *Interceding Against the Powers of Darkness* (Tulsa, Oklahoma: Terry Crist Ministries, 1990), 19.
5. Paul [David] Yonggi Cho, *Daniel: Insight on the Life and Dreams of the Prophet From Babylon* (Lake Mary, Florida: Creation House, 1990), 123.
6. Crist, *Interceding*, 18.
7. Crist, *Interceding*, 20-21.
8. C. Peter Wagner, *Confronting the Powers: How the New Testament Church Experienced the Power of Strategic-Level Spiritual Warfare* (Ventura, California: Regal Books, 1996), 149-150.
9. Wagner, *Confronting the Powers*, 149.
10. Wagner, *Confronting the Powers*, 152.

Section II

Guilty Hands and Unclean Hearts

Chapter 5

The Separation
of "Clergy" and "Laity"

arly one morning in April 1994, the Lord gave me a prophetic word in which He said, "*I am coming to wage war against the control spirit and every hindrance that holds My Church at arm's length from the presence and power of My Spirit.*"

The "control spirit" originated in the heart of satan, who aspired to bring all of Heaven under his personal rule. Selfish at its very heart, such a spirit disregards human free will and strives to dominate people and subject them to another's will and authority. It even dares to try to seize the things of God and bring them under human regulation and control. The control spirit has plagued us as a race ever since Adam and Eve tried to grab God's good gifts in Eden and turn them to their own selfish advantage.

Throughout history this propensity of man's fallen nature, fueled by the demonic forces of darkness specifically in the form of a control spirit, has been responsible for wars, oppression, subjugation and enslavement of entire nations under repressive rulers and regimes, "ethnic cleansing," and the genocide of millions of people. This destructive desire to control, dominate, and manipulate others is an innate part of our sinful nature and is the complete antithesis of life in the Kingdom of God and of everything He desires for us. Our Lord established His Church to be a community that would live in the world but operate under heavenly principles. Unfortunately, almost from the beginning the control spirit has been a problem in the Church as well as in the world. Consider these biblical examples.

Simon, a former magician in Samaria and a recent convert to Christ, was roundly condemned by Peter when he tried to buy from Peter and John the power to impart the Holy Spirit through the laying on of hands, as they did (see Acts 8:9-24). Simon was possibly influenced by a control spirit through which he sought Divine power and authority for his own benefit.

In Third John 9-10 the apostle writes of Diotrephes, a man in the church "who loves to be first among them," who challenged apostolic authority, forced his will and way on others in the church, and expelled those who disagreed with him. This is a classic example of self-ambition in the heart of man fueled by a demonic darkness often called a control spirit.

Paul and the other apostles had to contend repeatedly with a control spirit in the form of Judaizers. These were Jewish believers who taught and insisted that Gentile believers had to submit to and obey the Jewish law in order to be saved. This problem agitated the mostly Gentile church in Antioch to such a degree that they sent a delegation (led by Paul and Barnabas) to iron things out with the leaders of the church in Jerusalem. Later, when relating this trip in his letter to the Galatians, Paul described the troublemakers as "false brethren who had sneaked in to spy out our liberty which we have in Christ Jesus, in order to bring us into bondage" (Gal. 2:4). Some of you are saying, "Ouch!" by now. But sometimes truth hurts before it heals.

Freedom or Bondage?

A few years ago an amazing thing happened to me—I had eight dreams in one night, all on the same subject: the control spirit. In the last dream, I was handed a piece of paper, and I could read the scribbling on it. It stated, *"There are two roots to the control spirit: fear and unbelief."* That dream stunned me as I was awakened out of it. Ever since then I have sought the Lord to bring personal cleansing to me and have lifted up a cry in behalf of the Body of Christ, *"Forgive us, Father, for we have sinned!"*

A control spirit always brings bondage in its wake; those who allow it to have free reign in their lives trade their spiritual freedom in Christ for the chains of slavery to the will and opinions of men. This is contrary both to the will of Christ, who said, "If you abide in My word...you shall know the truth, and the truth shall make you *free*" (Jn. 8:31-32), and to the purpose of the Holy Spirit: "Now the Lord is the Spirit; and where the Spirit of the Lord is, there is *liberty*" (2 Cor. 3:17). Let me rephrase this, if you will allow me: "Where the Spirit is Lord, there is liberty." You see, we have a problem today. The Holy Spirit thinks He is God! Yes, you heard me right; our problem is not first with the devil. Our first problem is selfish ambition, fear, and unbelief in our hearts. Our next problem is that God is opposing us. Our last problem in reality is the demonic energy that locks up the masses into the state of being the "frozen chosen."

The truth of the matter is that for most of its history the Church has struggled with a controlling mind and heart that have appeared in any number of different manifestations. One of the most tragic of these, as well as one of the most costly in its consequences, is the centuries-old separation between "clergy" and "laity." This false distinction has marginalized the majority of Christians in almost every generation, leaving vast resources of human energy and devotion virtually untapped due to fear of entrusting the gifts, message, and ministry of the Church to the "unqualified" masses. Making matters worse, not only have those masses been afforded few opportunities to develop and use their gifts in ministry, but most of them also have lived their entire lives ignorant of their place and position in Christ as heirs of God as well as of God's purpose for them as fully functioning members of the Body of Christ.

From the very beginning Christ's will and design for His Church was for every believer to be a priest with a prophetic spirit on his or her life (see 1 Pet. 2:9). The purpose of the fivefold ministry gifts of Ephesians 4:11-13 was (and still is) to equip *all* the saints for the work of the ministry and to *build up* the Church into full maturity in Christ. Sadly, for most of its history the Church has not walked fully in these truths. As a result, the Church's witness to the world has been weak, the Church itself has been divided, and the fulfillment of Christ's command to evangelize the world has been hindered. For God's sake, may this change!

How did this happen? How did a Church founded on freedom in Christ and liberty in the Spirit end up bound in the shackles of a control spirit that has severely restricted most of its members from active involvement? A brief survey of Church history will shed some needed light.

Led by the Spirit

From the Day of Pentecost through its first few generations, the Church that Jesus Christ established had an infectious, spontaneous quality and was characterized by explosive growth throughout every region of the Roman Empire. This was due to the undeniable living presence of Christ in His Body through the Holy Spirit. In his excellent book, *Floods Upon the Dry Ground*, Charles P. Schmitt writes:

> "The most outstanding characteristics of the Church have always been the manifest presence and dynamic activity of Jesus Christ in its midst....And in the first century, Christ was manifestly present in His people! On the day of Pentecost He again came to them from His ascended glory in the power of His outpoured Spirit. By that Spirit He was active in them, spontaneously continuing to do His works and continuing to unfold His teachings through them as His Body....The resurrected Christ,

by the power of His Holy Spirit, was simply free to be Himself in His Church! In His Body He freely lived and moved and had His being."[1]

Simon Peter wrote of the Church, "You are a chosen race, a royal priesthood, a holy nation, a people for God's own possession..." (1 Pet. 2:9). The word *you* is all-inclusive, referring to *every* believer, not just a handful of select leader elites. In the Kingdom of God, we are *all* priests.

Christian believers are "the called-out ones"—an assembly of people who have been called into the spiritual family of God through faith in Christ as Savior and Lord. The Greek word for "church" is *ekklesia*, and it literally means "called out." In classical Greek *ekklesia* referred to a body of *free* citizens called together by a herald to an assembly for the purpose of dealing democratically with matters of common concern. The first Christians recognized themselves as "called out by God in Jesus Christ for a special purpose" and with a privileged status in Christ.[2]

Perhaps the most distinguishing characteristics of the New Testament Church were the unique love and unity that bound the believers together. Wherever the leadership of the Holy Spirit held sway, the presence of Christ in their midst removed man-made barriers and distinctions. In the Church all believers were *equal* in their inheritance; they were "one in Christ Jesus" (Gal. 3:28). No matter what their background, believers were bound together by "one Lord, one faith, one baptism" (Eph. 4:5) in the "unity of the Spirit in the bond of peace" (Eph. 4:3). They operated under the power of the Spirit, exercising spiritual gifts distributed to each of them by the Spirit as He willed (see 1 Cor. 12:1-11) and working together as many members of one Body (see 1 Cor. 12:12-31).

Christian historian Rufus M. Jones described life in the early Church this way:

"While this mystical stage of primitive Christianity lasted, the fellowship was an organism rather than an organization. The members had a common experience....They

79

were baptized into one Spirit....There was no rigid system. 'Custom' laid no heavy hand on anyone. Routine and sacred order had not come yet. There was large scope for spontaneity and personal initiative. Persons and gifts counted for everything. Procedure was fluid and not yet pattern-stamped and standardized. There was a place for the independent variable....No leader dominated the group meetings. No program was essential. The little body met as a community of the Spirit;...The exercises were charismatic, that is, due to the display of 'spiritual gifts' possessed by those who were present....They walked in the Spirit...a single body, a unified fellowship."[3]

Priests and Ministers

The early Church made no distinction between "clergy" and "laity." Any individual believer's position or function was determined by the spiritual gifts that were manifested in his or her life. Since every believer was a priest, every believer had direct access to the throne of God, could interpret the Word of God as the Spirit gave him understanding, and was directly responsible to God for his life and behavior. A priest ministers to God and to others in God's name. The priesthood of the believer means that *every* believer is a *minister*. Everyone who is called to Christ is called to the *ministry*.

According to Philip Schaff, a Church historian of the nineteenth century, the ministerial "office" was instituted by Christ and inaugurated by the Spirit at Pentecost as the "regular organ of the kingly power of Christ on earth in founding, maintaining, and extending the church." One's call and moral qualification came from the Spirit and had to be recognized and ratified by the church. "Yet, high as the sacred office is in its divine origin and import, it was separated by no impassable chasm from the body of believers. The Jewish and later Catholic antithesis of clergy and laity has no place in the apostolic age."[4]

80

Regarding the reference in First Peter 2:9 to a "royal priest-hood," Schaff states:

"It is remarkable, that Peter in particular should present the idea of the priesthood as the destiny of all, and apply the term…not to the ministerial order as distinct from the laity, but to the community; thus regarding every Christian congregation as a spiritual tribe of Levi, a peculiar people, holy to the Lord."[5]

Schaff concludes that "the temporal organization of the empirical church is to be a means (and not a hindrance, as it often is) for the actualization of the ideal republic of God when all Christians shall be prophets, priests, and kings, and fill all time and all space with his praise."[6]

Now, I do not want to bore some of you by overemphasizing minute details or by being overly technical. But bear with me for a while as I unfold some important concepts and views. I believe that the *institutional* Church was supposed to *enable* every member to function as a priest and minister; that was the ideal. Although that was the general pattern and character of the first-century Church, it never functioned correctly because of human sin and imperfection. With the passing of the first generation of Christians, however, a gradual change occurred in the attitude, organization, and governmental structure of the Church.

There were two main reasons for this change: the decline of the manifest presence of the Spirit in the lives of believers and the rise of dangerous heretical teachings that threatened the Church. Of the first, Lutheran historian Lars P. Qualben writes, "The enthusiastic prophetic element in early Christian life was gradually being replaced by a growing formalism in teaching and in worship….The specially 'gifted' became fewer….Instead of the immediate gifts of the Spirit, Christians rather relied on organizations and outward religious authority."[7]

The effort to combat heresy and false teachings was the second reason for the gradual shift away from the priesthood of every believer toward the separation of the "priests" (clergy) and the laity. Heresy was an early and continuing problem in the Church, and its presence caused Church leaders to recognize the importance of clarifying and establishing correct doctrinal teaching so that the congregations could distinguish between the true gospel and the false. This was and of course is an important issue. But when "fear of error" is the overriding motivation behind our reasoning, we will err. Gradually the churches developed the attitude that such teaching could be better accomplished if only one person was the recognized authority in each church. From this it was only a small step to adorning these individuals with *official* status as *clergy* (chosen ones) distinct from the *laity* (the masses).

Subtle Changes

The churches of the New Testament were led by "elders" (Greek, *presbuteros*) who were appointed by an apostle, apostolic team, or someone acting on an apostle's behalf (see Acts 14:23; Tit. 1:5), and they were referred to also as "overseers" (Greek, *episkopos*) or "bishops" (KJV, see Phil. 1:1). Each church had a council or college of elders providing leadership; there is no clear indication in the New Testament of any church being led or governed by a singular elder or bishop. This was already beginning to change by the end of the first century. Nevertheless, the New Testament pattern was team ministry. So stay with me as we expose and iron out some of the wrinkles in Church history.

Clement of Rome (c. A.D. 30–100) was the earliest of the post-apostolic writers and the first to suggest a distinction between clergy and laity. A disciple of Peter and probably a co-worker with Paul (see Phil. 4:3), Clement eventually became the leader of the church in Rome. He was so highly regarded in the early Church that his letter to the Corinthians, which was read aloud in many of the assemblies, was even included in one of the most ancient collections of the canon of Scripture.[8] Clement still understood a church to be governed by a college of elders, and he recognized only two offices in a church: bishops (which were synonymous with elders) and deacons. However, he identified these church leaders as "priests," thereby becoming "one of the first to distinguish between 'clergy' and 'laity,' a clear departure from the apostolic understanding of the priesthood of the whole Church."[9]

Polycarp, another post-apostolic leader and personal disciple of the apostle John, became the leader of the church at Smyrna and died a martyr's death around the middle of the second century. In a letter he wrote to the Philippian church he refers to presbyters and deacons as the only officers in the church. Like Clement, he also refers to the presbyters as "priests," thus making a subtle distinction between clergy and laity.[10]

Ignatius (A.D. 30–107), the "bishop" of Antioch, while on his way to a martyr's death in Rome, wrote seven letters to various churches in which he took the distinctive step of appealing to *one specific person* in each church whom he regarded as the *bishop* of that church, and exhorted the members of the congregations to be subject to their bishop and to the elders under him. Ignatius encouraged them to look upon their bishop as they would on *Christ Himself*,[11] and that the bishop presided in the *place of God*.[12]

These three examples illustrate the subtle shift in practice that was beginning to take place even before the end of the first century. Historian Lars P. Qualben sums it up this way:

"But the early church organization was not centered in office and in law, but in the special gifts of the Spirit....Toward the close of the first Christian century a change took place. A general lack of confidence in the special gifts of the Spirit, a desire for more specific order, and a pressing demand for proper safeguard against heresy resulted in a gradual transfer of the preaching, the teaching, and the administration of the Sacraments from the 'gifted men' to the local elders....The official functions were now performed by elders only. The ministry of the Word and the Sacraments became official, which marked the beginning of the division of the Christians into 'clergy' (chosen ones) and 'laity' (the masses)."[13]

This evolution of control continued over the next couple of centuries until authority in the churches became vested in one person, the "bishop," without whom no official or valid act of the congregation could be performed. This became the "normal" pattern for church structure and authority, which in many sectors of the Body of Christ has remained pretty much the same until our own day.

I hope it is clear by now that the separation between the clergy and laity that is so familiar to most of us was *not* the practice of the New Testament Church but a later development in a Church that was experiencing spiritual decline. Subsequent Church history is filled with evidence of the devastating effects that such a control spirit has had not only on the Church itself, but also on the peoples and nations that the Church has sought to reach with the gospel.

Left unchecked, a control spirit can cripple and even destroy a church. So how do we deal with it? How can we keep it from taking over? It is primarily a heart issue. The key is learning how to *release* rather than hold on; how to give back to God what He has given to us. It's an issue of faith and trust and of having a revelation of grace and mercy. These little keys will unlock the prison door that has held and continues to hold hundreds of thousands of God's people at arm's distance from the presence and power of His Spirit. Two biblical examples will help us understand what I mean.

No Greater Burden

When Paul and Barnabas and their companions arrived in Jerusalem from Antioch to resolve the Judaizer question, "the apostles and the elders came together to look into this matter" (Acts 15:6). After much debate, including testimonies from Peter, Paul, and Barnabas of the great work God was doing among the Gentiles, the council acknowledged the essential equality between Jewish and Gentile believers—that they were all "saved through the grace of the Lord Jesus" (Acts 15:11)—and that God had a purpose for the Gentiles that was much greater and broader than many in the Jerusalem church had realized at first (see Acts 15:7-31).

The council drafted a letter relating its conclusions and sent it to Antioch by way of a joint delegation consisting of Paul and Barnabas as well as Judas and Silas from the Jerusalem church—a visual symbol of the unity that had been reached. The "meat" of the letter read, "For it seemed good to the Holy Spirit and to us to lay upon you no greater burden than these essentials: that you abstain from things sacrificed to idols and from blood and from things strangled and from fornication; if you keep yourselves free from such things, you will do well. Farewell" (Acts 15:28-29).

Since at this time the mostly Jewish church in Jerusalem was still the largest and most influential church, it would have been easy for the apostles and elders to give in to a control spirit and attitude and try to force the Gentile believers to conform to Jewish standards and expectations. They did not do this, however; the Spirit of God in the heart of man won out. Under the leadership of the Holy Spirit, they let go of their prejudices and their preconceptions and *released* their Gentile brethren into the fullness of their freedom in Christ. In the years that followed, the churches at Antioch and later Ephesus became vibrant centers of evangelism and ministry through which all the known Gentile world was reached with the gospel.

My Father's Business

Probably no other people who ever walked the face of the earth went through a greater test of the control spirit than Mary and Joseph, the earthly parents of Jesus. Entrusted with the care and raising of the Son of God during His childhood, they then had to release Him to fulfill the purpose of His heavenly Father. They fed Him, clothed Him, taught Him the Scriptures, and took Him to the synagogue; Joseph even trained Him as a carpenter. Then, when the time was right, they who had raised Jesus as a son had to acknowledge Him as the Savior. Imagine that test! I think most of us would have flunked that one.

Their first real test came when Jesus was 12 years old. It was the Feast of the Passover and Jesus and His parents had made their usual pilgrimage to Jerusalem. After the festival was over, Mary and Joseph began the return trip to Nazareth, not knowing that Jesus had stayed behind in Jerusalem. Discovering after a day's journey that Jesus was not with them, Mary and Joseph hurried back to Jerusalem (see Lk. 2:41-45). After three days of searching, they found Jesus in the temple, "sitting in the midst of the teachers, both listening to them, and asking them questions" (Lk. 2:46). Although they were undoubtedly relieved, I can imagine that Mary's voice held more than a little exasperation as she said to Jesus, "Son, why have You treated us this way? Behold, Your father and I have been anxiously looking for You" (Lk. 2:48).

Jesus' reply was an indicator that things were beginning to change in His relationship with them. "And He said unto them, How is it that ye sought Me? wist [know] ye not that I must be about My Father's business?" (Lk. 2:49 KJV) Don't you imagine that as a father Joseph was cut to his heart by those words? Certainly Joseph loved God and knew that Jesus was God's Son with a Divine mission to fulfill, but he still must have felt a painful tug in the very depths of his being. I'm sure that Mary must have hurt deeply inside as well. After all, for 12 years Jesus had been "her" son, and now she was painfully reminded of what she had always known: He was God's Son and had a higher call and a prior allegiance. Even though Jesus returned to Nazareth with them and remained in subjection to them until He was fully of age, the first test had come. Mary and Joseph had to begin letting go of the controls and release Jesus to fulfill the purpose of His Father.

Mary's ultimate test came at the cross when she faced the challenge in her heart of giving back to God that which the one-time greatest event of all history had given to her. As a mother, she may have wanted to hold on to her baby—God's baby—but she had to let Him go and release Him to the Father. Three days later an even greater event for history took place when Jesus rose from the dead, killing death itself and winning forever forgiveness and eternal life for all who would repent and believe—including Mary herself.

Releasing the Church

As Christians at the beginning of the third millennium since Christ, we struggle with a legacy almost as old that says that the gifts, ministries, and service of the Church are reserved only for the "clergy"—the chosen, the elite, the trained, the "ordained"—whatever you want to call them. For years we have put too much emphasis on the concept of "going into full-time Christian service" (as opposed to "serving Christ" part-time?!), as if the only people who are *really* serving the Lord are those who devote all their time to the "professional" ministry. This is a completely false concept that is entirely foreign to the New Testament. Frankly, I want to see this mind-set which freezes people into passivity and inactivity, be destroyed. The fact is, *all* Christians are called to "full-time" Christian service, but this does not necessarily mean a full-time *vocation* in professional ministry. It means that Christ has called us to serve Him all the time in every walk of life, every day, everywhere we go, and in everything we do. We each have a destiny to fulfill!

The apostle Paul preached, established churches, and carried the gospel from one end of the Roman Empire to the other, but in one sense he was not a member of the "professional clergy." Paul made part of his living as a tentmaker (see Acts 18:1-3). There is scant evidence in the New Testament of *any* church leaders making their living as "professional" church workers. Paid, full-time ministers are a development of a later day.

Don't misunderstand me; I am not bashing professional clergy here (I am one)! And I am not promoting anarchy or just "doing what is right in our own eyes." What I am saying is that *there are no second-class citizens in the Kingdom of God!* Biblically, there is *no* hierarchy in the Church that you have to pass through to commune with Papa God. I'm a bit tired of the tier mentality: who is on the "church staff" and who is not; who is "gifted" and who is not; who is "called" and who is not. That sounds like spiritual downlines instead of the priesthood of all believers. *All* of us are called and gifted to serve Christ together and build the Kingdom of God.

One of the major hindrances to revival is that we have regulated, restricted, controlled, and limited who can do what in the Church rather than releasing people to function in the gifts, ministries, and service that Christ has called them to. Out of fear and unbelief and the desire to keep things "under control," we have forgotten the spirit (if not the words) of Jesus' commands: "Go [literally, 'having gone'] into all the world and preach the gospel to all creation....And these signs will accompany those who have believed..." (Mk. 16:15,17a); and "Go [literally, 'going therefore,' or 'as you go'] therefore and make disciples of all the nations..." (Mt. 28:19a).

The "fivefold ministry" gifts of apostle, prophet, evangelist, pastor, and teacher were given "for the equipping of the saints for the work of service, to the building up of the body of Christ" (Eph. 4:12). There are two dimensions here: an internal dimension of serving and building up each other as members of Christ's Body and an external dimension of serving others in Christ's name and building His Body by bringing lost people into His Kingdom. Success in either dimension requires *all* the saints to be equipped and functioning in ministry, not just the elite "chosen few." So, let's just do it for Jesus' sake!

New Paradigms for a New Millennium

Now let's touch another "sacred cow" for a moment. There is a long-standing mentality in much of the Church that says that unless you are "paid clergy" you do not or cannot function in the fivefold ministry gifts, or that you have to be someone "special" to operate in the Spirit. Frankly, that's "religious" hogwash! I am convinced that the Lord wants to shatter that mentality and turn our understanding upside down on this! Nowhere does the Word of God say that you cannot move in the gifts of healing and work at New York Life! Nowhere does the Bible teach that only the "well-educated" and the "ordained" can prophesy or preach the gospel!

The biblical pattern is "as you go, preach; as you go, make disciples." The world will never be won for Christ as long as the anointing stays within the four walls of the church building. God wants to break down those walls and pour out a great "market-place anointing." He wants to release a mighty army to carry the presence of Christ into the schools, the factories, and the public arena; He wants an army of anointed carpenters, chefs, and bus drivers; teachers, mechanics, and secretaries; doctors, lawyers, and engineers. There are new marketplace paradigms of the Kingdom of God emerging as we begin this new millennium.

In a 1998 interview about the Church in transition, Graham Cooke of United Christian Ministries in Southampton, England, had this to say about what God is doing in the Church today:

"He's messing with our structures, He's creating new paradigms and new prototypes of church, and He's wanting us...to put the church back into His control....We're heading to a place where God does fully own the Body of Christ and leadership does become what they should be...a broken group of people laying down their lives before God, taking on that father's anointing to release and empower and equip the Body of Christ to be what God wants them to be....

"A lot of leaders cling to their titles like apostle, prophet, bishop, reverend, minister, pastor; and those are not titles, they are functions. There is no hierarchy in the Body of Christ....In Scripture there are only three titles that God gives us:...servant...steward...bondslave. So you get promoted to different levels. You start off as a general servant. Then you get promoted down to being a steward. The critical issue with stewardship...is that when God begins to give you things as a steward, are you going to become a steward of those things for Him, or an owner of those things for yourself? Many leaders right now have an ownership grip on church, and not a stewardship grip on church."[14]

It is time for the "clergy-laity" mentality to let go of the controls and release *all* the saints (ordinary, everyday believers) of the Lord into their God-given places of ministry and service. For

89

many centuries members of the clergy and others in the hierarchy of church government have wrongfully repressed and held back millions of believers from reaching out to claim their rightful place in Kingdom work. As a member of the "clergy" I say, *"We have sinned! Father, forgive us!"* To all of you "marketplace people"— those who are trying every day to be "real" for Christ in the "real" world—I ask you to forgive us, the "clergy," for this great sin against you! Forgive us for holding you back, for not trusting you with the Spirit's anointing, for fearing that your impact could be greater than ours, and not allowing you to reach out for the fullness of your life in Christ!

Father, forgive us! Body of Christ, forgive us!

Reflection Questions

1. What does the term, *control spirit*, mean to you?

2. What is one of the barriers on the part of church leadership that hinders them from empowering the laity to do "the work of ministry"?

3. What is one of the barriers on the part of the laity that hinders them from taking their position in the world of being salt and light in society?

Recommended Reading

Floods Upon the Dry Ground by Charles Schmitt (Revival Press, 1998)

Images of Revival by Richard and Kathryn Riss (Revival Press, 1997)

Loving Monday by John D. Beckett (InterVarsity Press, 1998)

Endnotes

1. Charles P. Schmitt, *Floods Upon the Dry Ground* (Shippensburg, Pennsylvania: Revival Press, 1998), 4, 8.

2. Harold S. Songer, "Church," *Holman Bible Dictionary*, 1991. *Quick-Verse 4.0 Deluxe Bible Reference Collection*. CD-ROM. Parsons Technology, 1992–1996.

3. Rufus M. Jones, as quoted in Schmitt, *Floods Upon the Dry Ground*, 7-8.

4. Philip Schaff, *History of the Christian Church*, Vol. 1 (New York: Charles Scribner's Sons, 1882). Christian Classics Ethereal Library. 13 August 1999. <http://www.ccel.org/s/schaff/history/1_ch10.htm>.

5. Schaff, *History of the Christian Church*.

6. Schaff, *History of the Christian Church*.

7. Lars P. Qualben, *A History of the Christian Church* (New York: Thomas Nelson and Sons, 1933), 86, 96, as quoted in Schmitt, *Floods Upon the Dry Ground*, 16.

8. Schmitt, *Floods Upon the Dry Ground*, 23.

9. Schmitt, *Floods Upon the Dry Ground*, 23.

10. Schmitt, *Floods Upon the Dry Ground*, 24.

11. Ignatius, "The Epistle of Ignatius to the Ephesians," *The Ante-Nicene Fathers*, Vol. 1. Christian Classics Ethereal Library. 16 August 1999. <http://www.ccel.org/fathers2/ANF-01/anf01-16.htm#P1106_207779>.

12. Ignatius, "The Epistle of Ignatius to the Magnesians," *The Ante-Nicene Fathers*, Vol. 1. Christian Classics Ethereal Library. 16 August 1999. <http://www.ccel.org/fathers2/ANF-01/anf01-17.htm#P1394_249090>.

13. Qualben, *A History of the Christian Church*, 94-95, as quoted in Schmitt, *Floods Upon the Dry Ground*, 27.

14. Graham Cooke, "The Transitioning Church: Where Are We Now." Interview, April 21, 1998 (Greshem, Oregon: Second Wind, 1998).

Chapter 6

The Gender Gap

$\mathfrak{I}$t is my conviction that, historically, women are the most oppressed people group on the face of the earth. Although we acknowledge that this is certainly true in Muslim, Hindu, and many other non-Christian cultures, the tragic reality is that it is also true in the history of the Church. Much of the domination and subjugation of women in Western culture through the ages has been done in the name of Christ! *Father, forgive us!*

Great harm has been done to the Church and to the cause of the Kingdom of God in the earth because Christian women traditionally have been relegated to second-class status in the Body of Christ. According to Dr. Fuchsia Pickett, noted preacher, teacher, and author,

> "It is difficult to estimate the damage that has been done to the Body of Christ because of prejudice against gender. What giftings, ministries, consolations, and virtues have been inadvertently robbed from the Church because of strong prejudicial discrimination against the female gender. And what overt harm has been perpetrated on the Church because of women's harsh reactions against the

93

limitations placed upon them that frustrated their expression of the giftings of God in their lives."[1]

In his powerful book, *The Three Prejudices,* pastor Kelley Varner writes,

"Men are afraid of women. Women are afraid to be women. Great male preachers won't let females preach, dismissing them to the prayer room or nursery. At the same time these men unabashedly refer to themselves as the Bride of Christ!...

"The primary cause of male-female prejudice is insecurity, and the root of this weakness is the spirit of fear. Men and women are paranoid because they are unschooled in the Word of God. The Scriptures reveal the unique, divinely ordained roles of each gender. Outside of the knowledge of these truths, a great wall exists."[2]

What general, in going to war, would order 60 percent of his army to stay home? Yet, in effect this is exactly what happens so often in the life of the Church. Some years ago I read that 60 percent of all church members are women and that 80 percent of all intercessors are women. Does it not make sense then that we should recognize and release the largest part of God's army to wage war on His behalf and minister to a lost world in His name?

Author Paul K. Jewett framed the question this way:

"If...women are [no] less capable than men of piety, zeal, learning and whatever else seems necessary for the [ministry], then why...should the church not draw on the huge reserves which could pour into the priesthood if women were here, as in so many professions, put on the same footing with men?"[3]

That is an excellent question!

Can God Use a Woman?

It's hard for me to understand why women have been suppressed in the Church for so long, since the New Testament makes it clear that women were at the forefront of the birth and growth of the Church. Consider these Bible statistics:

- A Samaritan woman was one of the first to proclaim the gospel when she told the people of her village about Jesus (see Jn. 4:25-29,39).

- It was women who were the last to leave the cross (Jesus' disciples scattered when He was arrested). They also were the ones who watched to see where Jesus was buried (see Mk. 15:40-41,47).

- It was women who were the first to come to Jesus' tomb on the third day (see Mt. 28:1; Mk. 16:1-2; Lk. 23:55–24:1).

- It was women who were the first to declare that Christ was risen (see Mt. 28:5-10; Mk. 16:9-10; Lk. 24:5-10; Jn. 20:18).

- Women were part of the group in the upper room who "were continually devoting themselves to prayer" (Acts 1:14) in preparation for the outpouring of the Holy Spirit on the Day of Pentecost.

- It was a woman, Lydia, who was the first to respond to the gospel in Europe (see Acts 16:14).

In First Peter 3:7 the apostle charges Christian husbands to live with their wives "in an understanding way, as with a weaker vessel," but also to give them honor as a "fellow heir of the grace of life." "Fellow heir" certainly suggests equality, but what does Peter mean by "weaker vessel"? I don't believe that he is talking about a woman's physical strength, mental capabilities, or endurance; studies in recent years have demonstrated that women are equal to and often surpass men in any of these areas. No, I believe that Peter is referring to the woman's weaker social position of dependency—the trust she must place in someone else. This was certainly true for women in the society of Peter's day.

"Weakness" is not a liability in God's Kingdom; on the contrary, it is an *asset.* "God has chosen the foolish things of the world to shame the wise, and God has chosen the weak things of the world to shame the things which are strong" (1 Cor. 1:27). God has used many "weak" things to accomplish His purposes; the following is only a short list:

- a rod (see Ex. 4:2-4,17)
- an ass (see Num. 22:28)
- a ram's horn (see Josh. 6:5)
- an oxgoad (see Judg. 3:31)
- a tent peg—in the hand of a woman!—(see Judg. 4:21)
- a barley cake (see Judg. 7:13)
- clay pitchers (see Judg. 7:20)
- a millstone (see Judg. 9:53)
- the jawbone of an ass (see Judg. 15:15-16)
- ravens (see 1 Kings 17:4)
- a mantle (see 2 Kings 2:8)
- a jar of oil and empty vessels (see 2 Kings 4:2-7)
- a wind, a fish, a gourd, and a worm (see Jon. 1:4,17; 4:6-7)
- a cock (see Mk. 14:72)

Is it not possible, then, that God could use a woman? After all, if we get honest, we are all a bunch of "cracked pots"!

I am convinced that much of the Church's "traditional" view and attitude toward the role of women in the Body of Christ is at odds with the teaching of the Word of God. However, it is not my goal in this book to deal with this subject from the technical angle of detailed Scripture analysis and Greek word studies; many books are already available that do that much better than I could here. Instead, I want to present several clear examples both from

Scripture and from the history of the Church of women in ministerial and leadership roles.[4] As for me and my house—may humble yet bold, submissive yet powerful, gifted yet ethical women on
the front lines emerge once again!

Women of Faith in the Old Testament

Deborah (Judg. 4:1–5:31). Called both a prophetess and a judge,
Deborah lived around 1200 B.C.,[5] early in the time between Israel's
entrance into the Promised Land under Joshua and the establishment of the monarchy under Saul. "Now Deborah, a prophetess,
the wife of Lappidoth, was judging Israel at that time....and the
sons of Israel came up to her for judgment" (Judg. 4:4-5). This
means that she heard and decided cases brought to her by the people of Israel.[6]

At this time Israel had been under Canaanite oppression for
20 years (see Judg. 4:2-3). Under prophetic inspiration Deborah
told Barak, an Israelite general, that God would deliver the
Canaanites into his hand. At Barak's insistence, Deborah accompanied him to the battle, but she told him that Sisera, the Canaanite general, would be delivered into the hands of a woman (see
Judg. 4:6-9). The Israelites routed the Canaanites. Sisera fled on
foot and was killed by a woman named Jael, who drove a tent peg
through the side of his head as he slept (see Judg. 4:10-21). After
this great victory, Israel enjoyed peace for 40 years (see Judg. 5:31).

> "Deborah is described in Judges 5:7 as 'a mother in Israel'
> because of her role in delivering God's people....Some
> scholars believe that Deborah as a prophetess also com-
> posed the victory poem she and Barak sang in Judges 5.
> Deborah's authority under God was evidenced by
> Barak's desire to have her present with him in the army
> camp and by the testimony to her leadership in the song."[7]

This remarkable woman truly was an anointed servant of
God who led her people with courage and faith.

Huldah (2 Kings 22:14-20; 2 Chron. 34:22-28). Josiah, a godly king of Judah, was in the midst of carrying out sweeping spiritual reforms throughout the nation (see 2 Chron. 34:1-7). During the cleaning of the temple in preparation for repairing it, a copy of the Law of Moses was discovered (see 2 Chron. 34:8-15). Apparently, the people had turned so far away from God that most of them did not even know what the Law of Moses said. When it was read to Josiah, he tore his clothes in sorrow and repentance for how the people had disobeyed God (see 2 Chron. 34:16-19). He then ordered some of his advisers and servants to "inquire of the Lord for me and for those who are left in Israel and in Judah" (2 Chron. 34:21a).

For this important assignment the servants of the king sought out a *prophetess* named Huldah. Huldah prophesied that because the people of Judah had forsaken God and disobeyed His commands, great evil and judgment would come upon them. However, because Josiah had sought the Lord and been faithful to Him, God would delay this judgment until after Josiah's death so that he could go to his grave in peace (see 2 Chron. 34:22-28). A few years later Josiah died in battle and after a brief succession of evil kings, Judah was conquered by the Babylonians.

Brief as this reference is, Huldah's example is clear proof that the word of the Lord was given to *women* as well as to men and that their prophetic word was respected, even in a patriarchal society such as Israel.

Esther (The Book of Esther). The story of Esther dates from the time of Israel's exile and captivity. Esther was a Jewish orphan girl who was raised by her cousin, Mordecai, and who was later chosen to be queen to Ahasuerus, king of Persia. At the time of her coronation Ahasuerus did not know that Esther was Jewish, and she did not tell him, per instructions from Mordecai.

Haman, the prime minister, was a vain and evil-hearted man who harbored a deep hatred for the Jews, and especially for Mordecai, who refused to give him due homage. He hatched a plot to destroy the Jews—he induced the king to sign a decree that mandated death for anyone who would not bow to Haman. With this decree in his back pocket, Haman set a date for a general uprising across the land to wipe out the Jews.

Learning of the plot, Mordecai told Esther and urged her to tell the king. "If you remain silent at this time, relief and deliverance will arise for the Jews from another place and you and your father's house will perish. And who knows whether you have not attained royalty for such a time as this?" (Esther 4:14) This verse is the central focus of the Book of Esther. After three days of fasting Esther approached the king unsummoned, risking death by doing so. By law anyone who approached the king unsummoned was executed unless the king extended his scepter to him or her.

King Ahasuerus received Esther, though, and she obtained his permission to summon Haman for a private banquet where she exposed Haman's plot against her people. Haman was hanged on a gallows he had built for Mordecai and the king revoked the decree to destroy the Jews. On the appointed day, the Jews rose up against their enemies (Haman's allies) and destroyed them.

In a time of great crisis, God raised up a *woman* as His instrument of deliverance. Through her courageous and self-sacrificing boldness, God's people were saved.

Women of Faith in the New Testament

Priscilla (Acts 18:2,18,26; Rom. 16:3; 1 Cor. 16:19; 2 Tim. 4:19). Priscilla (or "Prisca") and her husband, Aquila, were Jewish Christians who fled to Corinth when Emperor Claudius expelled all the Jews from Rome. There they met and worked with Paul in their common trade of tent-making. Both Priscilla and Aquila were skilled teachers, at one point even instructing the eloquent and persuasive Apollos; they "explained to him the way of God more accurately" (Acts 18:26). Paul called them "fellow workers" with him in Christ Jesus (see Rom. 16:3), a term he applies equally to men and women throughout his letters. Priscilla and Aquila were active in proclaiming the gospel and in planting churches, even leading one in their home (see 1 Cor. 16:19). In four of the six occurrences of their names Priscilla is listed first, which is a possible indication of her particular prominence.

Lydia (Acts 16:14-15,40). The first recorded European convert to Christ, Lydia was a native of Thyatira who lived in Philippi. Her household became the nucleus of the church that Paul established in the city on his second missionary journey. Since all the churches at this time were house-churches, Lydia undoubtedly exercised some leadership in that congregation. That she was a "seller of purple" indicates that she was probably wealthy.

Nympha (Col. 4:15). Paul sends greetings to "Nympha and the church that is in her house." Nympha's house-church was probably located in Laodicea, and the phrasing of Paul's words suggests that she was a leader of that church, very possibly with pastoral-type responsibilities.

The four daughters of Philip the evangelist (Acts 21:8-9). Philip's daughters are called "prophetesses" and apparently provided ministry to the church at Caesarea. May daughters of purity and the prophetic emerge again this day! And may secure wives like the nameless wife of Phillip invest themselves into the purposes of God in the next generation. Who do you think nurtured that prophetic gift in those four daughters?

Euodia and Syntyche (Phil. 4:2-3). These two women served the church at Philippi, possibly as deacons or as leaders of house-churches that met in their respective homes. Paul commended them as fellow workers with him in the gospel. Their influence in the church was such that their disagreement with each other concerned Paul, to the point that he urged them to "live in harmony in the Lord."

Junia (Rom. 16:7). Some translations spell the name "Junias." Either way, the name is feminine in form. Paul calls Andronicus and Junias his "kinsmen" and "fellow prisoners, who are outstanding among the apostles." Early Christian leaders and writers were unanimous in the belief that Junias was a woman. John Crysostom (347–407) and Jerome (343–420) both refer to her as a female apostle.[8] She may have been the wife of Andronicus. At any rate, the fact that Paul calls her an apostle is certainly significant.

Phoebe (Rom. 16:1-2). Paul commends to the church at Rome this woman whom he calls "a helper of many, and of myself as well." He describes her as a "servant" (NAS, NIV) of the church at Cenchrea. Both the New American Standard and the New International Version indicate in footnotes that the word *deaconess* is an alternate translation, while the New Revised Standard Version actually uses the word *deacon* to describe Phoebe. The basic Greek word is *diakonos*, which means "servant, minister, or deacon." In Romans 16:1, in reference to Phoebe, the word appears in a *masculine* form, *diakonon*, which strongly suggests that it is the technical term for the *office* of deacon.[9] According to an early source Phoebe was well known throughout the Empire to Greeks, Romans, and barbarians alike, traveling extensively and preaching the gospel in foreign countries.[10] Phoebe obviously was a highly respected leader in the early Church. Personally, I love praying over women of valor and declaring, "I commend to you (fill in the blank) as a true servant of the Lord."

Women of Faith in the Medieval Church (A.D. 100–1400)

Marcella (325–410). An important teacher in the early Church, Marcella actively engaged in dialogue with heretics and brought many into a better understanding of Christian truth. She was highly regarded by Jerome, the translator of the *Vulgate*, the Latin version of the Bible used by the Roman Catholic Church for centuries. Once, when a dispute arose in Rome over the meaning of certain Scriptures, Jerome asked Marcella to settle it.[11] Born into a noble Roman family, Marcella turned her palatial home into a retreat for Bible study, teaching, and Christian activities, using her wealth and energy for benevolent work, prayer, and teaching the Scriptures to other Roman women.[12]

Paula (347–404). Like Marcella, Paula was born into an aristocratic Roman family. One of the wealthiest women of her day, she nevertheless gave it all away after her husband died and dedicated herself to a life of full service to God. She became known for her simplicity, poverty, and humility. Paula was also quite a scholar, mastering both Hebrew and Greek. With a solid grasp of the Bible, she often challenged Jerome with scriptural questions and provided fresh insights into the meanings of Bible passages.[13] Paula and her daughter Eustochium directly assisted Jerome in his translation of the Bible into Latin, revising and correcting his translations and making new Latin translations from the Hebrew and Greek texts. During her life Paula founded three convents and a monastery in Bethlehem, where biblical manuscripts were copied.[14]

Theodora (508–548). A woman of great learning and intellect, Theodora was the wife of the Christian emperor Justinian and was widely known as a moral reformer. Justinian was essentially the human head of the Church of his day and, as empress, Theodora shared his powers. Their reign together "was described as the most brilliant of the Byzantine Empire."[15]

Hildegard of Bingen (1098–1179). Known throughout Europe, this German abbess, mystic, and writer was an accomplished musician and theologian. She also was skilled in medicine, politics, and many other disciplines. Hildegard boldly challenged the sinfulness of the great men of her day, both in the Church and the state. People attributed many miracles to her during her lifetime.[16]

Women of Faith From the Reformation to the Present (1500–1900)

Anne Hutchinson (1591–1643). Raised in a Puritan household in England, Anne learned early in her life to read and think about the Bible for herself. She regularly took notes on the sermons of her pastor, John Cotton, and through diligent study acquired a theological education on her own. In 1634 she and her husband, William, followed Cotton to the Massachusetts Bay colony where they settled in Boston. Before long, Anne began opening her home to weekly gatherings of women to discuss the text and points of Cotton's sermons.[17] These meetings quickly became very popular and grew rapidly in size, eventually even including some men. Aside from being a skilled teacher of deep insight and personal spiritual commitment, Anne was the first female preacher in New England; she probably was the first anywhere in the American colonies. However, her success and "unwomanly" conduct brought opposition from the established male clergy in the colony. In 1638 she was banished.[18] Throughout all of this, Anne's husband remained supportive of her and her activities. The Hutchin sons moved to Rhode Island where there was greater religious freedom.

Margaret Fell (1614–1702) and the Quakers. Remembered as the "mother of Quakerism," Margaret Fell opened her English home, Swarthmoor Hall, as a refuge and place of renewal for persecuted Quakers for almost 50 years. At one point she was arrested for holding Quaker meetings in her home and spent four years in prison. After her release she and her daughters embarked on an itinerant preaching ministry. Some years after the death of her first husband, Judge Thomas Fell, Margaret married George Fox. Fox became one of the most prominent leaders of early Quakerism, and he fully supported her preaching ministry.[19] (*O Lord, would You raise many George Fox's today, who will put their hand in the middle of their wife's back and say, "Go for it. Do what God has put in your heart!"*)

These Quakers stressed the importance of the "Inner Light," which existed inside every person. Salvation came to those who followed their "inner light." Because this inner light was universal, Quakers refused to recognize standard social class distinctions between rich and poor or male and female. They also declined to apply deferential titles to themselves or anyone else, including rulers and civic leaders. This sense of equality caused Quakers to be particularly open to the full and active preaching ministry of women. For many Quaker women the "Inner Light" was a source of strength and power that enabled them to endure great physical hardship, defy established civic and religious authorities, and make autonomous decisions about their life's work, all for the sake of remaining true to their beliefs and conscience.[20]

Phoebe Worrall Palmer (1807–1874). Phoebe Palmer began her ministry in 1835 with the initiation of her "Tuesday Meetings for the Promotion of Holiness," which continued until her death 39 years later. These meetings became the center for the growing "Holiness" movement in America, which taught and sought Christian perfection through a "second blessing" of God's grace in sanctification. Annually during the 1850s Phoebe and her physician husband toured the eastern part of the United States and Canada visiting Methodist camp meetings and conducting their own Holiness revivals.[21] In the fall of 1857 the Palmers went to Hamilton, Ontario, where a planned afternoon prayer meeting turned into a ten-day revival meeting with 400 people converted to Christ. Similar successes characterized their meetings in New York City and in England, where they preached and worked for four years. The periodical *Guide to Holiness,* which Phoebe's husband, Walter, purchased in 1858, grew from 13,000 to 30,000 subscribers under her skilled editorship. All in all, it is estimated that Phoebe Palmer brought over 25,000 people to Christ during her lifetime.[22] Her ministry laid much of the groundwork for the Pentecostal outpouring of the early twentieth century.

Catherine Booth (1829–1890). Co-founder of the Salvation Army with her husband, William, Catherine Booth became one of the most famous and influential female preachers of her day, delivering her last sermon to an audience of 50,000 people.[23] The Booths were firm believers in the equality of women in every sphere of life. Even their marriage was based on this principle. Catherine was a very articulate defender of the right of women to preach: "If she have the necessary gifts, and feels herself called by the Spirit to preach, there is not a single word in the whole book of God to restrain her, but many, very many, to urge and encourage her. God says she SHALL do so, and Paul prescribed the manner in which she shall do it, and Phoebe, Junia, Philip's four daughters, and many other women, actually did preach and speak in the primitive churches."[24] William and Catherine Booth declared the "Women's Right to Preach the Gospel," and I say "yea and amen!"

Maria B. Woodworth-Etter (1844–1924). Like Carrie Judd Montgomery, Maria Woodworth-Etter's ministry began in the nineteenth-century Holiness movement and rose to even greater prominence in the early Pentecostal revival. Licensed to preach in 1884 by the Churches of God, her meetings began to draw national attention almost immediately. Unusual manifestations of God's power attended her meetings, including many healings and great numbers of conversions. In the early days of Pentecostalism she was in constant demand as a speaker. In 1918 she founded the Woodworth-Etter Tabernacle in Indianapolis, which she pastored until her death in 1924.[25]

Carrie Judd Montgomery (1858–1946). After receiving a miraculous physical healing herself, Carrie Montgomery went on to become a prominent healing evangelist. Her ministry grew out of the nineteenth century Holiness movement, but encompassed far more. In 1887 she became co-founder, with A.B. Simpson, of the Christian and Missionary Alliance. Carrie was a significant influence during the Pentecostal revival of the early 1900s, and she was ordained as a minister by the Assemblies of God in 1917. Her active ministry continued until her death in 1946.[26]

Kathryn Kuhlman (1907–1976). Regarded as one of the world's foremost healing evangelists, Kathryn Kuhlman began her ministry in 1923 as an ordained minister of the Evangelical Church Alliance. By the mid-1940s she was thriving as a preacher and radio evangelist in Pennsylvania. The powerful healing aspect of her ministry took off in 1947 and continued until her death in 1976.[27]

On a personal note, I remember seeing the last television broadcast of this unusual woman of God. She stated that God had first offered her gift to a man, but that he had refused. Then she went on to comment, "So God came to me—a woman. Someone ugly, despised, and a redhead at that! And I said yes." Availability is always the greatest ability.

So What About the Woman?

This survey is barely the tip of the iceberg in relating the role and place of women in the Church, but even this tiny bit is sufficient to show that from the very beginning God's plan has been for women to have full involvement in every aspect of the life of the Body of Christ. The fact that for the most part they have not been afforded that opportunity across two millennia of Church history is a sad situation that calls for heartbroken confession and abject repentance on the part of the men in the Church—and particularly the clergy.

A simple truth of history is that during times of revival women have entered more fully into the life and ministry of the Church in every area, including preaching, whereas during periods of spiritual decline the freedom and role of women in ministry have become more restricted. In other words, the degree to which women are released into the full ministry of the Church is a direct reflection of the degree to which the Church is in revival or decline. One reason for this is that during times of revival gender distinctions and clergy-laity distinctions become less important due to the increased sense of urgency that revival creates. In the pressing need for evangelism and missions, all available persons are put to work—whether men or women, clergy or laity, ordained or non-ordained, theologically educated or not. Under these circumstances what counts is one's call, not one's credentials. The early days of Pentecostalism is a good example. As author Edith Blumhofer writes,

"In the early Pentecostal movement, having the 'anointing' was far more important than one's sex. As evangelistic bands carried the full gospel across the country, women who were recognized as having the anointing of the Holy Spirit shared with men in the preaching ministry....A person's call—and how other believers viewed it—was far more important than [ministerial credentials]."[28]

Age-old traditions and entrenched mind-sets are not easy to change, but Christ is still Lord of His Church. He is bringing about in our day a new release of Christian women into the fullness of their lives as members of the Body of Christ. The ancient walls are crumbling; the rusty chains are falling off; old restrictions are being removed. The Lord is restoring His Church to the way He *really* wants it to be, not the way generations of Church leaders (mostly men) have *said* He wants it to be!

Evidence of this releasing of women can be seen across the full scope of the Church in virtually every group and denomination. One example is the Roman Catholic Church. In his *Letter to Women* published in June 1995, Pope John Paul II made this statement:

"Women's dignity has often been unacknowledged and their prerogatives misrepresented; they have often been relegated to the margins of society and even reduced to servitude....And if objective blame...has belonged to not just a few members of the Church, for this I am truly sorry. May this regret be transformed, on the part of the whole Church, into a renewed commitment of fidelity to the Gospel vision."[29]

In a later letter, the Pope had this to say concerning the place of women in ministry:

"Consecrated women...rightly aspire to have their identity, ability, mission and responsibility more clearly recognized, both in the awareness of the Church and in everyday life....It is therefore urgently necessary to take certain concrete steps, beginning by providing room for women to participate in different fields and at all levels, including decision-making processes, above all in matters which concern women themselves."[30]

A Paradigm Shift

Now, some of you might be ready to pull your hair out at this point—some for joy and others out of the thought, *Now you're going a bit too far this time, Jim Goll!* Well, let it be known that I didn't always have this view, understanding, or interpretation. At one point my wife asked my permission to do or say almost everything. She even covered her head just to join me in praying for someone! But then God came with His manifested presence and anointed a little, 5-foot, 3-inch package and made her into a holy volcano for God!

Yes, I am now married to an ordained woman preacher. So I understand to a degree the many different angles here. But as for me and my house, I decided to bless what I saw the Father doing.

This is not just something that has happened in our lives and ministry either. As I have the privilege of traveling the nations, I do get to see some overall trends of things that the Holy Spirit seems to be emphasizing. One of these is "giving honor to women."

While in Brazil in the fall of 1999, I was blessed to minister at the National Leadership Conference of the Church of Christ in Pires Do Rio, Brazil. It was a great blessing to be there and see what looks like the beginnings of authentic revival for that nation. At the last meeting of the Leadership gathering of 2,000 people, Senior Pastor Ulyssess called forward all the pastors' wives of this fast growing ministry. Then he proceeded, in their Portuguese language, to ask the women to forgive the men and the leadership of the church in particular for not receiving them as co-laborers in Christ. It was a very moving time as weeping broke out amongst the people and cleansing and healing began to flow. The time culminated then with all the pastors of this national movement laying hands on all the pastors' wives and publicly ordaining them as co-pastors with their husbands in the work of ministry. It was truly an awesome, holy, and historic moment.

So now with conviction and experience of having undergone that "paradigm shift," I make the following declarations.

Women of the Church, you have been shackled long enough! As a man in the Church I want to confess to you that we, the men of the Body of Christ, have feared you and have clung tightly to our rights, our positions, and our functions out of the fear that we would lose them to you. In our own insecurity and sin we have been unwilling to fully recognize your gifts, calling, and anointing in the Spirit or to accept you as full equals in the life and ministry of the Church. This might sound a bit brash, but in my opinion it's time for the "good ole boys' club" to come to an end!

Therefore, I ask you, the women, to forgive us for holding you back, for not being cheerleaders for you, for not helping to equip you, and for not releasing you to fulfill God's calling on your lives. Forgive us for paying only lip service to your value, your gifts, your call, and your anointing. Forgive us for treating you like second-class citizens of the Kingdom and for not recognizing your equal status with us.

Father, forgive us! We have sinned and acted wickedly! We have wrongfully bound our sisters, Your daughters, and held them back from full participation in the life of the Church of which they and we are equally a part. Forgive us, Lord, and release the light of revelation and change to come in Your Body. O Lord, release Your daughters!

Reflection Questions

1. What are some of the reasons women have been so oppressed and hindered from taking a greater role in Christian ministry?

2. In your opinion, what steps can be taken to bridge the gender gap?

3.   Stop right now and begin to confess before the Father the historical sin of the Church of men fearing women and women despising men for their actions.

Recommended Reading

Women on the Front Lines by Michal Ann Goll (Destiny Image, 1999)

Women of Destiny by Cindy Jacobs (Regal, 1998)

Women of Awakenings—The Historic Contribution of Women to Revival Movements by Lewis and Betty Drummond (Kregel Publications, 1997)

Endnotes

1.   Dr. Fuchsia Pickett, from the Foreword to "Part Two: Gender" in Kelley Varner, *The Three Prejudices* (Shippensburg, Pennsylvania: Destiny Image Publishers, 1997), 31.
2.   Varner, *The Three Prejudices*, 35-36.
3.   Paul K. Jewett, *The Ordination of Women* (Grand Rapids, Michigan: William. B. Eerdmans Publishing Co., 1980), 14, as quoted in Sheri R. Benvenuti, "Pentecostal Women in Ministry: Where Do We Go From Here?" *Cyberjournal for Pentecostal-Charismatic Research*, 14 Jan 1997: page 8. <http://www.fullnet.net/np/archives/cyberj/ben.html>.
4.   For additional inspiration from the lives of Christian women throughout history, let me recommend my wife's, Michal Ann's, book *Women on the Front Lines* (Shippensburg, Pennsylvania: Destiny Image Publishers, 1999).
5.   Pamela J. Scalise, "Deborah," *Holman Bible Dictionary*, 1991. *QuickVerse 4.0 Deluxe Bible Reference Collection*. CD-ROM. Parsons Technology, 1992–1996.
6.   Scalise, "Deborah," *Holman Bible Dictionary*.
7.   Scalise, "Deborah," *Holman Bible Dictionary*.
8.   Richard M. Riss, "Who's Who Among Women of the Word," *Spread the Fire*. Vol. 3, No. 5 (October 1997). 8 Dec. 1999. <http://www.tacf.org/stf/3-5/feature3.html>.

9. Stanley Grenz and Denise Kjesbo, *Women in the Church: A Biblical Theology of Women in Ministry* (Downers Grove, Illinois: InterVarsity Press, 1995), 88ff, cited in Glenn M. Miller, "Women's Roles in the Early Church," *The Christian Thinktank*, 20 Aug 1999. <http://www.webcom.com/~ctt/fem08.htm>.

10. Catherine Booth, "Female Teaching: Or, The Rev. A.A. Rees Versus Mrs. Palmer, Being a Reply to a Pamphlet by the Above Gentleman on the Sunderland Revival," *Victorian Women Writers Project: An Electronic Collection*, 1996. 20 Aug 1999. <http://www.indiana.edu/~letrs/vwwp/booth/femteach.html>.

11. Riss, "Who's Who Among Women of the Word," *Spread the Fire*.

12. Miller, "Women's Roles in the Early Church," *The Christian Thinktank*.

13. Miller, "Women's Roles in the Early Church," *The Christian Thinktank*.

14. Riss, "Who's Who Among Women of the Word," *Spread the Fire*.

15. Mary L. Hammack, *A Dictionary of Women in Church History* (Chicago, Illinois: Moody Press, 1984), 145.

16. Riss, "Who's Who Among Women of the Word," *Spread the Fire*.

17. Excerpted from Barbara J. MacHaffie, *Her Story: Women in Christian Tradition* (Philadelphia, Pennsylvania: Fortress Press, 1986).

18. Riss, "Who's Who Among Women of the Word," *Spread the Fire*.

19. Riss, "Who's Who Among Women of the Word," *Spread the Fire*.

20. Excerpted from MacHaffie, *Her Story: Women in Christian Tradition*.

21. Excerpted from MacHaffie, *Her Story: Women in Christian Tradition*.

22. Riss, "Who's Who Among Women of the Word," *Spread the Fire*.

23. Riss, "Who's Who Among Women of the Word" *Spread the Fire*.

24. Excerpted from MacHaffie, *Her Story: Women in Christian Tradition*.

25. Riss, "Who's Who Among Women of the Word," *Spread the Fire*.

26. Riss, "Who's Who Among Women of the Word," *Spread the Fire*.

27. Riss, "Who's Who Among Women of the Word," *Spread the Fire*.

28. Edith Blumhofer, *The Assemblies of God: A Popular History* (Springfield, Missouri: Gospel Publishing House, 1985), 137, as quoted in Benvenuti, "Pentecostal Women in Ministry," *Cyberjournal*.

29. Pope John Paul II, *Letter to Women*, June 1995, as quoted in Luigi Accattoli, *When a Pope Asks Forgiveness* (Boston, Massachusetts: Pauline Books and Media, 1998), 110.

30. Pope John Paul II, Apostolic Letter *Vita Consecrata*, March 1996, as quoted in Accattoli, *When a Pope Asks Forgiveness*, 114.

Chapter 7

The Genocide of the Jews

ne of the greatest blemishes on the garments of the Bride of Christ is our history of jealousy, hatred, persecution, and murder toward our elder brother, the Jewish people. The wounds cut deep; the blood-red stain runs dark and wide. Historically, the attitudes and actions of the Church toward the Jews have dishonored the holy name of Christ, distorted the true gospel of Christ, and all but destroyed any effective witness for Christ, leaving instead a centuries-old legacy of bitterness, suspicion, and hatred on both sides. Church, wake up! *Did we forget that our Messiah is Jewish?*

This prideful wedge between Christians and Jews must be removed for a couple of primary reasons. First, the dishonor that the Church has brought on the name of Jesus, as well as the misrepresentation of His character and grace, must be rectified. Second, the destiny of the Church is linked with the destiny of Israel. Despite what many theological camps teach and believe, God is *not* through with the Jewish people; the Church has *not* replaced Israel in the plan and purpose of God. The covenant promises that God made to the sons of Abraham still stand because "the gifts and the calling of God are irrevocable" (Rom. 11:29). Although the apostle Paul makes it clear that the *true* spiritual sons of Abraham are people of faith rather than law (see Gal. 3:1-7), he also speaks of a future *regathering* of the Jews (see Rom. 11). This regathering has both a physical fulfillment in the national state of Israel and a spiritual fulfillment in the veil of blindness dropping from their eyes as they joyfully embrace their Messiah.

Each of the areas I am specifically addressing in this book carry a weight and a burden on my heart. Perhaps this one beats the loudest within me at this juncture in my life. I want to see history rewritten—for *Father, we have sinned!*

One of the darkest chapters in the entire history of the Church was the period of the Crusades during the eleventh through thirteenth centuries. These armed campaigns to "liberate" the Holy Land from the "infidels" served as the vehicle for great atrocities that were perpetrated against Jews, Muslims, and Orthodox Christians. Such terrible cruelties occurred not only in the Holy Land, but also across Europe and Asia Minor—in every country through which the Crusaders passed on their way to Jerusalem. The savage, barbaric cruelty and brutality of those who acted in the "name" of Christ sowed seeds of fear, resentment, and mistrust toward "Christians" on the part of Jews and Muslims that continue to bear bitter fruit today, almost a millennium later.

A tragic example of this is the history of the nations that occupy the Balkan Peninsula in southern Europe. The various people groups of this region—the Croats, the Serbs, the Bosnians, and others—have endured political and religious turmoil for centuries. Ethnic hatred and religious prejudice have been constant sources of tension and unrest, and many wars have been fought on that soil.

I have been to these lands. I have prayer-walked their streets and opened my natural and spiritual eyes to take an honest look. Go with me now on a little historic journey.

In the summer of 1914 the assassination of Archduke Francis Ferdinand, the heir to the throne of Austria-Hungary, and of his wife by a Serbian nationalist in the city of Sarajevo was the spark that set off World War I, which claimed ten million lives. As the Kingdom of the Serbs, Croats, and Slovenes from 1918 until 1945, the region suffered terribly during World War II. From 1945 to the 1980s it existed as the Communist nation of Yugoslavia. Since the splintering of Yugoslavia, the nations of Slovenia, Croatia, Bosnia-Herzegovina, and Macedonia have declared their independence, while Serbia, Montenegro, and Vojvodina remain part of Yugoslavia. The 1980s and 1990s have witnessed one conflict after another in these countries, which have added an ominous new phrase—"ethnic cleansing"—to the world's vocabulary.

Along with my dear friend and evangelist Mahesh Chavda, I have stood in the very spot where Archduke Ferdinand was murdered. I have wept in identificational repentance until my being had nothing left within me.

The centuries-old conflict between these peoples is essentially religious in nature: Croatia is predominately Catholic, Serbia is Orthodox, Bosnia is Islamic. Many of the seeds were planted during the time of the Crusades. I am convinced that the unchristian behavior of the "Christian" Crusaders contributed to the creation of an atmosphere that has given demonic powers and territorial spirits a legal basis to operate. Because of this, I believe that there will be no final end to the ethnic and religious conflicts in this region (or in the Middle East) until the Church rises up in true heartfelt identificational intercession and repents for the atrocities of the Crusades. Christian confession and repentance for these are long overdue. *Father, forgive us!*

The Reconciliation Walk

But new history is being written! On July 15, 1999, the residents of Jerusalem witnessed the culmination of the "Reconciliation Walk," a four-year event during which groups of ordinary Christians retraced on foot the routes taken by the first Crusaders, talking with Jews, Muslims, and Orthodox Christians along the way and apologizing for the inhumanity of the Crusades. The date was significant: It was 900 years to the day since the city of Jerusalem fell to the Crusaders. Participants in the Walk met with leaders of the Muslim, Jewish, and Eastern (Orthodox) communities in Jerusalem and offered the apology.

The Reconciliation Walk represents identification in intercession and confession of generational sin in action. According to Lynn Green, the organizer and director of the Reconciliation Walk, the idea grew out of a conversation between two young people who were concerned about the unease and tension that exists between Christians, Muslims, and Jews, and the part that the Crusades played in creating this tension.[1] The purpose of the Walk was to "bring Christians face to face with Muslims and Jews with a simple message of regret and confession."[2]

Everything about the Walk was timed to coincide with the nine hundredth anniversary of the First Crusade. It officially began on November 27, 1995, with a day of prayer at Clermont-Ferrand in France. It was the same place and the same day 900 years ago when Pope Urban II issued the initial call that launched the First Crusade.[3]

> "Then in the spring of 1996, a few small groups of walkers started traveling from Germany and France, up the Rhine and down the Danube, with others going via Italy and the Balkans, thus retracing the footsteps taken by the first Crusaders....They...concentrate[d] on asking forgiveness from the remaining Jewish citizens and praying in towns and cities like Cologne, Mainz and Worms, where so many Jews were slaughtered during the First Crusade."[4]

As the Walk progressed, the number of participants grew. In 1997 and 1998 the walkers trekked throughout Turkey, and in 1999 made their way through Syria and Lebanon to Israel. By the time the Walk concluded in Jerusalem in July 1999, hundreds of Christians from many different countries had taken part, some walking for a few days, others for a few weeks, and still others for several months at a time.

Each walker was equipped with a statement, written in the local language for the region he was in, apologizing for the way "Christians" misrepresented Christ during the Crusades. The statement read as follows:

"Nine hundred years ago, our forefathers carried the name of Jesus Christ in battle across the Middle East. Fueled by fear, greed and hatred, they betrayed the name of Christ by conducting themselves in a manner contrary to His wishes and character. The Crusaders lifted the banner of the Cross above your people. By this act they corrupted its true meaning of reconciliation, forgiveness and selfless love.

"On the anniversary of the first Crusade we also carry the name of Christ. We wish to retrace the footsteps of the Crusaders in apology for their deeds and in demonstration of the true meaning of the Cross. We deeply regret the atrocities committed in the name of Christ by our predecessors. We renounce greed, hatred and fear, and condemn all violence done in the name of Jesus Christ.

"Where they were motivated by hatred and prejudice, we offer love and brotherhood. Jesus the Messiah came to give life. Forgive us for allowing His name to be associated with death. Please accept again the true meaning of the Messiah's words:

"The Spirit of the Lord is upon me, because He has anointed me to bring good news to the poor. He has sent me to proclaim release to the captive, and recovery of sight to the blind, to let the oppressed go free, to proclaim the year of the Lord's favour."[5]

Mark Elliott, a personal friend of mine from the Nashville, Tennessee, area, was in Jerusalem for the conclusion of the Reconciliation Walk. He expressed the heart of all the walkers when he said, "To people of the Middle East, there has been no greater inhumanity, no greater evil than when the Christians brought their Crusade. The bitter root of the Crusades has festered 900 years. But Jesus said, 'Blessed are the peacemakers.' We want to be peacemakers."[6]

The Roots of Anti-Semitism in the Church

How serious is the problem? Do we as Christians really need to take such a radical step as was demonstrated in the Reconciliation Walk? How did a Church founded on love, joy, peace, grace, and mercy end up with such a legacy of bitterness, fear, and hatred?

The ugly truth is that the roots of anti-Semitism—the hatred of the Jews—extend far back into the early years of Church history. Realize that truth in one area does not mean that you have light and truth in all areas. Many of the most respected and influential leaders of the Church in its first few centuries, as godly and devoted to Christ as they may have been, nevertheless had huge blind spots when it came to the Jews. Their prejudice, and in some cases hatred, of the Jews set a precedent of thought and attitude that has influenced the Church's treatment of the Jews ever since. The reasons for this anti-Semitic sentiment are many and involve social, cultural, demonic, as well as theological aspects.

In the very beginning, the Church was exclusively Jewish: Jesus was a Jew and so were all His disciples. All the believers present in the upper room on the Day of Pentecost were Jews, and for almost ten years after Pentecost, the gospel was preached to Jews exclusively. Early Christian worship borrowed its worship style and practices from those of the synagogue. In its earliest days, the Church of Jesus Christ was very Jewish in flavor. In fact, the Bible that we have today—both the Old and the New Testaments—was written by Jews! Our origins are Jewish. There "just ain't no way of gettin' around" that one.

Gradually, however, the gospel began to spread to non-Jews. Philip preached to the Samaritans and won many converts; then he spoke to an Ethiopian government official, who also believed (see Acts 8:5-13,26-39). Peter preached Christ in the home of Cornelius, a Roman centurion, whose entire household believed along with him (see Acts 10). As the "apostle to the Gentiles," Paul, with his companions Barnabas and later Silas, proclaimed Christ far and wide across the Roman Empire, bringing Gentiles to Christ by the thousands. (Yet even Paul was in the practice of preaching to the Jews first in any city that he entered.)

Thus, even before the end of the first century, there were more Gentiles than Jews in the Church. Because Gentile believers were not required to observe Jewish law and practices, the Church as a whole began to lose its Jewish flavor, becoming more distinctly Gentile in culture and custom. This "Gentilization" of the Church, plus a declining number of Jewish believers as well as an increasingly implacable opposition and hostility to the gospel by the Jewish people as a whole, helped plant seeds of anti-Jewish sentiment in the hearts of many believers, particularly Church leaders. Another contributing factor was the decline of the manifest presence of the Holy Spirit in Church life and a greater dependence on human reason (see Chapter 5). When the mind of man becomes exalted over the spirit/heart of man, it gives darkness an opportunity to enter and, if unchallenged, to spread and prevail.

One significant event in the second century was the spark that ignited the rise of anti-Semitism in the Church. The Jews for the most part had rejected Jesus, and devout Jews were still looking for their Messiah, whom they believed would be a political and military deliverer. In A.D. 132 many of them thought that they had found him in a man named Simon Bar Kochba. Although many Jews followed Bar Kochba, the Jews who had believed in Jesus as the Messiah did not. For this reason Bar Kochba killed many of them, regarding them as enemies, heretics, and traitors. This action outraged the Church as a whole, which began then to harbor bitterness toward the Jewish people.[7]

Jewish Christians, feeling increasingly alienated on the one hand by a Gentile Church that had begun to distrust their Jewishness and on the other hand by a Jewish society that ostracized them for their failure to support Bar Kochba, established two Messianic sects, the Ebionites and the Nazarenes, in an attempt to establish congregations that were essentially Jewish in culture. By the middle of the fifth century, however, these groups had disappeared.[8]

The Christian Church, now completely Gentile in identity, became less and less tolerant of anything relating to its Jewish roots. During the second century, Church leaders began to take an uncompromising stance against anything Jewish. As a result, they began to interpret Scripture in a new way, particularly where Israel was concerned:

- The promises of blessing to Israel in the Hebrew Scriptures were now seen as the *exclusive* property of the Church.

- God had cursed and rejected Israel, and the Church was now the "true" or "new" Israel.

- The Jews killed Jesus; therefore, all Jews everywhere forever were responsible for His death.[9]

Bitter Fruit From a Bitter Root

The bitter seeds of anti-Semitism that were planted early in the life of the Church bore increasingly bitter fruit across the generations. Sadly, this is clear in some of the writings of the early Church Fathers. By and large, these men were admirable in their godliness and devotion to Christ, so it is all the more painful today to read their forceful diatribes against the Jews.

Origen (185–254), a brilliant and noted biblical scholar and theologian, wrote,

"On account of their unbelief and other insults which they heaped upon Jesus, the Jews will not only suffer more than others in the judgment...but have even already endured such sufferings....And the calamities they have suffered because they were *a most wicked nation*, which although guilty of many other sins, yet has been punished so severely for none as for those that were committed against *our* Jesus."[10]

Gregory of Nyssa (331–396) described the Jews as such:

"Slayers of the Lord, murderers of the prophets, adversaries of God, men who show contempt for the Law, foes of grace, enemies of their fathers' faith, advocates of the Devil, brood of vipers, slanderers, scoffers, men whose minds are in darkness, leaven of the Pharisees, assembly of demons, sinners, wicked men, stoners, and haters of righteousness."[11]

John Chrysostom (347–407), patriarch of Constantinople, whose name means "golden-mouthed," was known as a bright, gentle, sensitive person, yet he was an eloquent and powerful preacher. He has come down through history with a reputation as one of the greatest of the Church Fathers, yet he too had a horrendous blind spot where the Jews were concerned:

"The synagogue is worse than a brothel...it is the den of scoundrels and the repair of wild beasts...the temple of demons devoted to idolatrous cults...the refuge of brigands and debauchees, and the cavern of devils. [It is] a criminal assembly of Jews...a place of meeting for the assassins of Christ...a house worse than a drinking shop...a den of thieves; a house of ill fame, a dwelling of iniquity, the refuge of devils, a gulf and abyss of perdition....I would say the same thing about [the Jews'] souls....As for me, I hate the synagogue....I hate the Jews for the same reason."[12]

Whew! With vitriolic words like these coming from the mouths and the pens of the leaders, is it any wonder that the Church as a whole learned to fear, hate, and despise the Jewish people?

Our Bloodstained Hands

By the time of the Crusades, anti-Semitism was thoroughly entrenched in the beliefs and attitudes of the Church. In the middle of the eleventh century, the Byzantine Empire was the greatest

Christian power base in the world at the time. During this time, however, its capital at Constantinople (headquarters of the Eastern Orthodox Church) was threatened by the Seljuk Turks, a nomadic race of shepherds from central Asia who had converted to Islam as they migrated westwards. The defeat of the Byzantine army by the Turks in 1071 put the city of Constantinople at great risk. In addition, the Turks were ambushing Christian pilgrims on their way to Jerusalem. The emperor and patriarch in Constantinople appealed to Pope Urban II in Rome for help.

On November 27, 1095, Pope Urban called the Western Church to arms for the liberation of the Holy Land. For all who pledged themselves to the Crusade, the Pope promised forgiveness of their sins and direct passage to Heaven (no Purgatory). The First Crusade did not consist of a disciplined army of trained soldiers, but instead...

> "a mobile riot of thousands of peasants...dominated by superstitions, easily manipulated and desperate to do something that would smooth the road to heaven.

> "The first and second waves of Crusaders murdered, raped and plundered their way up the Rhine and down the Danube as they headed for Jerusalem. They especially targeted the Jewish communities, whom the Crusaders saw as the infidel in their midst; thousands of Jews were wiped out in Europe. Many Jewish scholars refer to these events as the *first holocaust.*"[13]

Nearly four years later, in June 1099, the Crusaders reached Jerusalem. They finally captured the city on July 15, indiscriminately slaughtering men, women, and children throughout the day and night. The following morning, the "Christians" discovered 6,000 Jews who had fled to the synagogue for safety. The Crusaders set the synagogue on fire and burned them alive. Meanwhile, the Muslims who had survived fled to the Mosque of al Aqsa in the southeastern quarter of the city. The Crusaders broke the doors down and massacred an estimated 30,000 Muslims.[14]

Periodically throughout the Middle Ages (and in succeeding centuries as well), Jews in the "Christian" nations of Europe were faced with three choices: conversion (forced baptism), expulsion, or death. Most Jews chose either to be expelled or to die rather than convert (martyrs are not found only in the Church!). In addition, Jews of the Middle Ages were victims of many other cruelties and slanders perpetrated by the "Christian" West. Consider these examples:

- *Blood Libel*, a myth that began in England in 1144, alleged that Jews regularly murdered Christian children at Passover and used their blood in preparing the unleavened bread (*matzoh*).

- *The Black Death*, an endemic bubonic plague in the fourteenth century that wiped out a quarter of the population of Europe, was blamed on the Jews of Europe and Asia. Enraged and frightened mobs killed many Jews despite a bull (formal document) from the Pope declaring that the Jews were not responsible.

- *The Inquisition*, designed by the Catholic Church in the thirteenth century to suppress heresy, became a tool of persecution against the Jews. Jews were pressed to convert; if they refused, they were killed. The Spanish Inquisition (est. 1478) sought to discover and punish converted Jews and Muslims who showed signs of reverting back to their old religions and practices. Victims were tortured until they confessed, then burned at the stake.

In the face of such hideous brutality, atrocities, and vicious, outrageous lies from those in the "Church," is it any wonder that Jews and Muslims learned to hate and despise Christians?

Martin Luther and the Jews

One of the true shining lights of Christian history was the Augustinian monk *Martin Luther (1483–1546)*, whose courageous stand for the doctrine of justification by faith in Christ alone defied the Roman Catholic Church and gave birth to the Protestant Reformation in Germany and across northern Europe. Early on Luther reached out in kindness to the Jews, hoping that they would be attracted to a Christian faith that had been set free from the bondage and error of the Catholic Church. Luther had little respect for the Church leadership of his day, calling them "fools" and "coarse blockheads." Concerning their treatment of the Jews, Luther wrote in 1523, "...if I had been a Jew and had seen such idiots and blockheads ruling and teaching the Christian religion, I would rather have been a sow than a Christian. For they have dealt with the Jews as if they were dogs and not human beings."[15]

German Jews proved no more willing, however, to convert to Luther's "brand" of Christianity than they had to Catholicism, which created increasing frustration for the fiery ex-monk. In addition, he became outraged over some blasphemous anti-Christian literature written by Jews. These factors, coupled with age and illness, caused a tragic change of heart in Luther's attitude toward the end of his life, and he lashed out at the Jews in some of the most poisonous words that had been penned up to that time.

> "What shall we Christians do with this damned, rejected race of Jews?...First, their synagogues should be set on fire...Secondly, their homes should likewise be broken down and destroyed....Thirdly, they should be deprived of their prayer-books and Talmuds...Fourthly, their rabbis must be forbidden under threat of death to teach any more...Fifthly, passport and traveling privileges should be absolutely forbidden to the Jews....Sixthly, they ought to be stopped from usury [charging interest on loans]....Seventhly, let the young and strong Jews and Jewesses be given the flail, the ax, the hoe, the spade, the distaff, and spindle, and let them earn their bread by the sweat of their noses...We ought to drive the rascally lazy bones out of our system....Therefore away with them....

"To sum up, dear princes and nobles who have Jews in your domains, if this advice of mine does not suit you, then find a better one so that you and we may all be free of this insufferable devilish burden—the Jews."[16]

Sadly, the story does not end with mere words. These sentiments and others like them have influenced "Christian" attitudes toward Jews ever since. During the 1930s and 40s Luther's "advice" was taken to heart and acted upon by the Nazi government of Germany, which found a "better" way to be free of the "insufferable devilish burden" of the Jews. By the time it was all over in May 1945, much of Europe lay in ruins and six million Jewish men, women, and children—fully one third of the Jewish population of Europe—were dead.

Church, we have Jewish blood all over our hands! Father, forgive us!

The Future of Israel and the Church

If we want to see the fullness of God's glory and purpose come in the earth, then the blight and stain of anti-Semitism must be removed from the heart and soul of the Church. Contrary to what the proponents of "replacement theology" teach, God still has plans for the nation of Israel and the Jewish people. In recent years approximately 800,000 Russian-speaking Jews have left the "land of the North" and returned to the land of Israel. Ancient Bible prophecies are beginning to be fulfilled. An indigenous Messianic movement is beginning in Israel and the nations in this generation.

Does God have a plan? Yes, the destiny of Israel and the destiny of the Christian Church are inseparably linked! God chose the Jews to be the people through whom the Messiah and Savior of the world would come. Even though the majority of Jews rejected Jesus when He appeared—and have continued to do so—God's covenant promises still apply. Always remember, when man is faithless, God remains faithful. Aren't you glad for that?

In Second Corinthians 3:15 Paul writes of a "veil" over the hearts of the Jews that blinds them to the truth of the gospel. In Romans he says that "a partial hardening has happened to Israel until the fulness of the Gentiles has come in; and thus all Israel will be saved" (Rom. 11:25b-26a). The day is coming when those of the nation of Israel who have rejected Yeshua, their Messiah, will be brought around. The veil will be lifted from their hearts and they will believe. Zechariah prophesied,

And I will pour out on the house of David and on the inhabitants of Jerusalem, the Spirit of grace and of supplication, so that they will look on Me whom they have pierced; and they will mourn for Him, as one mourns for an only son, and they will weep bitterly over Him, like the bitter weeping over a first-born (Zechariah 12:10).

God's redemptive plan for all people—Jews and Gentiles alike—centers around Jesus Christ, His only begotten Son. It always has. Everything in the law and the covenant—the sacrifices, the priestly functions, the tabernacle and temple worship, the feasts—point to Jesus Christ, whose death and resurrection brought them to completion. Jesus said, "Do not think that I came to abolish the Law or the Prophets; I did not come to abolish, but to fulfill. For truly I say to you, until heaven and earth pass away, not the smallest letter or stroke shall pass away from the Law, until all is accomplished" (Mt. 5:17-18). Christ is the One in whom "all is accomplished." Simon Peter, filled with the Holy Spirit as he stood before the Jewish high court, said of Jesus: "And there is salvation in no one else; for there is no other name under heaven that has been given among men, by which we must be saved" (Acts 4:12).

Natural and Spiritual Restoration

The restoration of Israel, both nationally and spiritually, is part of God's end-time plan for the ages.

For I will take you from the nations, gather you from all the lands, and bring you into your own land. Then I will sprinkle clean water on you, and you will be clean; I will cleanse you from all your filthiness and from all your idols. Moreover, I will give you a new heart and put a new spirit within you; and

*I will remove the heart of stone from your flesh and give you a
heart of flesh* (Ezekiel 36:24-26).

National restoration has already occurred; in 1998 Israel celebrated its Jubilee—50 years—of existence once more among the
nations of the earth. Spiritual restoration—the turning of the Jews
to faith in their Messiah, Yeshua (Jesus)—will occur as the "fulness
of the Gentiles" is completed. In recent years through the International Festivals of Jewish Worship and Dance, I have seen with my
own eyes as many as 50,000 Jews place their faith in Jesus as their
Messiah in the former Soviet Union.

I am convinced that a major reason for the historic veil of spiritual blindness on the hearts of Jews is the anti-Semitic prejudice
of the Church. By our actions and attitudes toward the Jews, we
have hidden and veiled the true Christ from their view. For centuries, when Jews have looked to the Church, instead of meeting
the Christ of love, mercy, grace, compassion, and forgiveness, they
have met bigotry, slander, violence, hatred, persecution, and murder. As Christians, we bear a major responsibility for the veil of
unbelief that separates the Jewish people from their Messiah.

We must repent for the sins and crimes of the "Church" against
the Jewish people. Only through confession and repentance of this
great generational sin can we break and remove the legal basis for
the demonic forces behind the spiritual blindness of the Jews and
the separation between Jews and Christians. But this is not just a
historic sin of yesterday; it continues to today. Across the nations
this prideful, arrogant anti-Semitic spirit is on the rise. Yes, even in
the United States of America the ugly head of anti-Semitism has
been arising again. Whether it has been burning synagogues in
Sacramento, California, or shooting in Chicago or Los Angeles,
this ugly monster has been raising its head again in our day.
Therefore, my heart explodes all the more within me, weeping for
mercy and a time of change. *Have mercy, Father, for we have sinned!*

As a follower of Christ and a member of His Body, the Church, I now openly confess to my Jewish friends that we have sinned against you! Please forgive us for our actions, our attitudes, our traditions, our fears, our suspicion, our hatred, and our theological misinterpretations that have caused you such agony and anguish and hindered you from coming forth into your destiny. I ask you in Yeshua's name, please forgive us!

Father, we have sinned! Father, forgive us! Forgive us for our prejudice and hatred toward the Jews, Your chosen ones who are the "apple" of Your eye (see Zech. 2:8). Forgive us for the Crusades and the Inquisition, for the pogroms and the slander. Forgive us for the Holocaust, particularly for our silence and inaction. Forgive us for the six million dead. Forgive us, Lord, for harboring these prideful attitudes and actions to this day. Cleanse us and remove this stain from the heart and soul of Your Church.

Cleanse our hearts, O God. Give us Your heart for the Jewish people. Remove the veil from their hearts that their eyes might be opened to see and embrace Yeshua, Your Son and their Messiah! Restore Your people and bring in the harvest for the honor of Your great name in all the earth!

Reflection Questions

1. Recite one of the historical sad statements of a prominent Church leader against the Jewish people.

2. When man is faithless, does God remain faithful? Give a scriptural basis for your answer and explain.

3. What are the biblical promises for the Jewish people that yet remain to be fulfilled?

Recommended Reading

Our Hands Are Stained With Blood by Michael L. Brown (Destiny Image, 1992)

Jewish Roots by Dan Juster (Destiny Image, 1995)

Endnotes

1. Leyla Tavsanoglu, "Towards Peace Reconciliation Walk," an interview with Lynn Green published in the Turkish newspaper *Cumhuriyet*, October 11, 1996. 24 Aug 1999. <http://www.reconciliationwalk. org/cumhuriyet961011.htm>.
2. Quoted from the Reconciliation Walk official website. 24 Aug 1999. <http://www.reconciliationwalk.org/walk/htm>.
3. Reconciliation Walk. 24 Aug 1999. <http://www.reconciliationwalk. org/walk/htm>.
4. Reconciliation Walk. 24 Aug 1999. <http://www.reconciliationwalk. org/walk/htm>.
5. Reconciliation Walk. 24 Aug 1999. <http://www.reconciliationwalk. org/walk/htm>.
6. Ray Waddle, "Christians apologizing for Crusades," *The Tennessean*, June 27, 1999.
7. Gary M. Grobman, "Classical and Christian Anti-Semitism," 1990. 11 Feb 1999. <http://remember.org/History.root.classical.html>.
8. Grobman, "Classical and Christian Anti-Semitism."
9. Grobman, "Classical and Christian Anti-Semitism."
10. Origen, "Against Celsus," as quoted in Sandra S. Williams, "The Origins of Christian Anti-Semitism," 1993. 11 Feb 1999. <http://ddi.digital.net/~billw/ANTI/anti-semitism.html>. Emphasis added.
11. As quoted in Williams, "The Origins of Christian Anti-Semitism."
12. As quoted in Michael L. Brown, *Our Hands Are Stained With Blood* (Shippensburg, Pennsylvania: Destiny Image Publishers, 1992), 10.
13. Reconciliation Walk. 24 Aug 1999. <http://www.reconciliationwalk. org/crusades.htm>. Emphasis added.
14. Reconciliation Walk. 24 Aug 1999. <http://www.reconciliationwalk. org/crusades.htm>.
15. Martin Luther, *That Jesus Christ was Born a Jew*, as quoted in Michael L. Brown, *Our Hands Are Stained With Blood*, 14.
16. Martin Luther, *Concerning the Jews and Their Lies*, as quoted in Brown, *Our Hands Are Stained With Blood*, 14-15.

Chapter 8

The First Nations Massacre

On the morning of February 6, 1992, a historic meeting—the first of its kind in this nation—took place in Kansas City, Missouri. Leaders from 50 different denominations in the city met with the chiefs of the five Native American tribes who had formerly inhabited the land now occupied by the new residents of Kansas City. For the church leaders the purpose of the meeting was simple, yet profound: to ask God's forgiveness and the forgiveness of the five tribes for the sins and wrongs committed against them in years past by those in the Kansas City metropolitan area.[1]

Sponsored by a local interdenominational prayer ministry called Ministries of New Life, this landmark event, "A Day of Repentance and Reconciliation," was the culmination of two years of research and planning.[2] My family and I were living in Kansas City at the time and, representing Ministry to the Nations, I had the privilege of not only attending this event but also being one of many believers participating in the citywide prayer movement that preceded it. More than 200 people attended the event. During the meeting itself, intercessors all over the city were praying.[3]

Following music from the choir of Haskell Indian Junior College, a representative of a group called Reconciliation Ministries recited a list of sins committed by the white man against the Native Americans of the area:

"broken treaties...merciless plundering of tribal land...13 million buffalo slaughtered to force the Native Americans through starvation to leave Kansas and Missouri...digging up their loved ones and selling articles buried with them...instigating quarrels among the tribes...plying discouraged tribes with whiskey to extract from them what little money they had...eventually taking from them all land that had been promised to them perpetually and driving them to Oklahoma."[4]

Brief histories of each of the tribes were shared, after which the chiefs in attendance delivered remarks on behalf of their tribes: the Delaware, the Kansa, the Osage, the Shawnee, and the Wyandotte. Following this, prayers of repentance were offered by three pastors representing the evangelical, liturgical, and charismatic branches of the Church. In response to these prayers, Chief Charles O. Tillman of the Osage, representing all the chiefs present, responded,

"I just want to say that this is a new beginning, and we must not look back. I read a scripture that said that when the Lord forgives He forgets about it. Those are powerful words. And in that, we forgive you, and you forgive us. It's two-sided, everything that's happened in the past, we know that."[5]

At the close of the meeting, a local pastor pronounced a blessing on the Native American leaders and their nations, and one of the chiefs reciprocated by blessing the assembly on behalf of the Indian Nations. Everyone then joined in singing the Lord's Prayer while a young woman from the Wyandotte tribe interpreted in Indian sign language.[6] The entire proceeding touched everyone who was present, and an atmosphere of reconciliation and unity filled the room. It indeed was a privilege to be present and witness such a historic event.

Overturning the Past

This landmark meeting in Kansas City is an excellent example of the kind of identification, confession, and repentance of generational sin that is so critical today for healing the offenses, injustices, and abuses of the past. Although such a gathering cannot by itself undo the past or resolve all the problems, it is a vital first step. Honest confession, sincere repentance, and a heartfelt cry for forgiveness can go a long way in softening anger, relieving resentment, and opening an avenue for reconciliation. Most people prefer harmony to discord. Clearing the air through humble confession and repentance helps remove the bases for estrangement and helps establish common ground for working together. It allows the Holy Spirit to bring about genuine reconciliation, which is always the desire and expression of God's heart.

Aside from being the first of its kind in the nation, the Kansas City gathering was significant for other reasons as well. That region of the country is part of what is called the "heartland of America." The condition of the heart determines the health of the body. As with any city or geographical region, God wants to pour out His heart there and bring healing. The Kansas City area has two particularly tragic legacies from its past to overcome. One is the treatment Native Americans received at the hands of the "whites," and the other deals with slavery.

During the decade immediately preceding the Civil War, violence broke out along the Missouri-Kansas border between pro-slavery and anti-slavery factions. Missouri was a slave state, and advocates of slavery wanted Kansas to enter the Union as a slave state also. Opponents of slavery fought this vigorously. Eventually Kansas was admitted as a free state in 1861, but the violence, murder, bloodshed, and lawlessness of the border fighting earned the region the grim nickname of "bloody Kansas."

All these things brought curses of division, slander, hatred, and murder onto the land that in turn gave demonic powers the legal basis to operate. True unity and reconciliation are possible only if confession and repentance are made for the atrocities and violence of the past. The "Day of Repentance and Reconciliation" was an important step in that direction. In the preceding year, 1991, Ministries of New Life sponsored a similar meeting for reconciliation between blacks and whites in which white church leaders humbled themselves before their black brethren and sought forgiveness for the injustices of slavery and racial prejudice.

Such events as these serve to begin the process of healing and reconciliation. Since that event in Kansas City in 1992, similar gatherings have taken place in other cities and regions where more repentance and apologies have been made to Native Americans—the First Nations People—for their treatment at the hands of European American immigrants.

Called to Be Reconcilers

As Christians, we are called to be reconcilers. "Now all these things are from God, who reconciled us to Himself through Christ, and gave us the ministry of reconciliation, namely, that God was in Christ reconciling the world to Himself, not counting their trespasses against them, and He has committed to us the word of reconciliation" (2 Cor. 5:18-19). Just as God seeks to reconcile the world to Himself through Christ, so we should urge lost people to be reconciled to God.

But in order to be effective we ourselves must be right with God, and this means that we must also be right with others. The apostle Paul wrote, "If possible, so far as it depends on you, be at peace with all men" (Rom. 12:18). Jesus said, "If therefore you are presenting your offering at the altar, and there remember that your brother has something against you, leave your offering there before the altar, and go your way; first be reconciled to your brother, and then come and present your offering" (Mt. 5:23-24). John stated the matter very plainly: "If someone says, 'I love God,' and hates his brother, he is a liar; for the one who does not love his brother whom he has seen, cannot love God whom he has not seen" (1 Jn. 4:20).

The focus in all three of these Scripture passages is that *we are to take the initiative*. If we want to see genuine reconciliation in our day, we must be willing to take the first step. We cannot ignore the sins and injustices of the past. That's what identification in intercession and confession of generational sin are all about.

Remember Sand Creek

For the most part, the history of "white" European American dealings with Native American people is a sad and sorry tale of lies, deceit, corruption, betrayal, cheating, subjugation, humiliation, and annihilation. To be sure, both sides committed wrongs and atrocities, and there were many "whites" who treated the Indians with honesty, integrity, respect, and compassion. By and large, however, it is a dismal record. Confession and repentance by American Caucasian Christians are needed because this ill treatment was primarily at the hands of people raised in the culture, traditions, beliefs, and social and moral values of European Christianity, and in many cases it happened with the direct involvement or at least the tacit support and approval of these so-called American "Christians."

In 1836, Texans fighting for independence from Mexico rallied to the cry, "Remember the Alamo!" Americans rushing to enlist in the war against Spain in 1898 were exhorted to "Remember the *Maine!*" In December 1941, our entire nation geared up for war to the call, "Remember Pearl Harbor!" If Native Americans had a "battle cry" to memorialize their experiences with "European" America, it would be, "Remember Sand Creek!" For many Native Americans there is no greater source of offense and bitterness than this action in Colorado on November 29, 1864, by elements of the U.S. Army under the command of a former

Methodist minister against a village of Cheyenne and Arapaho Indians, many of whom were women and children.

Prelude to Tragedy

After several years of mounting tensions, by the fall of 1864 a practical state of war existed in Colorado between the Indians and the white settlers. The Indians had become increasingly concerned and frustrated that the whites were taking over traditional hunting grounds, plowing up the land, and raising cattle on grasslands needed by the buffalo. Whites, on the other hand, were angry and fearful over the increasing number of raids by small bands of Indians who robbed farms and stole cattle, horses, and food. The murders of a rancher and his family by Indians in June 1864 had brought the anger, fear, and panic to a fever pitch.

Governor John Evans, who believed that a general Indian uprising was underway, sought to break it up by informing the tribes that if they wanted peace, provisions, and security, then they should report to certain forts and place themselves under the protection of the army garrisons there. Unfortunately, misunderstandings between Indians and soldiers inflamed the situation until major raids by the Indians on wagon trains and ranches left as many as 200 whites dead.

Colonel John M. Chivington, commander of the Military District of Colorado and a former Methodist minister, was ordered by General Samuel Curtis to deliver up the "bad" Indians and see to it that stolen stock was restored and hostages secured. Chivington was to make no peace with the Indians without orders from Curtis.[7]

At about the same time Chivington and Governor Evans met with Black Kettle, White Antelope, and several other chiefs near Denver. Chivington advised them that peace required that they lay down their arms and submit to military authority. Major Wynkoop, the commanding officer of Fort Lyon, had promised Black Kettle earlier that any Indians who reported to Fort Lyon wanting peace would be protected and safe from attack.

In early November, a band of 650-700 Cheyennes and Arapahos under Chiefs Black Kettle, White Antelope, Left Hand, and War Bonnet camped beside Sand Creek, as directed by Major Anthony, the new commanding officer of Fort Lyon. These Indians wanted peace with the whites and believed that they were under military protection. However, Major Anthony was not as sympathetic toward the Indians as Major Wynkoop was. He had no authority to negotiate peace, nor did he seek it; he did, however, advise Chivington of the location of Black Kettle and his band.

At dawn on November 29, 1864, Chivington and his command arrived on the ridge above the Cheyenne-Arapaho village on Sand Creek. Chivington's latest orders from General Curtis were, "Pursue everywhere and chastise the Cheyennes and Arapaho; pay no attention to district lines. No presents must be made and no peace concluded without my consent." Chivington himself, although a staunch opponent of slavery, was no lover of Indians. When several officers protested the upcoming attack on the grounds that Major Wynkoop had promised protection for Black Kettle and his people, Chivington reportedly said,

> "The Cheyenne nation has been waging bloody war against the whites...Black Kettle is their principal chief. They have been guilty of arson, murder, rape, and fiendish torture, not even sparing women and little children. I believe it is right and honorable to use any means under God's heaven to kill Indians who kill and torture women and children. Damn any man who is in sympathy with them."[8]

Chivington's command consisted of 750 volunteers, mostly rough, undisciplined, independent-minded men from the Colorado mining camps who had enlisted for 100 days. So far they had seen no action. Their enlistments were almost up, so they were itching for a fight.

The Battle of Sand Creek

Chivington attacked around 6:00 a.m., just after dawn. The battle raged most of the day, ending around 4:00 p.m. The exact course of the battle, as well as the specific conduct of the soldiers under Chivington's command, have been the source of controversy and debate ever since. Initially Chivington and his men were considered heroes. Before long, however, amid accusations of massacre and mutilation, demands were made for inquiries into the military actions at Sand Creek. One Army investigation was inconclusive. Two Congressional hearings painted Chivington and his men as villains who attacked a peaceful village of Indians who believed they were under military protection, indiscriminately slaughtering men, women, and children and scalping and mutilating their bodies.

Eyewitness testimonies shed some light on what happened that cold November morning.

> "I...saw that Black Kettle had a large American flag tied to the end of a long lodge pole, and was standing in front of his lodge, holding the pole, with the flag fluttering in the gray light of winter dawn. I heard him call to the people not to be afraid, that the soldiers would not hurt them; then the troops opened fire from two sides of the camp."[9]

> "I think there were thirty-five braves and some old men, about sixty in all...after the firing the warriors put the squaws and children together, and surrounded them to protect them. I saw five squaws under a bank for shelter. When the troops came up to them, they ran out...and begged for mercy, but the soldiers shot them all....There seemed to be indiscriminate slaughter of men, women and children. There were some thirty or forty squaws collected in a hole for protection; they sent out a little girl about six years old with a white flag on a stick. She...was shot and killed. All the squaws in that hole were afterwards killed....Everyone I saw dead was scalped....I saw a number of infants in arms, killed with their mothers."[10]

> "In going over the battlefield the next day I did not see a body of man, woman or child but was scalped and in

many instances their bodies were mutilated in the most horrible manners."[11]

Because the Cheyennes carried away their wounded and many of their dead, it was never completely clear exactly how many Indians died at Sand Creek or how many warriors there were in comparison to old men, women, and children. Colonel Chivington, in his first report to General Curtis, called Sand Creek "one of the bloodiest Indian battles ever fought on these plains" and claimed that 500 Indians had died. Other estimates ranged between 69 and 450. Testimony regarding the number of women and children in the village ranged from a few to as many as two-thirds of the camp. Whatever happened that day, "there can be little doubt that Sand Creek occurred because of white incursions, government mismanagement, broken treaties and the fact that there were not only 'bad' white men but also 'bad' Indians."[12]

Although there are two sides (or more) to every story, most accounts of the battle at Sand Creek agree that as many as 200 Cheyenne and Arapaho, two-thirds of them women and children, were brutally killed and that many of the bodies were savagely mutilated.

Repenting for Sand Creek

Regardless of the specifics, the incident at Sand Creek still stands (along with the massacre of 250 Indians at Wounded Knee, South Dakota, on December 29, 1890), as one of the most infamous and shameful events in the history of white American and Native American relations. Immediately after Sand Creek enraged Indians went on the warpath, and news of the killings and mutilations shocked white Americans all across the country. No *official* apology has ever been offered. It is long overdue.

On April 22, 1996, the United Methodist Church, recognizing its link to the Sand Creek tragedy through the "Fighting Parson," Methodist lay preacher John Chivington, took an important step toward reconciliation. Meeting in Denver, the United Methodist General Conference adopted a resolution apologizing for the Sand

Creek massacre and proposing a healing service of reconciliation. Rev. Alvin Deer stated, "The United Methodist Church delegation has recognized this was a tragedy in U.S. history that needed to be addressed. With the General Conference meeting in Denver, it was the most appropriate time to deal with the tragedy."[13]

John Dawson is the international director of Urban Missions for Youth With a Mission (YWAM) and founder of the International Reconciliation Coalition. On January 14, 1993, he participated in a Coalition-sponsored reconciliation gathering at the Sand Creek massacre site in Colorado. Everyone in attendance was a believer and a mature intercessor. He described what took place:

> "I looked around the circle at the inheritors of this legacy. Some had deep roots in Colorado, both Indian and European. Some represented families with generations of involvement with the U.S. Army....I suggested that we make confession and ask forgiveness in the presence of the Lord and our Native American brothers. There were many tears. Prayers were heartfelt and deeply honest.
>
> "One woman stretched herself out in the sand, touching the feet of an Indian pastor; deeply ashamed she wept for the lost generation that was cut off in this place. The sense of loss was upon us all; the beauty of what might have been had these two peoples walked together in integrity; the generations of alcoholism, suicide and despair that could have been avoided if a culture with the gospel in its roots had exemplified rather than defamed Jesus to a spiritually hungry people."[14]

A carefully prepared confession itemized the injustices committed. It covered four categories (paraphrased below), and each concluded with a specific request for forgiveness:

- *Government—military.*
  Confession of dishonest actions by government agents and business interests that cheated Indians out of their rightful land and property; government

failure to enforce more than 300 treaties; government failure to resolve the Sand Creek massacre. *"For the wrongs committed, for the related betrayals of your trust, and for the atrocity of Sand Creek, we offer our apology and ask for forgiveness."*

- *Social injustices—prejudices.*
  Removal of Indian children from their homes, often forever, to make them "white"; subjection of Indians to blatant prejudice and subservient positions in society; violation of Indian graves and selling of artifacts. *"We apologize for these wrongs and injustices, and ask for forgiveness."*

- *Sins of those bearing Christ's name.*
  Frequent attitudes of superiority on the part of Christian missionaries; imposition of Western culture along with the gospel; economic exploitation of Indian children; John Chivington's unfeeling actions toward Indians at Sand Creek. *"For the destructiveness of zeal without wisdom, and the misguided and insensitive ways in which the Church has dealt with you, we ask your forgiveness."*

- *Violation of stewardship of the land.*
  Indians, who possessed the land by the first right of occupancy lost the right to large parts of their land due to the greed and dishonesty of white businessmen, miners, and land speculators in direct defiance of treaty rights; wanton destruction of buffalo herds, the mainstay of food, clothing, and shelter for the plains Indians, which, through starvation, forced them onto reservations. *"For the wrongs committed in the illegal taking of land, for the government's unwillingness to enforce legal treaty rights, and for the hundreds of Indian lives taken in defense of these treaty rights, we ask for forgiveness."*[15]

The Reconciliation Coalition has provided us with a wonderful model for identificational confession and repentance; it is specific, direct, and comprehensive, expressing full acceptance of responsibility and a genuine desire for forgiveness and reconciliation. As far as John Dawson is concerned, the issue is critical for the future of the American Church:

> "Reconciliation with Native Americans, especially, is foundational. There is a hindrance to God's blessing on this nation as long as this wound remains unhealed. Without the embrace and blessing of the 'host' people, Americans will fall short of apprehending both their identity and their destiny....If the American Church is ever to reach its full potential, reconciliation between European Americans and Native Americans is non-negotiable."[16]

The Macedonian Call

One of the things that makes the dismal record of European American treatment of the Indians especially tragic is that many of the earliest colonists were motivated to come to these shores by a desire to evangelize the native peoples. The Massachusetts Bay Colony, established by the Puritans in 1630, adopted a seal that pictured an American Indian saying, *"Come over and help us,"* a direct reference to Paul's *"Macedonian call"* in Acts 16:9-10. Conversion of Indians to Christ was a specific goal written into the charters of early New England settlements. Cultural clashes, pervading attitudes of "superiority" on the part of the Europeans, and general resistance to conversion on the part of the Indians caused problems from the outset. There were some bright lights, however.

John Eliot (1604–1690), a Puritan minister educated in England at Cambridge University, arrived in Boston in 1631. Together with family and friends from England, he organized the First Church of Roxbury, Massachusetts, in 1632, which he pastored for 58 years. Two years into this ministry, Eliot began working among the Algonquin Indians. His many years of hard, diligent labor to reach them for Christ earned him the title, "Apostle to the Indians." He even learned their language so he could preach Christ to them without an interpreter. As a result, many Indians came to Christ, and Eliot helped them establish villages where more than 1,000 "Praying Indians" lived and learned about the Lord. He issued a series of "Eliot's Indian Tracts" to help the Indians grow in the faith. Eliot's most significant contribution, however, was his eight-year effort to translate the Bible into Algonquin. When it appeared in 1663, it was the first complete Bible of any kind published in the New World.[17]

Although frail and sickly for most of his short life, *David Brainerd (1718–1747)* was a bright light for Christ among the Indians of New York, New Jersey, and eastern Pennsylvania. Converted to Christ while a student at Yale University, Brainerd began his ministry among the Indians in April 1743. In four-and-a-half short years of missionary work before tuberculosis took his life at the age of 29, Brainerd sought to master the language and culture of the Indians and traveled hundreds of miles through forests and over mountains on horseback and on foot to preach and minister to them. He spent literally hours at a time, day after day, in prayer for the Indians—often standing or kneeling in the snow. It is thought that by the end of his brief ministry as many as one-sixth of the Indian population within the scope of his influence had been won to Christ. Brainerd's journal of his years with the Indians, published two years after his death, has been a source of inspiration, conviction, and challenge to generations of believers, including many who answered God's call to missionary service after reading it.

An 1833 issue of the *Christian Advocate and Journal* tells the story of four Indians from west of the Rocky Mountains who traveled 3,000 miles to St. Louis. Why? They had heard that the white people knew the proper way to worship the Great Spirit and that they had a book that contained directions. Two of the Indians dropped dead from disease and exhaustion as soon as they reached the city, but the other two were well received and treated in high style. At the end of their visit, one of the Indians, named Ta-Wis-Sis-Sim-Nim, said these words:

> "My people sent me to get the white man's Book of Heaven. You took me where you allow your women to dance, as we do not ours, and the Book was not there. You showed me images of the Great Spirit and pictures of the Good Land beyond, but the Book was not among them to tell me the way. I am going back the long trail to my people in the dark land. You make my feet heavy with gifts, and my moccasins will grow old in carrying them, and yet the Book is not among them. When I tell my poor, blind people, after one more snow, in the big council, that I did not bring the Book, no word will be spoken by our old men or by our young braves. One by one, they will rise up and go out in silence. My people will die in darkness, and they will go a long path to other hunting grounds. No white man will go with them, and no white man's Book to make the way plain. I have no more words."[18]

Talk about a "Macedonian call"! What a marvelous opportunity! What a tragic failure! The appearance of these words convicted many of God's people, and around a hundred missionaries answered the call to take the gospel to the Indians. Among them were Dr. Marcus and Narcissa Whitman and Rev. Henry and Eliza Spalding, who traveled to the Oregon territory in 1836 and established missions among the Cayuse and Nez Perce Indians. In 1847 the Whitmans and 11 others were killed by the very Indians they had been trying to reach for 11 years.

A Humble Confession

As a white American Christian of European descent, I ask the First Nations People—the Native American brothers and sisters—to forgive us for our colonialization, for our prideful entry, for our cultural arrogance! Forgive us for the exploitation, the lies, the betrayal, the murder, the theft of your land, the destruction of your way of life, and the contempt for your dignity! Forgive us for showing you a Christianity without Christ, a "form of godliness" but without its power; for talking about the way, but not showing you the way.

Father, we have sinned! Father, forgive us! O Lord, raise up again in this generation your John Eliots and David Brainerds, your Marcus and Narcissa Whitmans and Henry and Eliza Spaldings! Father, lift the burden and stain of injustice we bear for our sins against our Native American brethren! Raise up again among them more faithful ambassadors for Christ of their own. Help us together to heal the wounds and build bridges and move as one people into the destiny we share as Your children!

Reflection Questions

1. What is one of the great historical wounds in America's history against the First Nations People?

2. What sins committed against the Native North American Indians do you believe that you could begin to confess before the Father in behalf of our (your) nation?

3. If you stood right now before one of the First Nations People, what would you have to say as a Christian?

Recommended Reading

Healing America's Wounds by John Dawson (Regal, 1994)

Can You Feel the Mountains Tremble? A Healing The Land Handbook by Dr. Suugiina (Inuit Ministries International, 1999)

Five Hundred Years of Bad Haircuts by Richard Twiss (Wiconi International, 1996)

Endnotes

1. Albert Rountree, "Why Should We Christians Repent for the Sins Committed by Others in Years Past?" *New Life* newsletter (Ministries of New Life, n.d.), 5.
2. Bette Armstrong, "A Day of Repentance and Reconciliation," *New Life* newsletter (Ministries of New Life, n.d.), 1.
3. Armstrong, "A Day of Repentance and Reconciliation," *New Life* newsletter, 1.
4. Armstrong, "A Day of Repentance and Reconciliation," *New Life* newsletter, 2.
5. Armstrong, "A Day of Repentance and Reconciliation," *New Life* newsletter, 4.
6. Armstrong, "A Day of Repentance and Reconciliation," *New Life* newsletter, 4.
7. J. Jay Myers, "The Notorious Fight at Sand Creek," *WildWest*, December, 1998. 2 Feb 1999. <http://www.thehistorynet.com/WildWest/articles/1998/1298_text.htm>.
8. Myers, "The Notorious Fight at Sand Creek," *WildWest*.
9. George Bent to George E. Hyde, April 14, 1906 (Coe Collection, Yale University), as quoted in John Dawson, *Healing America's Wounds* (Ventura, California: Regal Books, 1994), 146.
10. Robert Bent, U.S. Congress 39th 2nd session, Senate Report 156, pages 73, 96, as quoted in Dawson, *Healing America's Wounds*, 146-147.
11. Lieutenant James Conner, U.S. Congress 39th 2nd session, Senate Report 156, page 53, as quoted in Dawson, *Healing America's Wounds*, 147.
12. Myers, "The Notorious Fight at Sand Creek," *WildWest*.
13. "Delegates apologize for 1864 Sand Creek Massacre led by Methodist lay preacher," *United Methodist Daily News*, April 22, 1996. 1 Sep 1999. <http://www.umc.org/gencon/news/massacre.html>.
14. Dawson, *Healing America's Wounds*, 148.
15. Dawson, *Healing America's Wounds*, 151-154.
16. John Dawson, "Happy Trails or Trail of Tears?" *Reconciliation Wednesday, A Weekly Forum on Current Issues*, June 12, 1996. 8 Feb 1999. <http://www.execpc.com/logos/eliot.htm>.

17. "The Eliot Indian Bible," *Logos Christian Resource Pages*. 2 Sept 1999.
     <http://www.execpc.com/logos/eliot.htm>.
18. "A Call for Missionaries," taken from *A Voice in the Wilderness*,
     March, 1998. 2 Sept 1999. <http://www.worldmissions.org/
     clipper/Missions/ACallForMissionaries.html>.

Chapter 9

The Enslavement of a People

All across the Body of Christ a yearning, passionate cry to God is growing: "Thy kingdom come. Thy will be done in earth, as it is in heaven" (Mt. 6:10 KJV). We long for the glory of the Lord to fill the earth. More and more of the people of God are pleading along with John, "And the Spirit and the bride say, 'Come.'...Amen. Come, Lord Jesus" (Rev. 22:17a,20b).

Christ, our Bridegroom, will return to receive His Church...a Bride pure and spotless, holy and innocent, beautifully adorned, with an unfeigned and undivided adoration for Him. The Scriptures indicate that the Bride will be ready *before* He comes for her; He will not make her ready *after* He comes. " 'Let us rejoice and be glad and give the glory to Him, for the marriage of the Lamb has come and His bride has *made herself* ready.' And it was given to her to clothe herself in fine linen, bright and clean; for the *fine linen is the righteous acts of the saints*" (Rev. 19:7-8). The conditions under which the Lord will receive His Church *when* He returns will be in place in the Church *before* He returns. So let's get out our Holy Ghost ironing board and press out some of the wrinkles that are in the Bride's dress, for Jesus' sake!

One of those conditions—one of the "righteous acts of the saints"—is unity. It is perhaps the most important one of all. Jesus made this clear when He prayed,

*I do not ask in behalf of these alone, but for those also who believe in Me through their word; **that they may all be one;** even as Thou, Father, art in Me, and I in Thee, that they also may be in Us; that the world may believe that Thou didst send Me. And the glory which Thou hast given Me I have given to them; **that they may be one, just as We are one;** I in them, and Thou in Me, **that they may be perfected in unity,** that the world may know that Thou didst send Me, and didst love them, even as Thou didst love Me (John 17:20-23).*

Christ wants His Church to walk in the same unity that He enjoys with the Father. Perfect harmony exists within the Godhead; there is a complete oneness between Father, Son, and Holy Spirit. No competition, jealousy, or pushing for position there! And that is how the Godhead wants us to walk with each other. That oneness is to be reflected in the life and witness of the Church.

Paul reiterated the theme of unity in several of his letters. "There is neither Jew nor Greek, there is neither slave nor free man, there is neither male nor female; for you are all one in Christ Jesus" (Gal. 3:28). "And beyond all these things put on love, which is the perfect bond of unity" (Col. 3:14). "I...entreat you to walk in a manner worthy of the calling with which you have been called...being diligent to preserve the unity of the Spirit in the bond of peace" (Eph. 4:1,3). "And He gave some as apostles, and some as prophets, and some as evangelists, and some as pastors and teachers, for the equipping of the saints for the work of service, to the building up of the body of Christ; until we all attain to the unity of the faith..." (Eph. 4:11-13).

Clearly the unity of *all* believers is both the burning desire and the demand of our Lord. Yet today there are many things that we have allowed to separate us into different camps. From the very beginning satan has followed a strategy of "divide and conquer" to cripple the Church. His intention has been to trip us up and cause us to fight among ourselves instead of focusing on the commission that Christ gave us to make disciples of all nations. We are divided over theology, doctrine, and denominational perspectives, as well as over baptismal methodology, communion, and spiritual gifts. These are bad enough because they make it difficult for us to find common ground on which to work together. Worse still, however, is that we are divided along *racial* lines.

Racism: A Deadly Disease

Racism is probably the most virulent malignancy infecting American society today, with black-white antagonism being its most potent form. From 1619, when the first 20 African slaves were sold in Jamestown, Virginia, until the end of the Civil War nearly 250 years later, the ugly specter of slavery cast a grim shadow over our land. Although President Abraham Lincoln's Emancipation Proclamation of 1863, the Union victory in 1865, and passage of the thirteenth Amendment to the Constitution in December 1865 secured the physical freedom of the slaves, the "Jim Crow" laws passed and enforced by the white majority effectively kept black Americans bound politically, socially, and economically for another century. The Civil Rights movement of the 1950s and 60s brought an end to the dominance of "Jim Crow," but more than 30 years later many of the dreams and goals of African-Americans for complete equality remain dreadfully unfulfilled. For more than three centuries prejudice and discrimination have festered in our land, frequently erupting into violence and tragedy. As we cross over the threshold ino the new millennium the problem is still very much with us.

The sin and injustice of white-black racism in general, and slavery in particular, has had devastating effects on both sides. For many blacks it has created a legacy of bitterness, anger, hopelessness, and despair. This is seen most clearly in the cycles of poverty, crime, and broken homes in the inner cities of our major urban areas. Writing from the African-American perspective, pastor and author Michael Goings states,

"We battle an ethnic inferiority complex developed over several hundred years of dehumanizing slavery, subsequent racism, segregation, and discrimination. As a result, most African-Americans face a formidable battle to find equality in their own minds—a fight many lose before they ever reach the marketplace or job site."[1]

On the other hand, many whites struggle with feelings of guilt, self-inflicted or otherwise. Sometimes it is guilt by association: "I'm guilty because I'm white," which often leads to attitudes of defensiveness, resentment, and self-protection. In their extreme form, these attitudes are reflected in the vehemence of white supremacist groups and in the rise of white-against-black "hate crimes."

The evil seed of racism bears bitter fruit. As Michael Goings writes,

"Racism is the mother of bigotry, discrimination, 'Jim Crowism' (discrimination against African Americans by 'legal' means or sanctions), Nazism, the 'white supremacy' movement, anti-Semitism, apartheid, and the Black Muslim movement. All of these belief systems and ideologies spring from an attitude of superiority over others who are different....This same evil and deep-rooted belief is still ingrained in the minds of many whites in America and South Africa, respectively perpetuating discrimination and apartheid in these nations."[2]

Racism is based on ignorance. Ignorance breeds fear, which gives birth to hatred. All of these—ignorance, fear, and hatred— are contrary to the will and the Spirit of God. As pastor and author Kelley Varner writes,

"God hates racism in any form—it is sin. Racism is rooted in degeneracy, pride, superior attitudes, ignorance, and fear. Unregenerate Adamic flesh is the soil from which racism springs. Included here are pride of place (social status), pride of face (physical attributes), pride of grace (religious or denominational traditions), and pride of race (based on skin color or ethnicity)."[3]

Michael Goings defines racism as "racial attitudes, beliefs, and false concepts of ethnic superiority," and has identified three forms of racism according to their sources:[4]

1. *Hereditary racism.*
   Racist attitudes passed down from parent to child, from one generation to the next, often in the guise of religious instruction.

2. *Environmental racism.*
   Racist attitudes caused by the overpowering influence of one's environment and association (such as hate groups and racist organizations).

3. *Reactionary/reverse racism.*
   Racist attitudes triggered in a suppressed minority by ill treatment and acts of racism inflicted by members of other dominant groups.

The divisiveness and destructiveness of racism in our land should cut to the heart of every sensitive and reasonable American, regardless of race. We who call ourselves Christians, and especially we who are "pale faced," should feel an even greater sense of responsibility. We are responsible in large part for these atrocities since throughout our nation's history many segments of the institutional "white" American Church have aided and abetted the existence and perpetuation of racism in America. But, as believers in Christ, we have been given the ministry of reconciliation. Therefore, to my fellow "white" brothers and sisters I say, *"Our hands are not clean! Father, forgive us!"*

Slavery: America's National Shame

From 1619, when the first slaves stood on the block in Jamestown, Virginia, until 1807, when the United States banned the further importation of slaves, well over three million African men, women, and children were brought to these shores against their will and sold into lives of permanent servitude. Stolen from their homes and families, these captives were crammed aboard ships especially fitted out to transport as many slaves as possible. Every inch of space below decks was utilized. The conditions were unspeakable. Flat on their backs, shackled hand and foot with no space between them, and unable to move, the slaves were often forced to lie in their own excrement for days at a time during a voyage lasting several weeks. The stench must have been incredible. In the heat, stale air, and accumulated filth, hundreds of thousands did not survive the trip. Those who died were simply and unceremoniously dumped over the side like so much driftwood.

Those slaves who lived to stand on the auction block faced a bleak future with little hope. Terrified and unable to speak the language of their captors, they had no rights, no redress under the law, and no one to stand for them. They simply were treated as property to be bought and sold at will. Even family ties meant nothing; countless times families were torn apart as children and even husbands and wives were sold to different owners, never to see each other again. All children born to slaves were automatically considered slaves as well. Unless they escaped, were able to buy their freedom, or were freed by their masters, slaves were in bondage for life. Because they were "property," slaves could be (and routinely were) willed to successive generations of owners.

Slave life was hard, particularly on the southern plantations. The majority of slaves were field hands who labored from sunrise to sunset six days a week (sometimes seven, depending on the plantation owner). Punishment for infractions was often harsh and terribly brutal. Runaway slaves who were recaptured usually faced at least a severe whipping. Sometimes they were maimed in a manner that would make it difficult for them to run away again. Another punishment was to be "sold down the river"—sold to another owner—which usually meant an even worse situation for the slave. Being "sold down the river" became a euphemism for a slave's worst nightmare, especially for those with families.

Although in the beginning slavery existed in both northern and southern states, strong abolitionist sentiment arose particularly in the North. Even though states north of the Mason-Dixon line gradually abolished slavery, federal laws continued to support the institution until the Civil War. One reason is that for many years prior to the Civil War, the United States Congress was controlled by Southern interests. A Fugitive Slave law, passed in 1793, provided for the return of runaway slaves to their owners from any state into which they had fled, even if that state was a free state. The Missouri Compromise of 1820 admitted my native born state of Missouri to the Union as a slave state, Maine as a free state, and outlawed slavery in every state or territory (except Missouri) north of 36°30' latitude.

As northern states eventually abolished slavery altogether, they also relaxed enforcement of the 1793 Fugitive Slave law. The Underground Railroad also did much to nullify the effects of the law. The Compromise of 1850 admitted California as a slave state and abolished slavery in the District of Columbia. It also strengthened the 1793 Fugitive Slave law by stating that since slaves were officially property and that ownership of property extended across state lines, slave owners were within their rights to cross state lines in order to retrieve their runaway slaves. Furthermore, law enforcement officials charged with the public trust to protect person and property were held responsible for the capture and return of slaves to their owners. One consequence of this law was that it became much easier to capture blacks, ex-slaves or not, and ship them south in chains. In this way many "free" blacks were charged with being runaways and taken into bondage. The U.S. Supreme Court upheld this trend in its 1857 Dred Scott decision, ruling that slaves were property, even if they were living in a free state, and that Congress had no authority to forbid slaveholding. The whole slavery issue was decided permanently just a few years later in the fiery cauldron of the Civil War, at the cost (on both sides) of 562,130 dead and 418,206 wounded.

The Blindness of the "White" American Church

Now hold on to your hat, because I'm about to make some weighty statements. The enslavement of African-Americans for nearly 250 years, and their subsequent disfranchisement socially, politically, and economically, remains one of the greatest "generational sins" of America. Confession and repentance on this issue are doubly important for we who are Caucasian American Christians because, to a great degree, the "white" Church in America has been very cooperative, first in the legitimization of slavery and second in the perpetuation of racial stereotypes and segregation. We stand guilty!

One of the reasons so many white Americans accepted slavery for so long is because many churches supported it in their teaching. There were notable exceptions, of course. For example, the Quakers were adamantly opposed to slavery on spiritual and moral grounds, as were the Mennonites and many other groups and individuals. In general, the people and churches of the more industrialized northern United States were less inclined to support slavery than those in the South did. The agriculturally based economy of the southern states depended heavily on slave labor. Slavery was knit into the very social, economic, and religious framework of Southern culture. Southern churches acknowledged the "necessity" of the "peculiar institution." Southern preachers supported slavery on supposed scriptural grounds. Typical of their "biblical" arguments were these:

- Slavery was an accepted reality in the Bible, in both the Old and New Testaments. Jesus, Paul, Peter, John, and other biblical leaders, teachers and writers had ample opportunity to denounce slavery if it was so evil, yet they did not. Therefore, it is an acceptable practice.

- Africans were inherently inferior, created by God specifically as a "servant race." Among other things, this was based on the supposed "curse of Ham," one of Noah's sons, through whom the Negro "race" is descended.

- Because they were "inferior," the Negro race needed for their own good the regulation, control, and guidance of the "higher" and more "enlightened" white people.

Many southern Americans saw slavery not only as acceptable and necessary for their society, but also as an institution established and sanctioned by God. During his inaugural address as provisional President of the Confederate States of America, Jefferson Davis said,

"[Slavery] was established by decree of Almighty God...it is sanctioned in the Bible, in both Testaments, from Genesis to Revelation...it has existed in all ages, has been found among the people of the highest civilization, and in nations of the highest proficiency in the arts."[5]

The Reverend Alexander Campbell said, "There is not one verse in the Bible inhibiting slavery, but many regulating it. It is not then, we conclude, immoral."[6] The Reverend R. Furman, a Baptist in South Carolina, had this to say: "The right of holding slaves is clearly established in the Holy Scriptures, both by precept and example."[7]

These quotes are typical of what most southern Americans, including many, many Christians, believed. Yes, often our "cultural lenses" taint how we read God's instruction manual. Slavery was thoroughly entrenched in Southern society and culture. Hereditary and environmental racist influences blinded them (I must now say *us*, as I am now a resident of a southern state) to the gross immorality and injustice of slavery as well as to the inconsistency of a pro-slavery stance with the true message of the gospel.

In the years since the end of the Civil War, many segments of the "white" Church in America have perpetuated racial stereotypes and encouraged racial separation, even in church. Dr. Martin Luther King, Jr., once said that the most segregated hour in

America is 11:00 on Sunday morning. Although much progress has been made, after 30 years Dr. King's statement is just as true in many ways as when he first made it.

On the surface, the American racial landscape today looks much different than it did even 50 years ago. Desegregation and equal opportunity are the laws of the land in education, housing, employment, public facilities, and virtually every other area of life, yet racial tension between blacks and whites is on the rise. African-American church buildings have been burned to the ground. The problem actually seems to be escalating. Why? One reason is that "integration" only addresses the surface, or the appearance, of the race problem. True racial harmony cannot be achieved by any law or legislation. Nor can it be accomplished through "sensitivity" training or "cultural diversity" classes. Racial harmony requires reconciliation of the differences that divide us, and reconciliation is a matter of the *heart*. It is also the ministry of the true Church. The answer to racism is found only in the liberating gospel of Jesus Christ.

Rough Road to Reconciliation

The road to reconciliation will not, is not, and never has been, an easy one. There is a lot of baggage to deal with on both sides. White American Christians have the legacy of a Church that in many ways and for many years, has been an obstacle standing in the way of blacks, both by supporting slavery and by hindering blacks' full spiritual, social, and economic development.

In the earliest years of slavery, a general practice existed that discouraged evangelizing slaves in the belief that a pagan slave would be a better slave—a more controllable slave—than a Christian slave would. Many slave owners who took this position were Christians and church members in good standing. Some even believed that blacks were sub-human and did not have souls to save! There was also the moral dilemma at the thought of a Christian slave owner keeping a fellow Christian in bondage. As concern for the "souls" of slaves grew, evangelizing them became more accepted, but laws were passed expressly stating that a slave's conversion to Christ was *not* automatically grounds for setting him free. For many, this removed both the moral dilemma and the economic risk of bringing slaves to Christ.

Over the course of the years, many African-Americans, both slave and free, did become authentic Christians. They were touched by God in many of the same revivals that swept through white America: the First Great Awakening of the 1730s and 40s, the second Great Awakening of the 1790s and early 1800s, and subsequent movements. Although mostly illiterate at first (educating slaves was generally forbidden as well), believing slaves developed a vibrant faith with a style of worship and expression uniquely their own, and the gospel spread readily through many slave communities. However, due to fear of slave insurrections, in most places slaves were forbidden to congregate together in any numbers, even for worship. Often slaves were taken to their master's church where they sat shackled together in specially designated pews. Many slaves defied the rules, however, and risked severe punishment to sneak off into the woods to attend secret prayer meetings and worship services with other slaves. Imagine, this is part of our "American history"!

On the other hand, many slaves rejected the "white man's religion" because they clearly saw the hypocrisy between what Christianity taught and the lifestyles and practices of the white Christians whom they knew.

As the number of African-American Christians grew, many of the traditionally "white" denominations, particularly the Methodists and Baptists, were flooded with black members. The white leadership of these denominations sought to limit black members' involvement by prohibiting them from holding any positions of leadership or authority with any kind of decision-making power. This helped precipitate not only separate black and white churches in the same denominations, but also the formation of completely independent, all-black denominations, thus widening the rift between black and white Christians. That rift still remains today, and it is only just now beginning to close.

But it's a two-sided street. Reconciliation is difficult also because of the accumulated hurt and anger among blacks due to generations of bigotry and injustice (not to mention the reactionary guilt and defensiveness of many whites). In *Healing America's Wounds*, John Dawson provides an excellent discussion of this.

> "When a people have been oppressed and wounded and the yoke is lifted, when the circumstances finally change, the emancipation of their souls is not immediate. The first generation, those who are free but carrying the memory of hurt, are often too numb to be angry....The past is literally unspeakable, and...they are reluctant to talk about it....
>
> "This means that the second generation...are often relatively ignorant of the suffering that overshadows the recent past. It is often the third generation that stumbles across the awful truth in their search for understanding about identity: the unspeakable is spoken about and anger and bitterness surface into the public domain. This also means that the grandchildren of the oppressor often face the greatest hostility and rejection from elements of the offended people group, leaving them bewildered and struggling for an appropriate response."[8]

Breaking the Bonds of Racism

One key to racial reconciliation is understanding the false premise that lies behind racism: that "races" are genetically distinct and specific and that some "races" are inherently superior to others. This is a complete and total fiction with its roots in a time long before knowledge of modern biology, propped up by generations of people who needed to justify their enslavement and persecution of people who were superficially different from them. Once again, John Dawson says it well:

"Biologically, there are no races. So-called racial characteristics vary so much from individual to individual that all attempts at establishing distinct biological units that deserve classification are arbitrary. Each person has tens of thousands of different genes. At the genetic level, human beings are incredibly diverse in a way that transcends geographic dispersion. Therefore, what we call a race is a classification of culture, having more to do with tribal membership or national citizenship than any real genetic distinction.

"For some reason, skin color has been the defining characteristic in cross-cultural relationships. No personal physical feature, except gender, has made such an impact on the fates of individuals and people groups, yet pigmentation is a relatively superficial thing."[9]

If there is any issue that keeps the American Church from reaching its greatest potential, it is racism. Until we resolve this problem at a *heart* level, we will not see the fullness of God in our midst and our ministry. As Dawson says, "If racism is the thing more than any other that reveals the spiritual poverty of the American Church, let's take up this issue as the first order of public confession."[10] I give a hearty "Amen!"

Racial reconciliation calls not only for confession of sin, but also for the courage and the willingness to enter into dialogue with one another on more than a surface level. We need to learn to *talk* to each other honestly and openly about the hurt and the anger, the fear and the resentment, the bitterness and the misunderstanding that divide us.

Efforts are underway in many parts of the country. The Promise Keepers groups have made great strides in this direction with their ethnically diverse meetings nationwide. A few years ago while I was still living in Kansas City, white pastors and other church leaders gathered with their black brethren for a time of reconciliation. During that time the white leaders confessed the sins of the white Church against the blacks and asked for forgiveness. Similar gatherings have been held in other cities.

In some cases there have been denominational recognition of responsibility. For example, the Southern Baptist Convention, the largest Protestant denomination in America (it had split with northern Baptists in 1845 over the slavery issue), has in recent years adopted several resolutions at its annual meetings expressing regret and apology for racist policies and practices of the past. It should be noted too that Southern Baptist ranks include substantial numbers of African-Americans and a small but growing number of interracial churches.

A Bold Step

In 1992 two Baptist pastors in St. Paul, Minnesota—one white and the other black—began talking together about how their churches might work toward racial reconciliation. The effort was sparked when Dave Johnson, the white pastor, saw on television the riots and racial unrest in Los Angeles that followed the acquittal of four police officers in the beating of black motorist Rodney King. Johnson felt inadequate for the task of addressing the spiritual needs of the racially mixed neighborhood around his church. Black pastor Ron Smith had similar concerns.

As the two men met and prayed together, they began to understand and appreciate each other at a much deeper level. Johnson realized more than ever before how much of an advantage his white skin was, and Smith faced his deep fear of being betrayed by a white man. They exchanged pulpits occasionally. Finally, in August 1993, the two congregations—Johnson's Park Baptist Church and Smith's Open Door Baptist Church—worshiped together a few times. Members of the two congregations met and talked.

In late 1994 the two churches entered into a four-month experiment of worshiping together every Sunday. They wrestled with many questions: worship styles, types of music, decorum in the services. In February 1998 the two churches formally merged into the Unity Baptist Church, with Johnson and Smith serving as co-pastors. One significant fact is that although people in both churches felt uncomfortable in the combined church, the vast majority of them also favored merging. According to Pastor Johnson, "They felt God wanted us to be this way. The new way. Together." The way is still rocky at times. Pastor Ron Smith says, "We're not where we want to be. But we're on the way. God has knitted us together. We're going to make it."[11]

The creation of Unity Baptist Church goes beyond mere integration and taps into the true power of racial reconciliation in Christ. There is a big difference.

> "[Integration] removes formal barriers, primarily laws, that keep people apart, but leaves intact the centuries-old images, beliefs and cultural barriers that divide people— the miles-high walls in our hearts and minds. In racial reconciliation, individuals consciously strive to overcome the legacy of racism, first by forging genuine bonds with at least one person of a different race."[12]

There is a crying need in America today for racial reconciliation. We could tear other pages out of history and consider issues concerning the Chinese, Irish, Polish, Japanese, and many other nationalities. But to heal America's wounds, we must begin at one of our greatest historic sins and stains—the fear, prejudice, and pride between white and black Christians. The hideous shadow of slavery and its legacy of racial hostility and violence must be banished from the land.

As a white European Christian, I ask my African-American brothers and sisters to forgive us for denying to you the love of Christ we claimed for ourselves and shared among ourselves. Forgive us for our blindness, our prejudice, and our spiritual arrogance. Forgive us for our contempt of your culture, your identity, and your personhood. Forgive us for so often denying your essential worth in the eyes of God and man. Forgive us, my friends! We need you!

We have sinned! Father, forgive us! Forgive us, Your Caucasian children, for our bigotry and injustice toward our brothers and sisters of African descent—people also created in Your image and likeness and precious in Your sight. Forgive us for our arrogance and for our pride of place, our pride of face, our pride of grace, and our pride of race. Cleanse our hearts of any trace of prejudice and renew a right spirit within us. Lord, lead us boldly into reconciliation and unity with all believers, so that we may, as Your Bride, be prepared for Your coming—pure and spotless, holy and innocent, and undivided in our love. May it ever be so! Heal our wounds. Amen. Come, Lord Jesus!

Reflection Questions

1. What motivated the European settlers in North America to enslave the African peoples?

2. What does the word *prejudice* mean to you and what fuels it, in your opinion?

3. What was one of the great historic atrocities done in the United States that you could confess as sin before our Father in Jesus' name?

Recommended Reading
The Three Prejudices by Kelley Varner (Destiny Image, 1997)
Right or Reconciled? by Joseph Garlington (Destiny Image, 1998)

Endnotes

1. Michael E. Goings, *Free at Last? The Reality of Racism in the Church* (Shippensburg, Pennsylvania: Treasure House, 1995), 10.
2. Goings, *Free at Last?*, 5.
3. Kelley Varner, *The Three Prejudices* (Shippensburg, Pennsylvania: Destiny Image Publishers, 1997), 110-111.
4. Goings, *Free at Last?*, 6-10.

5. Quoted in "What the Bible says about Slavery." 10 Sep 1999. <http://www.religioustolerance.org/sla_bibl.htm>.
6. Quoted in "What the Bible says about Slavery."
7. Quoted in "What the Bible says about Slavery."
8. John Dawson, *Healing America's Wounds* (Ventura, California: Regal Books, 1994), 184-185.
9. Dawson, *Healing America's Wounds*, 205.
10. Dawson, *Healing America's Wounds*, 209.
11. Frank Clancy, "How One Small Church Bridges the Racial Divide," *USA Weekend*, September 10-12, 1999, 6-8.
12. Clancy, "How One Small Church," 6.

Chapter 10

The Sins of Greed and Idolatry

There can be little doubt that the United States of America is one of the most blessed nations in all history. Our natural resources and standard of living are second to none; our abundance of food, conveniences, and the general affluence of our citizens make us the envy of the world. For more than 200 years this country truly has been a beacon of freedom shining in the eyes of oppressed peoples everywhere. Millions the world over who have desired a better life for themselves and their children have sought to come to these shores to fulfill their dream. Missionary zeal and a hunger for religious freedom fired the hearts of many of the earliest settlers of this land. Certainly God's hand was behind the establishment of a nation that has demonstrated before the world a level of personal, national, and religious liberty never before achieved. Some would even dare to claim that all our great abundance is a sure sign of God's favor.

On the surface everything looks fine. Things are not always as they seem, however. All is not well after all. A closer look reveals cracks in the polished veneer of our prosperity. Lurking just below the surface is a society in the grip of rapacious greed, all-consuming selfishness, shallow materialism, empty humanism, and for many, grinding poverty. Even though the poor of America are wealthy by the standards of Third World nations, that does not diminish the reality and the national shame of genuine poverty in the richest nation on earth. Millions of Americans observe a "practical atheism"—giving lip service to God but living as though His existence makes no difference at all. Sanctity of life has given way to debates on "quality" of life while the value of life for the aged and the infirm, the mentally deficient, and the unborn have been degraded. Clearly, something is terribly wrong. *Lord, have mercy upon us!*

America "thrives" on consumerism. Nationwide, credit card debt has never been higher; nor has the incidence of personal bankruptcy. Our national debt—the highest ever—and uncontrolled deficit spending threaten to mortgage our children's tomorrow while fueling higher taxes today. For the past several years a popular mantra has been, "It's the economy, stupid!" *as if personal material prosperity is all that matters.* Whatever happened to honor, honesty, integrity, morality, ethics, and character? They have been sacrificed on the altar of ambition, greed, lust, indulgence, hedonism, political expediency, and personal convenience.

This points out the potential peril of prosperity. Luke 12:48 says that "from everyone who has been given much shall much be required." Blessings and opportunity also carry risks. As a nation our responsibility before God is great because of the greatness of His blessings toward us. There exists a very real danger of perverting our prosperity, of pursuing prosperity as an end in itself, forgetting that what God has given He can just as easily take away.

Speaking frankly, America has a love affair with Mammon. We worship at his altar, commit our lives to the pursuit of his values, and seek to build our society and culture according to his standards. As a nation we have sold our souls to this hedonistic spirit. *Father, forgive us!*

No Man Can Serve Two Masters

Judging from the four Gospels, during His earthly ministry Jesus had more to say about money, our use of it, and our attitude toward it than about any other single subject. The attention Jesus gave to this subject indicates both the power of its appeal to human consciousness and the potential danger of that appeal. Nowhere is this seen more clearly than in Jesus' encounter with the rich young ruler (see Mt. 19:16-22).

You remember the story. A personable young man approached Jesus one day and asked what he needed to do to obtain eternal life. Jesus reminded him to obey the commandments. When the young man assured Jesus that he did obey them, Jesus released a specific requirement laced with stumbling blocks: "If you wish to be complete, go and sell your possessions and give to the poor, and you shall have treasure in heaven; and come, follow Me" (Mt. 19:21). At these words the young man "went away grieved" because he "owned much property" (verse 22).

This encounter gave Jesus an opportunity to teach His disciples how hard it is for a rich man to enter the Kingdom of heaven. It is not hard because he is rich, but because of the danger that his wealth will rival God in his affections. In His call to the rich young ruler to give up his possessions, Jesus was not condemning the young man's prosperity; rather, He understood that the man's commitment to his wealth in his heart prevented him from committing his life to God. The young man's choice revealed where his heart really was—bound in covetousness.

Jesus devoted much of His Sermon on the Mount to this same subject, warning against the pursuit of the wrong kind of treasure.

> *Do not lay up for yourselves treasures upon earth, where moth and rust destroy, and where thieves break in and steal. But lay up for yourselves treasures in heaven, where neither moth nor rust destroys, and where thieves do not break in or steal; for where your treasure is, there will your heart be also....No one can serve two masters; for either he will hate the one and love*

*the other, or he will hold to one and despise the other. You can-
not serve God and mammon* (Matthew 6:19-21,24).

What Jesus is saying here is that we cannot have divided loy-
alties. Either we serve God or we serve Mammon; we cannot do
both. We tend to think of the word *mammon* as simply a synonym
for *wealth* or *money*. In reality, the truth goes much deeper. Mammon is a word of Chaldean origin that came to mean "wealth per-
sonified" or "avarice deified."[1] In other words, mammon is greed
or covetousness elevated to the status of a god. This is not merely
an abstract concept, however; there is a *principality* involved here.
As Dr. C. Peter Wagner writes,

> "Covetousness is allegiance to a false god named Mam-
> mon. *Mamona* is an Aramaic term for wealth. First centu-
> ry rabbis considered *Mamona* a demonic being and a rival
> of God. That is why the NIV translated Jesus' words in
> Luke 16:13: 'You cannot serve both God and Money
> [Mammon].' It is correct to capitalize 'Money' or 'Mam-
> mon' because it is a proper name. Mammon is a person,
> not a thing or an urge or an attitude....When Jesus men-
> tioned Mammon, it was in the context of not being able to
> serve two masters. Serving any supernatural master in
> the demonic world, like Mammon, is hard-core idolatry."[2]

Hard-core idolatry? In America? It is the tragic truth. Our
national obsession with Mammon—the accumulation of wealth
and the pursuit of pleasure and plenty—as the *driving force of our
lives* reveals that idolatry is deeply embedded in our society. The
damning indictment that we must face is this: *The United States of
America is an idolatrous nation!*

No Other Gods?

Throughout His Word, God has made His feelings about idolatry perfectly clear: He *hates* it! The first two commandments deal
specifically with the subject, and their placement at the head of the
list indicates that they are fundamental—they are foundational for
everything that follows.

*You shall have no other gods before Me. You shall not make for
yourself an idol, or any likeness of what is in heaven above or
on the earth beneath or in the water under the earth. You shall
not worship them or serve them; for I, the Lord your God, am
a jealous God...* (Exodus 20:3-5).

God will brook no rivals. His prohibition of idolatry is
straightforward; there are to be no carved images of celestial bodies or supernatural beings (heaven above), land creatures (the
earth beneath), or sea creatures (the water under the earth). That
covers the entire created realm, both natural and supernatural.
God alone is to be worshiped and served.

Biblically speaking, idolatry refers to the actual worship of
someone or something other than God. In his excellent booklet
Hard-Core Idolatry, Dr. C. Peter Wagner writes,

"Idolatry is worshiping, serving, pledging allegiance to,
doing acts of obeisance to, paying homage to, forming
alliances with, making covenants with, seeking power
from, or in any other way exalting any supernatural
being other than God. The supernatural beings refer to
angels, cherubim, seraphim, Satan, principalities, powers, deities, territorial spirits, goddesses, and demonic
beings on any other level."[3]

Dr. Wagner further adds,

"[Idolatry] is about worshiping beings in the invisible
world, which often leads to a special recognition of tan
gible objects ('carved images' or idols), in the visible
world. What you see in the visible world is a person bowing down or making a sacrifice or burning incense either
to an image of some kind or to a feature of creation like
the sun, a mountain, a rock, or a river. What is actually
taking place behind the scenes is a spiritual transaction
with one or more spirit beings in the invisible world. This
is what I am calling 'hard-core idolatry.' "[4]

Many believers would be quick to point out that there is no power in an inert image of wood or stone. That's true enough. So what's the danger? The danger lies not in the image or idol itself, but in the demonic spirit that it represents. Listen to the words of the apostle Paul: "What do I mean then? That a thing sacrificed to idols is anything, or that an idol is anything? No, but I say that the things which the Gentiles sacrifice, *they sacrifice to demons*, and not to God; and I do not want you to become sharers in demons" (1 Cor. 10:19-20).

According to Paul, then, idolatry is worshiping, sacrificing to, or serving a demonic being. America's allegiance to Mammon certainly falls into this category. Consider a society in which one teenager kills another teenager for his $200 pair of sneakers or where the weak and powerless are routinely trod upon, abused, and dispossessed by the more fortunate in their endless striving for more, more, more.

A Bloodthirsty "God"

Worship of Mammon is not the only form of idolatry in the land. There is another that is even more hideous; it is a new, modern manifestation of an age-old blood cult. Idolatry involves the worship of demons. The Old Testament is full of references to idolatry, but it contains only four clear-cut references to demons.[5] Each of these four refer to idolatrous practices in Israel and occur in the context of making sacrifices to demons, which involves the shedding of innocent blood. It is the shedding of blood that empowers the demonic forces behind the idols. In some cases children were the innocent victims:

> [They] *served their idols, which became a snare to them. They even sacrificed their sons and their daughters to the demons, and shed innocent blood, the blood of their sons and their daughters, whom they sacrificed to the idols of Canaan; and the land was polluted with the blood* (Psalm 106:36-38).

The Old Testament also contains eight references to Molech, a false deity (demon) identified as the "god" of the Ammonites.[6] He was a grim and bloodthirsty principality whose worship rituals apparently involved human sacrifice, particularly that of children. First Kings 11:7 describes Molech as "the detestable idol of the sons of Ammon." Apparently there were some within the nation of Israel who served Molech. "And they built the high places of Baal that are in the valley of Ben-hinnom to cause their sons and their daughters to pass through the fire to Molech, which I had not commanded them nor had it entered My mind that they should do this abomination, to cause Judah to sin" (Jer. 32:35).

"To pass through the fire" is the reference to human sacrifice to Molech, although the exact process is not clear. According to some rabbinic writers, a bronze statue in the form of a man but with the head of an ox was used. Children were placed inside the statue, which was then heated from below. Loud, pounding drums drowned out the cries and screams of the children.[7]

No wonder such a twisted "worship" practice would be an "abomination" to God! Innocent children by the thousands were sacrificed horribly to sate the blood lust of a demonic "god." Contrast this with the Son of God, who said, "Let the little children come to Me, and do not hinder them, for the kingdom of heaven belongs to such as these" (Mt. 19:14 NIV). Jesus then placed His hands on them and blessed them.

The bloodthirsty "spirit of Molech" has been alive in every age, including our own. In the "civilized" Western world of today, it is the driving force behind the burgeoning abortion industry. Because of the U.S. Supreme Court decision in *Roe v. Wade* in 1973, the United States now has the most liberal abortion laws of any nation in the world. Since that infamous ruling 26 years ago, an estimated *37 million* unborn children have been killed in the womb. This equates to *4,000 abortions a day or one every 24 seconds!*[8] These figures are for the United States alone; they do not include abortions performed in other countries.

According to abortion statistical studies as recent as 1995, you find additional startling news. The abortion rate is virtually the same among Protestant young women in the United States as it is among non-churched women.[9] Something is terribly wrong here! The sin is as great in the Church as it is in the world! *Father, have mercy on us Your people!*

Were these 37 million abortions "medically necessary"? Hardly. To listen to the pro-choice people you would think that abortion is a "right" that is absolutely essential to the physical health of women. Abortion is "justified" to preserve the life of the mother, to prevent a "defective" child, or in cases of rape or incest. According to Dr. C. Everett Koop, former U.S. Surgeon General, this is a fallacious argument. "Even if these were valid reasons, they would account for only 2 percent of all abortions. A full 98 percent of abortions occur for reasons of convenience and economy."[10]

"Convenience and economy"? What's wrong with us? Since 1973, 37 million unborn babies have been sacrificed at the bloody altar of Molech for reasons inspired by the spirit of Mammon! It is a "holocaust" that, in numbers alone, dwarfs that of the Nazi genocide of Jews and other "undesirables" in the 1930s and 40s. There is no way under the sun to justify such deliberate termination of human life at any level, much less the all but incomprehensible scale occurring in our country. Dr. James Dobson of *Focus on the Family* expressed it well when he wrote,

> "No rationalization can justify detaching a healthy little human being from its place of safety and leaving him or her to suffocate on a porcelain table. No social or financial considerations can assuage our collective guilt for destroying lives which were being fashioned in the image of God Himself. Throughout the Gospels, Jesus revealed a tenderness toward boys and girls ('Suffer the little children to come unto Me'), and some of His most frightening warnings were addressed to those who would hurt them. How can He hold us blameless for our wanton feticide and infanticide? As the Lord said to

Cain, who had killed Abel, 'Your brother's blood calls to me from the ground!' (Genesis 4:10)"[11]

As a nation, our sins are great. Dark is the stain that we cannot hide. Unless we turn and repent (and my hope and prayer is that we do), certain judgment awaits. How else could a holy, just, and righteous God respond to our wickedness and idolatry? I believe that some of America's greatest destiny awaits us. But we must remove the blockades so that the promise can yet come forth. *We have sinned! Father, forgive us!*

Heartless in the Heartland

A telltale indicator of the spiritual and moral health of any nation is how it treats its poor. This is because, historically and traditionally, the poor have been the dispossessed people who lack power, influence, or any practical voice in the affairs of society, particularly those areas that directly concern them. Often they are pawns of the state, manipulated even by their "advocates," whose support for the poor is seen primarily as a means to achieve other political or social agendas. Because they have little power or influence, the "have-nots" many times receive injustice, unfair treatment, oppression, or exploitation at the hands of the "haves."

This country has countless laws on the books that are designed to aid the poor; it also has many government agencies and programs at the federal, state, and local levels. Across the country thousands of non-profit and church-based organizations also seek to minister to the needs of the poor. A new cry from radical believers for Jesus is beginning to emerge. Yet while all these efforts are undoubtedly doing some good, as a nation our overall record with the poor of our land stinks. You heard me correctly. It is repugnant! Thirty years and billions of dollars later, America's "war on poverty" still has not been won. The poor are still with us in greater numbers than before, and those numbers grow every day.

How can this be? How can there be a rising number of poor people in the richest nation on earth? What does this say about our national character? I believe that the problem lies in the fact that, despite all the money, programs, and outward efforts on behalf of the poor, as a nation we suffer from a lack of genuine concern and compassion for them.

We need to take a close look at ourselves and ask ourselves what we *really* think about the poor. There is a widespread attitude that says poor people *choose* to be poor; that they would rather be supported by others or by the government than support themselves. Another "popular" belief is that poor people have brought their poverty on themselves by their own actions or lifestyle, and therefore they deserve whatever they get. Many say that the poor are a "drag" on society, taking much but giving nothing in return. Still others feel that poverty is the will of God for some; that God has *chosen* some people to be poor or that their poverty is His "punishment" for their sins.

All these attitudes become excuses for not dealing with the very real problem of poverty in America. I am convinced that this is another symptom of our national sin of worshiping and serving Mammon. Many of the major problems in the United States can be linked to the fact that, as a nation, we have generally neglected and abused our poor. In our covetousness and greed, in our drive for personal comfort and convenience, in our daily fight to "get ours" and to "look out for number one," we have no room in our hearts for the poor. They are an inconvenience, an embarrassing reminder that all is not well in the heartland. We do not have God's eyes or God's heart for the poor. *O Lord, take the blinders off our hearts and minds, for Jesus' sake, I pray.*

Pure and Undefiled Religion

Speaking to a gathering of youth in Strasbourg, France, on October 8, 1988, Pope John Paul II said,

> "The earth belongs to God, but it has been given to all human beings. It is not God's will that some waste while others go hungry; that some have abundance because their soil is fertile, while others are destitute because they

do not have this good fortune. It should not be that the rich and the strong enjoy privileges while injustice is reserved for the poor and the disabled....

"Does the Church assert this strongly enough? Perhaps not. The members of the Church have their weaknesses as well. We are the Church, you and I."[12]

With this statement the Pope expressed not only the basic injustice of poverty in the midst of plenty, but also the responsibility that the Church bears historically for not denouncing the injustice strongly enough or addressing the problem of poverty vigorously enough.

At the heart of God-pleasing faith is a concern and compassion for the poor and oppressed. This is not because such a concern earns God's favor, but because it is a reflection of God's heart and only those who know God can reflect His heart. Compassion for the poor is a natural outgrowth of "saving faith," one fruit of a redeemed life. James, the brother of our Lord, expressed it this way: "This is pure and undefiled religion in the sight of our God and Father, to visit orphans and widows in their distress, and to keep oneself unstained by the world" (Jas. 1:27).

"Orphans and widows" represented the lowest strata of society, the poorest of the poor. They are without power or influence, without anyone to plead their cause, and with usually little opportunity to better their situation. God's people are called to minister to just such as these. We receive our marching orders from Christ, who said of His own mission: "The Spirit of the Lord is on Me, because He has anointed Me to preach good news to the poor. He has sent Me to proclaim freedom for the prisoners and recovery of sight for the blind, to release the oppressed, to proclaim the year of the Lord's favor" (Lk. 4:18-19 NIV). Throughout His ministry Jesus identified with the poor and dispossessed of society. His identification was so complete that He said that to provide for or to deny "the least of these" was to provide for or to deny Him (see Mt. 25:40,45).

If there is anything that the Bible makes clear, it is God's heart for the poor.

- *God cares for the poor.*
  "If there is a poor man with you, one of your brothers…you shall not harden your heart, nor close your hand from your poor brother; but you shall freely open your hand to him, and shall generously lend him sufficient for his need in whatever he lacks" (Deut. 15:7-8).

- *God defends the poor.*
  "Who executes justice for the oppressed; who gives food to the hungry. The Lord sets the prisoners free. The Lord opens the eyes of the blind; the Lord raises up those who are bowed down; the Lord loves the righteous; the Lord protects the strangers; He supports the fatherless and the widow; but He thwarts the way of the wicked" (Ps. 146:7-9).

- *God loves the poor.*
  "He who oppresses the poor reproaches his Maker, but he who is gracious to the needy honors Him" (Prov. 14:31).

- *God judges those who close their hearts and ears to the poor.*
  "Therefore, because you impose heavy rent on the poor and exact a tribute of grain from them, though you have built houses of well-hewn stone, yet you will not live in them; you have planted pleasant vineyards, yet you will not drink their wine. For I know your transgressions are many and your sins are great, you who distress the righteous and accept bribes, and turn aside the poor in the gate" (Amos 5:11-12).

Cultivating God's Heart for the Poor

Before the American Church can be truly effective in dealing with the idolatry in our land and in cultivating God's heart for the poor, we must acknowledge and confess that we have been part of the problem.

Idolatry in the Church? Yes! One evidence of this is the popularity of the often called "prosperity theology." Some appear to teach that if we do such-and-such, if we jump through the right hoops or recite certain promises long enough, that God has *obligated* Himself to bless us *materially.* Indeed, many Scriptures do promise that the people of God will prosper—Psalm 1 is a good example—but the primary thrust of these promises is *spiritual* prosperity. He may *choose* to bless you with substantial wealth, and frequently does, but He is not obligated to do so. This kind of demanding, self-centered teaching is nothing other than the spirit of Mammon gaining a foothold in the Church. Now, don't misunderstand me. We need a genuine faith movement! But it is faith toward the God of promise, not wishful, self-centered arm-twisting, that we need.

Another evidence of idolatry is when churches put their own prosperity ahead of the genuine needs of people around them. Jim Wallis, editor-in-chief of *Sojourners* magazine, made this biting statement: "In a world where most people are poor, a rich church is living testimony of idol worship. The mere possession of such wealth is proof of serving money. Accumulating wealth while brothers and sisters are in poverty is evidence of sin in the church's life."[13]

Chris Heuertz, executive director of Word Made Flesh, a Christian organization committed to serving Christ among the "poorest of the poor," has identified six issues that hinder the Church from ministering effectively among the poor:[14]

- *Isolation.*
  The Church often isolates itself from the poor, worshiping in a "soundproof glass sanctuary" while ignoring the cries of the needy. We also isolate the poor by communicating the message that they are not welcome.

- *Fractured Community.*
  The Church is fractured into many different denominations and sects. The poor need community. We can't expect the poor to join us until we can offer them the community they need.

- *Selfishness.*
  Too often the Church has been "tightfisted and stingy." We must learn to reach out in willingness to share the financial blessings we have received from God.

- *Paternalism.*
  There is a prevailing attitude in the Church that the poor are unable to help themselves. In reality they often are unable to change their circumstances, which is different. We must approach our ministry to the poor with a spirit of humility that encourages them to stand on their own two feet.

- *Forgotten Mission.*
  When Jesus came, He focused His ministry on the poor, modeling the kind of ministry that His Church was to carry out. Often the Church today seems more interested in ease and convenience than in making disciples.

- *Partiality.*
  The Church readily confesses love for a lost and dying world but has yet to really comprehend what it means to love a suffering world. When we look at the poor and needy, do we wish for them the *very best*, or do we expect them to be satisfied with our leftovers?

In his book *Liberating the Church*, Howard Snyder addresses the challenge that the Church faces in reaching out to the poor. He states that the Church must both work *for* the poor and be *of* the poor, in the sense of making the poor its "special concern in evangelism, justice ministries and way of life."[15] Furthermore, he says that the Church "cannot be of the poor unless it is *among* the poor."[16] Snyder then identifies four things the Church must do to reach the poor:[17]

- *The Church must identify with and learn from the poor.*
  This involves learning to see life from the point of view of the poor, learning to identify with *God's* point of view toward the poor, and learning to deal with our prejudice against the poor.

- *The Church must defend the cause of the poor.*
  We can do this in two ways. First we can work to provide relief for the poor and help them improve their own lives; and second we can examine our own lifestyles in order to be more responsible in the way we live.

- *The Church must offer Christ to the poor.*
  The poor need the gospel as much as anyone else does, and "offering Christ to the poor can be done with integrity only by those who take the side of the poor and learn from them."

- *The Church must be a reconciled and reconciling community of and with the poor.*
  As the Church identifies with and works among the poor, defending their cause and presenting Christ to them, the basis is laid for the Christian revolution. We are not to be the Church of the poor against the rich and middle class, but the Church of all peoples standing on the side of the oppressed.

Destroying Our Idols

Over the past six chapters I have talked about specific generational and historic sins that we as Christians need to address in our land: the clergy-laity separation; the gender gap; the need for reconciliation with Jews, the First Nations People (Native Americans), and African-Americans; and the problems of greed and idolatry. This is by no means a comprehensive list of the obstacles and barriers that stand in the way of spiritual awakening and revival in our land; they only represent the major issues that the Holy Spirit has laid on my heart to address.

Of the six issues discussed, I placed the greed and idolatry problem last because it is the most subtle and critical. Until we take seriously the problem of idolatry in America and deal with it in a biblical manner, we will not see full awakening and revival come. Much insight has been gained in recent years and much high-level strategic spiritual warfare has taken place with a heart to reclaim the cities of our land for God. Unless we deal with the idolatry problem, though, we will see little real lasting success. Dr. C. Peter Wagner makes this very clear:

> "The finest of our leaders may competently apply all the excellent insights that God has given us for city transformation over the last few years on the highest levels in our cities, but if we do not also deal a significant and simultaneous blow to idolatry, we will not see our dream for city transformation come true."[18]

My brothers and sisters, the day is almost spent. It's time to take a stand! The Lord is looking for those who will stand in the gap before Him for the land, that He not destroy it (see Ezek. 22:30). We need to cleanse our own hearts first and then stand in the gap for our families, our friends, our neighbors, our schools, our cities, and our nation. Let's take a stand together for God's light to shine by removing satan's legal basis to blind us by confessing our historic sins.

We have sinned! Father, forgive us! Forgive us for the greed, for the covetousness that runs rampant in our land! Forgive us as a nation for squandering Your blessings and for turning from Your high call to serve the spirit of Mammon! Forgive us for our monstrous holocaust of the unborn—children created in Your image and precious in Your sight sacrificed in the spirit of Molech for the sake of greed and convenience! Forgive us for neglecting the poor and needy around us, for despising their dignity and demeaning their worth. Forgive us for not displaying Your heart for the poor.

182

Lord, help us to strip away the idols in our heart and in our national consciousness. Give us Your heart for the poor—a heart of love, compassion, and mercy. Let us minister in a spirit that renounces greed and covetousness. Deliver our land from false altars of worship and enlighten our hearts that we may honor You as the one true God and worship You alone! Father, let Your glory fill our land! May the best be yet to come.

Reflection Questions

1. Give a definition for "hard-core idolatry."

2. How do you see the sins of idolatry and greed to be connected?

3. What are the demonic spirits behind the abortion industry in America?

Recommended Reading

Hard-Core Idolatry by C. Peter Wagner (Wagner Institute for Practical Learning, 1999)
When You Were Formed in Secret by Gary Bergel (pamphlet by Intercessors for America, 1980, 1998)

Endnotes

1. James Strong, *Strong's Exhaustive Concordance of the Bible* (Peabody, Massachusetts: Hendrickson Publishers, n.d.), *mammon*, #G3126.

2. C. Peter Wagner, *Hard-Core Idolatry: Facing the Facts* (Colorado Springs, Colorado: Wagner Institute for Practical Ministry, 1998), 17.

3. Wagner, *Hard-Core Idolatry*, 11-12.

4. Wagner, *Hard-Core Idolatry*, 12.

5. These are Leviticus 17:7; Deuteronomy 32:17; Second Chronicles 11:15; and Psalm 106:36-38. Of course, this does not include references to satan in the Book of Job or to lucifer in Isaiah 14:12 (KJV only).

6. These are Leviticus 18:21; 20:2-5; First Kings 11:7; Second Kings 23:10; and Jeremiah 32:35.

7. Paul E. Robertson, "Molech," *Holman Bible Dictionary* (Nashville, Tennessee: Holman Bible Publishers, 1991). *QuickVerse 4.0 Deluxe Bible Reference Collection.* CD-ROM. Parsons Technology, 1992–1996.
8. Gary Bergel, *Abortion in America* (Leesburg, Virginia: Intercessors for America, 1998), II-4.
9. This statistical information was posted by Intercessors for America from the original Henshaw/Kost Abortion Patients survey done in 1994-95.
10. C. Everett Koop, "...at the Crossroads," in Bergel, *Abortion in America*, II-7.
11. James C. Dobson, "Abortion & the Future..." in Bergel, *Abortion in America*, II-7.
12. Pope John Paul II, as quoted in Luigi Accattoli, *When a Pope Asks Forgiveness* (Boston, Massachusetts: Pauline Books and Media, 1998), 166.
13. Jim Wallis, as quoted in Howard Snyder, *Liberating the Church* (Basingstoke, Hants, United Kingdom: Marshall Paperbacks, 1983), 209.
14. Chris Heuertz, "Discovering Holiness in Ministry Among the Poor," in Randy Clark, comp., *Power, Holiness, and Evangelism* (Shippensburg, Pennsylvania: Destiny Image Publishers, 1999), 80-85.
15. Snyder, *Liberating the Church*, 240.
16. Snyder, *Liberating the Church*, 240.
17. Snyder, *Liberating the Church*, 241-245.
18. Wagner, *Hard-Core Idolatry*, 34.

Section III

The Cure of All Evils

Chapter 11

Praying With Insight

The great nineteenth-century English poet Tennyson once wrote, "More things are wrought by prayer than this world dreams of."[1] How right he was. Prayer is the key, the secret behind every advance of the Kingdom of God in the earth. Remember, little keys open big doors. Every great revival of the Church, every breakthrough of the gospel into new areas or people groups, every defeat of a demonic stronghold has been preceded by a protracted season of prayer from committed, ordinary believers.

Prayer preceded Pentecost, when the Church was baptized with spiritual power. In fact, there never has been, nor ever will be, a prayerless Pentecost. Prayer delivered Peter from prison (see Acts 12:1-17). Prayer prepared Paul and Barnabas in Antioch to preach the gospel and plant churches across the Roman Empire—and even into Europe. The eighteenth-century Moravian community on the Saxony estate of Count Nikolaus Ludwig von Zinzendorf entered into a 24-hour-a-day prayer vigil that continued unbroken for more than 100 years, and they birthed an evangelical missionary movement that was unequaled until our own day. The First and Second Great Awakenings, the Pentecostal movement, the Argentinean revival of the 1950s and later—all these were born through prayer. As I stated in my first book, *The Lost Art of Intercession*, "What goes up, must come down!"

One of the most exciting and significant characteristics of the current move of God in renewal and revival of His people is that He is restoring to the Church an understanding of prayer's centrality in everything we do. In our zeal to be about our Lord's work, we sometimes neglect prayer—shortchanging our ministry and effectiveness in the process. Our efforts are fruitless without God's action to bring about His purpose, and God's action is linked to our prayers. John Wesley once said, "God does everything by prayer, and nothing without it." In his dynamic book *The Hidden Power of Prayer and Fasting*, my dear friend Mahesh Chavda, who certainly has experience with both, writes,

> "The Lord is opening our eyes to the simple truth that prayer is where everything begins and ends in the realm of the Spirit. It is here that everything is accomplished. Prayer is the true genetic code of the Church. We have received other mutant genes that have caused us to evolve away from God's true design for His Body. *Nothing that God is going to do will happen without prayer.*"[2]

Although the call of the Church is to make disciples, the central activity of the Church is prayer. One of satan's primary strategies is to distract the Church—to divert us from our central focus. Prayer is the conduit through which both the wisdom to know the will and ways of God and the power to do the work of God are imparted. Through the dynamic moving of the Holy Spirit today the Church is rediscovering prayer.

We are in a war zone. We are born in war and we are born for war. Battle lines have been drawn and a historic conflict is underway. The combat is not between flesh-and-blood adversaries, however; it is a spiritual war. Paul certainly recognized this. "For we are not wrestling with flesh and blood [contending only with physical opponents], but against the despotisms, against the powers, against [the master spirits who are] the world rulers of this present darkness, against the spirit forces of wickedness in the heavenly (supernatural) sphere" (Eph. 6:12 AMP). "For though we walk (live) in the flesh, we are not carrying on our warfare according to the flesh and using mere human weapons. For the weapons of our warfare are not physical [weapons of flesh and blood], but they are mighty before God for the overthrow and destruction of strongholds" (2 Cor. 10:3-4 AMP). Our chief weapon is prayer, which has the power not only to destroy the works of the enemy but also to "refute arguments and theories and reasonings and every proud and lofty thing that sets itself up against the [true] knowledge of God" (2 Cor. 10:5a AMP).

In readjusting the Church's focus on prayer, the Lord is both restoring old methods and revealing new applications to prayer, both individual and corporate. One of the significant characteristics of this is the practice of praying with insight.

Insight, Discernment, and Wisdom

What does "praying with insight" mean? It means praying from the perspective of knowledge or understanding regarding the circumstances of the person or situation you are praying for. *Insight* is the power to see below the surface of a situation, to discern the inner nature or truth of something that is not immediately apparent. Although asking questions and doing research often sheds light on a situation, true insight is essentially a spiritual quality. As such it has its source in God: "I have more insight than all my teachers, for Thy testimonies are my meditation" (Ps. 119:99); "In all wisdom and insight He made known to us the mystery of His will..." (Eph. 1:8b-9).

Similar to insight in source and meaning is *discernment*, the ability to comprehend that which is obscure, to distinguish or discriminate (in the positive sense) between good and evil, true and false, right and wrong, especially where (on the surface at least) the differences are very subtle. "And this I pray, that your love may abound still more and more in real knowledge and all discernment, so that you may approve the things that are excellent..." (Phil. 1:9-10).

God rewards those who seek a discerning spirit:

For if you cry for discernment, lift your voice for understanding; if you seek her as silver, and search for her as for hidden treasures; then you will discern the fear of the Lord, and discover the knowledge of God. For the Lord gives wisdom; from His mouth come knowledge and understanding (Proverbs 2:3-6).

God was pleased when Solomon sought the discernment and judgment to be a wise ruler:

And it was pleasing in the sight of the Lord that Solomon had asked this thing. And God said to him, "Because you have asked this thing and have not asked for yourself long life, nor have asked riches for yourself, nor have you asked for the life of your enemies, but have asked for yourself discernment to understand justice, behold, I have done according to your words. Behold, I have given you a wise and discerning heart, so that there has been no one like you before you, nor shall one like you arise after you" (1 Kings 3:10-12).

Wisdom is a quality related to insight and discernment, and it too comes from God. It is the ability to discern inner qualities and relationships and to make practical application of experience, knowledge, and information. God challenged Job with the rhetorical question, "Who has put wisdom in the innermost being, or has given understanding to the mind?" (Job 38:36) James exhorted his readers to depend on God for wisdom in living: "But if any of you lacks wisdom, let him ask of God, who gives to all men generously and without reproach, and it will be given to him" (Jas. 1:5).

The knowledge and fear of the Lord is the most fundamental evidence of wisdom. In fact, it is the starting place: "The fear of the Lord is the beginning of knowledge; fools despise wisdom and instruction" (Prov. 1:7); "The fear of the Lord is the instruction for wisdom, and before honor comes humility" (Prov. 15:33).

Insight, discernment, wisdom—all are critical qualities for effective prayer. God has called us to be a people of prayer and our churches to be houses of prayer. He has invited us to join Him in His redemptive plan for the world. God gives insight because whenever He gets ready to move, He reveals His plans to those who are seeking Him. "Then you shall see this, and your heart shall be glad, and your bones shall flourish like the new grass; and *the hand of the Lord shall be made known to His servants*, but He shall be indignant toward His enemies" (Is. 66:14); "Surely the Lord God does nothing unless *He reveals His secret counsel to His servants the prophets*" (Amos 3:7).

Ever go hunting? There are three basic steps: Ready, aim, fire! In prayer and spiritual warfare we have to first "get ready—get prepared!" You might need to clean out your gun before you attempt to fire it again. After you clean and oil your gun, you next take aim. This is where you set your sights with careful, proper steady gaze. This deals with the subject of "praying with insight." Your focus is clear. Your aim is steady. Then, finally, after preparing your weapon and taking aim through the lens of the Holy Spirit, you pull the trigger and FIRE! But without the right "sight," you might hit the wrong thing!

Praying with insight is a key strategy that the Lord is restoring to His Church in these days. But just as there are different types of military weapons, so there are many different forms of prayer in God's warchest, such as praying on-site, prayer-walking, prayer watches, prayer and fasting, reminding God of His Word, etc.

Praying On-Site

On-site prayer is a fresh application of an ancient practice that the Holy Spirit is reviving in our generation. The ancient Israelites under Joshua circled the city of Jericho for seven days as God had commanded, and He delivered the city into their hands. In July 1999, more than 400 members of the Reconciliation Walk (see Chapter 7) gathered in Jerusalem where they lined the wall of the Old City, joined hands, and prayed for the city and its people.

Praying on-site is not an exercise for the spiritual "elite" (if there is such a thing); it is a movement among everyday believers. There is no set pattern or prepackaged "formula." The styles and approaches are as unique and varied as the people involved, ranging from carefully planned strategies to spontaneous Spirit-given prompts; from lofty appeals to pinpointed petitions; from a sharp focus on family and neighborhood to broader intercession for an entire campus, city, or nation.

Everyday believers are praying house by house in their neighborhoods, spreading God's love by being lighthouses of prayer. Churches of different backgrounds are coming together and spreading out to pray for diverse neighborhoods. Students are marching in quiet prayer through their high schools and college campuses. Consider, for example, the annual "See You at the Pole." What began with one youth group in Texas has over the last decade expanded to include thousands of Christian students on hundreds of public school campuses across the nation. Together they gather around their school's flagpole to pray for each other, for their fellow students, for their teachers and administrators, and for their schools.

Praying on-site is directed, purposeful intercession, typically for a preset period of time, conducted in the very places we expect our prayers to be answered. It is insightful prayer, with research and geographical identification combined with dependency on the Holy Spirit's guidance to determine the specific needs and issues. In other words, it is responsive, researched, and revealed insight. A good example of this is the gathering of believers for repentance and reconciliation on the site of the Sand Creek massacre (see Chapter 8).

On-site intercession is a refreshing, creative expression of prayer that should supplement but never replace regular prayer meetings. As refreshment, it carries several significant benefits:

- *It thaws the ice.*
  We get so used to the comfortable four walls of our churches that we tend to forget what it is like to be the salt of the earth and the light of the world. Praying on-site helps us begin to cross boundaries into more effective ministry.

- *It helps us overcome fear.*
  On-site prayer forces us out of our comfort zones and into the world. The mutual support of those who pray with us helps us gain confidence and boldness.

- *It helps us identify with our surroundings.*
  As we pray on-site for a city or a nation or whatever, we begin to develop a love for that place. There is a sense of personal ownership and identification that would not exist when praying from a distance.

- *It helps us get God's heart.*
  We begin to feel His pulse for the city, His love and compassion for the region. We begin to discern His mind and desire for the people.

- *It helps us confess sin.*
  Once we have God's heart for an area we can move in authentic confession of sin, either for those of our own generation or of generations that have gone before.

- *It helps us proclaim God's promises.*
  As we move in identification and confession, we can speak God's promises and desired blessings for the people and region over which we are praying.

- *It helps us worship God.*
  One of the highest and greatest things that we can do is worship and praise God in an open, public setting,

particularly in places where curses have been pronounced or where tragedies have occurred.

Practical applications of prayer are proceeding forth in various cities where united prayer of the watchmen on the walls is
being submitted to the pastoral and apostolic eldership networks.
The day of independent prayer ministries is coming to a close.
"Gatekeepers and watchmen" must walk together. Some great
applications have intercessors praying over every public school
facility in their cities. Others are praying on location at police
precincts, church facilities, and county and state capital buildings.
Awesome!

A Biblical Precedent

There is biblical precedent for on-site prayer. I've already
mentioned the Israelites at the city of Jericho. The Gospels of Luke
and Matthew provide several examples from the life of Jesus. In
Luke chapter 13, Jesus is making His way toward Jerusalem,
where He will be crucified. In His heart and mind He is already
there, and He laments over the city:

> *O Jerusalem, Jerusalem, the city that kills the prophets and*
> *stones those sent to her! How often I wanted to gather your*
> *children together, just as a hen gathers her brood under her*
> *wings, and you would not have it! Behold, your house is left to*
> *you desolate; and I say to you, you shall not see Me until the*
> *time comes when you say, "Blessed is He who comes in the*
> *name of the Lord!"* (Luke 13:34-35)

A few days later, at the time of His "triumphal entry" into
Jerusalem on the back of a donkey, Jesus was again moved by the
spiritual blindness of the city:

> *And when He approached, He saw the city and wept over it,*
> *saying, "If you had known in this day, even you, the things*
> *which make for peace! But now they have been hidden from*
> *your eyes. For the days shall come upon you when your ene-*
> *mies will throw up a bank before you, and surround you, and*
> *hem you in on every side, and will level you to the ground and*

your children within you, and they will not leave in you one stone upon another, because you did not recognize the time of your visitation" (Luke 19:41-44).

Matthew gives us a compelling picture of Jesus, at the sight of great need, crying out for laborers:

> *And Jesus was going about all the cities and the villages, teaching in their synagogues, and proclaiming the gospel of the kingdom, and healing every kind of disease and every kind of sickness. And seeing the multitudes, He felt compassion for them, because they were distressed and downcast like sheep without a shepherd. Then He said to His disciples, "The harvest is plentiful, but the workers are few. Therefore beseech the Lord of the harvest to send out workers into His harvest"* (Matthew 9:35-38).

What are we to do when we pray on-site? It could be any number of things. We may pray for laborers to be released as Jesus did or for God to give us His heart concerning the city or region. It might be a prayer of repentance or of grieving. The situation might call for a prayer of proclamation where we "kneel on the promises," or declare God's promises, or claim His purposes for the area.

Prayer-Walking

Very similar to praying on-site, prayer-walking is another fresh expression of intercession that is occurring more and more frequently within the Body of Christ. It may be as simple in scope as stepping out your front door and walking the streets of your neighborhood, praying for the people you meet as well as for those you can't see behind the closed doors of their homes. On the other hand, it might be a carefully planned campaign to cover an entire city by walking intercessors who lift up to God cries of repentance and pleas for mercy as they walk.

On an even larger scale is the international March for Jesus movement, an annual event that emphasizes the power of praise in the streets. In recent years more than 60,000 people took part in Europe in strategic praise and prayer. Beginning in London, England, they crossed to the Continent and walked hundreds of kilometers, ending up in Berlin, Germany. It was a great public demonstration and proclamation of praise to the Lord. The Reconciliation Walk mentioned in Chapter 7 is another great example on a similar scale.

In Nashville, Tennessee, commonly known as Music City U.S.A., over the years a team of people have done research on the history of this city for prayer purposes. Stephen Mansfield, Senior Pastor of Belmont Church, compiled this research in a manual entitled *Releasing Destiny—A Spiritual Warfare Manual for Nashville and Country Music*. The following is a partial list of strategic places where prayer walks and on-site locational prayer are encouraged to take place on an on-going basis.[3]

- *The Parathenon.*
  This monument is the object of civic pride, a temple that houses a goddess of cities and military strategy, and it is a known site for prostitution and homosexuality. Nashville derives its title, the "Athens of the South," as a result of this monument.

- *Ryman Auditorium.*
  "The Mother Church of Country Music" is important not only as the symbolic home of country music, but also as a building inspired by the Revival of 1885 led by Sam Jones. The building originally was called the "Union Gospel Tabernacle."

- *Third National Bank Building.*
  This building is on the site of the old Maxwell House Hotel. The Hotel was the spot where the Ku Klux Klan held its first national strategy meeting in 1867. It was attended by KKK leaders from all over the South.

- *The "Old" Vanderbilt University Campus.*
  Vanderbilt University was founded in the 1870s by Methodists to train Christian leaders and to serve as a healing institution between North and South. It has, unfortunately, become extremely liberal in recent years.

- *The Hermitage Area.*
  This area is not only important as the home of Andrew Jackson, but also because the Trail of Tears wound right through its southern portions.

- *Battlefields.*
  The significant sites of the Battle of Nashville can be found all over southern Nashville, as well as one of the bloodiest battles fought in the War Between the States in Franklin, Tennessee.

Remember, though, that anywhere God leads you to pray is strategic! Just do it!

Prayer Watches

A prayer watch is a sustained prayer vigil over an extended period of time. Keeping a "watch" for the Lord is a thoroughly biblical principle. "O my Strength, I watch for You; You, O God, are my fortress" (Ps. 59:9 NIV); "But as for me, I will watch expectantly for the Lord; I will wait for the God of my salvation. My God will hear me" (Mic. 7:7).

Part of keeping the *watch* of the Lord is learning to *wait* on the Lord. "Wait for the Lord; be strong, and let your heart take courage; yes, wait for the Lord" (Ps. 27:14); "Wait for the Lord, and keep His way, and He will exalt you to inherit the land; when the wicked are cut off, you will see it" (Ps. 37:34). Now *that's* a powerful and encouraging promise for believers who want to reclaim the land from the enemy!

197

The discipline of a prayer watch can help us tap into the mind and heart of God as well as build spiritual strength and maturity. On the night before He died, when Jesus found Peter, James and John sleeping after He had asked them to "keep watch with Me," He said to them, "So, you men could not keep watch with Me for one hour? Keep watching and praying, that you may not enter into temptation; the spirit is willing, but the flesh is weak" (Mt. 26:40b-41). God's promise for those who watch and wait is sure: "Yet those who wait for the Lord will gain new strength; they will mount up with wings like eagles, they will run and not get tired, they will walk and not become weary" (Is. 40:31).

I believe the definitive example of a prayer watch would have to be that of the Moravians, whom I mentioned earlier. In the first chapter of my book *The Lost Art of Intercession* I dealt with the Moravians at some length. Concerning their prayer watch I wrote:

> "The Moravians' over 100-year prayer vigil and global missionary exploits marked one of the purest moves of the Spirit in church history, and it radically changed the expression of Christianity in their age. Many leaders today feel that virtually every great missionary endeavor of the eighteenth and nineteenth centuries—regardless of denominational affiliation—was in a very real sense part of the fruit of the Moravians' sacrificial service and prophetic intercessory prayer. Their influence continues to be felt even in our day."[4]

My visit in 1993 to Herrnhut, the historic Moravian community, was a watershed event for me. As we prayed at the cemetery where hundreds of these dear faithful saints were buried, the Lord spoke to me as He did to Ezekiel: "Son of man, can these bones live?" My answer was the same as Ezekiel's: "O Sovereign Lord, You alone know" (Ezek. 37:3 NIV). That day a powerful spirit of intercession struck us all and I realized that God wanted to blow this spirit of prayer out into the nations. Indeed, these bones *can* live! *O Lord, let the bones rattle! Let them shake! Let the promises of those who walked before us be given to us today!*

One of the best contemporary examples I know of a prayer watch is the Watch of the Lord™ established by Mahesh and Bonnie Chavda at All Nations Church in Charlotte, North Carolina. Mahesh describes how it came about:

"The Watch of the Lord™ began in January of 1995 when the Lord said to us, 'Watch with Me.' In response we invited about 20 people to spend from 10:00 p.m. Friday until 6:00 a.m. Saturday keeping the 'night watch,' which is going without sleep for spiritual reasons.

"We waited on God in worship and prayer, and shared in communion through Jesus' body and blood represented in the Lord's Supper. Every Friday since then, we have done the same. We have celebrated the watch with thousands of watchmen present. Watch groups have now sprung up throughout the United States and around the globe. We find ourselves in the midst of a renewed visitation that is manifesting the glory of the Lord!"[5]

Prayer and Fasting

Fasting is another powerful prayer practice that is seeing a great revival in these days. Except for scattered brief periods of time or extraordinary individuals, for much of the history of the Church fasting has been tucked away in the closet of the outdated fashions of spiritual clothing. In recent years, however, more and more people have begun to take it out of mothballs, smooth it out, and dust it off. Many of these bold souls are discovering that fasting combined with prayer is a powerhouse punch, able to deliver a solid one-two knockout blow to the enemy. It also opens the channel for a greater outpouring of the glory, power, and presence of God.

Fasting is the discipline of going without food for certain specified periods of time for spiritual reasons. The length and type of fast will vary according to the individual and the situation. I will not attempt to give a detailed discussion of fasting here; there are numerous books and other resources readily available that deal with the subject much better than I can. One of the best, in my opinion, is *The Hidden Power of Prayer and Fasting* by Mahesh Chavda. I want to share just a few basic points from his book to clarify a little bit of this whole area of fasting.

Why *should* we fast, anyway? Mahesh gives nine reasons:[6]

1. We fast in obedience to God's Word.

2. We fast to humble ourselves before God and to obtain His grace and power.

3. We fast to overcome temptations in areas that keep us from moving into God's power.

4. We fast to be purified from sin (and to help others become purified as well).

5. We fast to become weak before God so God's power can be strong.

6. We fast to obtain God's support in order to accomplish His will.

7. We fast in times of crisis.

8. We fast when seeking God's direction.

9. We fast for understanding and divine revelation.

Beyond the reasons for fasting are the *benefits* of fasting. Mahesh lists seven.[7] He says that when we fast,

1. We humble ourselves.

2. We see life's priorities more clearly.

3. We see balance return to areas of our lives where there is imbalance.

4. Our selfish ambition and pride begin to be washed away.

5. We become more sensitive to God's Spirit, and the nine gifts of the Holy Spirit work more effectively in our lives.

6. Our hidden areas of weakness or susceptibility rise to the surface so that God can deal with them.

7. God makes us more unselfish.

Reclaiming Our Christian Heritage

One of the things I like to do is locational prayer at national, governmental, and historical sites. I have prayed with people in the Boston Bay area and at Plymouth Rock, where the Pilgrims landed. I have prayed at Federation Hall in New York City, where George Washington was inaugurated. I have followed the path that he took afterwards on his horse; where he went to church; and where he knelt in prayer dedicating himself and this country to the Lord. I have taken the very prayers of George Washington as they were written down and prayed them back to the Lord, standing in the gap and reminding God of the covenant that our forefathers made for this land. As Christians we need to reclaim our nation's Christian heritage.

Despite claims to the contrary by the secularists and historical revisionists of the past 40 years, the United States of America *was* founded as a Christian nation. By 1778, 11 of the 13 colonies had constitutions stipulating that no one could hold public office who did not acknowledge faith in Christ, the ultimate authority of the Bible, and the certainty of the final judgment. Fifty-three of the 55 delegates to the Constitutional Convention of the United States were professing Christians. Ninety-four percent of the significant writings of the founding fathers upheld the supreme authority of the Bible. In 1892 and again in 1931 the United States Supreme Court affirmed that America was established as a Christian nation. In 1952, the Court stated that the First Amendment was never intended to keep religion separate from affairs of the state, but only to prevent any one religion or denomination from running the country.[8]

All of this began to change in 1962 when the Supreme Court removed audible prayer and Bible reading from the public schools of America, along with copies of the Ten Commandments. This has led to a "domino effect":

> "Since 1962, Secular Humanism, Atheism, and Satanism were all declared by the Court to be religions equivalent to Christianity, and to be tax-deductible for contributors. Such religious pluralism has brought us to a complete reversal of the mind of our founding fathers toward the God of the Bible."[9]

The overall result of all this has been a grave deterioration of the spiritual, moral, and ethical fiber of this country. Add to that the accumulated generational sins of our history with regard to the First Nations People (the Native Americans); with African-Americans; with Japanese-Americans during World War II; and with other minority groups—plus the divisions in the American Church as well as our general silence and inaction concerning the moral and spiritual problems of our land—and it then becomes easy to understand why our sin and guilt as a nation are so great and why identificational intercession, confession, repentance, and reconciliation are so critical.

This is also why learning to pray with insight is so important. "Only as the church is restored to its New Testament heritage of 'simplicity and purity of devotion to Christ' (2 Cor. 11:3) can our nation begin to be restored to its Christian foundations."[10]

John Dawson relates eight important points to remember as we seek to be intercessors and reconcilers and to reclaim our land for the Lord:[11]

1. *Become a worshiper.*
   Jesus should be the focus of our hearts.

2. *Take the opportunity of confession, with identification, when we find it.*

3. *Release forgiveness and refrain from judgment.*

4. *Receive God's gifts of friendship.*
   Welcome all whom God sends to walk beside us.

5. *Join united efforts.*
   Get involved in crossover ministries that unite different groups.

6. *Look around.*
   Be curious. Learn to celebrate the diversity in our nation.

7. *Discern the Body of Christ.*
   Value the contributions of groups beyond our own.

8. *Hold our ground.*
   The enemy's opposition will be fierce, but God's grace is sufficient.

It's time to clean the sights on our prayer guns. No more "friendly fire" in the Kingdom of God! Let's seek the Lord for insight, discernment, and the fear of the Lord. Then, and only then, will our aim be accurate to hit the bull's eye on God's target and win.

We have sinned! Father, forgive us! Forgive us for our failure to pray and for our silence while our neighbors and our cities wander in darkness! Stir our hearts, Father! Fill us with the knowledge of Your heart and mind for our nation! Give us insight, discernment, and wisdom, that we may rise up in prophetic intercession and see the curse lifted from our land and the river of Your forgiveness, redemption, and restoration flow from shore to shore! "Let justice roll down like waters and righteousness like an everflowing stream" (Amos 5:24).

Reflection Questions

1. What does it mean to pray with insight?

2. What is "prayer-walking," and what is its value?

3. What are some locations in your city where you and other believers could do on-site locational prayer?

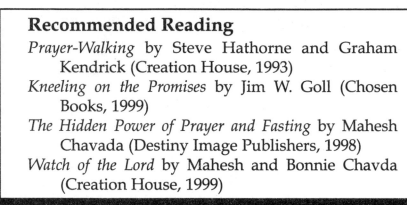

Recommended Reading

Prayer-Walking by Steve Hathorne and Graham Kendrick (Creation House, 1993)

Kneeling on the Promises by Jim W. Goll (Chosen Books, 1999)

The Hidden Power of Prayer and Fasting by Mahesh Chavada (Destiny Image Publishers, 1998)

Watch of the Lord by Mahesh and Bonnie Chavda (Creation House, 1999)

Endnotes

1. Quoted in John Bartlett, *Bartlett's Familiar Quotations*, 16th ed., Justin Kaplan, ed. (New York: Little, Brown and Company, 1992), 459:27.

2. Mahesh Chavda, *The Hidden Power of Prayer and Fasting* (Shippensburg, Pennsylvania: Destiny Image Publishers, 1998), 132. Emphasis in the original.

3. Material referred to here are from Stephen Mansfield, "Praying: On Location," *Releasing Destiny* (Nashville, Tennessee: Daniel 1 School of Ministry, 1993), 55-56.

4. Jim W. Goll, *The Lost Art of Intercession* (Shippensburg, Pennsylvania: Revival Press, 1997), 4.

5. Chavda, *The Hidden Power of Prayer and Fasting*, 148, note 2.

6. Chavda, *The Hidden Power of Prayer and Fasting*, 37-49.

7. Chavda, *The Hidden Power of Prayer and Fasting*, 118-120.

8. Facts cited in Albert Rountree, "Was America Established as a Christian Nation by God?", *New Life* newsletter (Ministries of New Life, May, 1992), 1-2.

9. Rountree, "Was America Established as a Christian Nation by God?", *New Life* newsletter, 2.

10. Rountree, "Was America Established as a Christian Nation by God?", *New Life* newsletter, 2.
11. John Dawson, *Healing America's Wounds* (Ventura, California: Regal Books, 1994), 269-278.

Chapter 12

Worship Warfare

It's time for the Church to go on the offensive!

et's get out of our comfortable pew-sitting and do something for Jesus' sake! For far too long the Church has been taking a beating from the enemy. He has intimidated us, divided us, and diverted us from our mission. He has shot arrows of doubt, fear, and condemnation our way. He has attempted to silence us by arraying the forces of secular society and government against us. He has sought to steal from us the knowledge of our heritage and position in Christ. He has tried to make us despair of victory.

The tide is turning, however. God is calling forth in this generation a great army of intercessors and bridal warriors to carry the battle right into the enemy's camp. He has raised up a mighty prayer movement unlike anything we have ever seen before. Intercessors at all levels are discerning the historic reasons why demonic strongholds have the legal basis to remain. Then, as we meet God's conditions of confession and repentance for both our own sins as well as those of earlier generations, He sends in spiritual "smart bombs" to target enemy strongholds, lift the curse on the land, and break the shackles of spiritual bondage.

From the beginning the Church has been the instrument, the Body through whom Christ is working, to fulfill the Father's plan and shed abroad His glory in the earth. This is why He is cleansing us, redirecting our focus, and restoring us to our fundamental ministries of worship, prayer, and praise. Worship has been described as the "missing jewel" of the Church. In recent years churches all across the spectrum have been rediscovering worship and are finding that it is a fundamental basis for successful spiritual warfare. Just as a lens focuses light into a coherent point, so worship focuses our energy where God wants it to go.

Just how is worship fundamental to spiritual warfare? We can understand this better by looking at three related concepts: worship, thanksgiving, and praise.

True Worship

One of the most well-known biblical accounts of worship is found in chapter 6 of Isaiah:

> *In the year of King Uzziah's death, I saw the Lord sitting on a throne, lofty and exalted, with the train of His robe filling the temple. Seraphim stood above Him, each having six wings; with two he covered his face, and with two he covered his feet, and with two he flew. And one called out to another and said, "Holy, Holy, Holy, is the Lord of hosts, the whole earth is full of His glory." And the foundations of the thresholds trembled at the voice of him who called out, while the temple was filling with smoke* (Isaiah 6:1-4).

Isaiah's vision tells us three very important things about worship. *First*, worship is primarily an inward attitude of the heart that is exhibited through the outward posture of the body. The seraphim covered their faces and feet with four of their wings. This signified their humility in worship before God. The word *worship* can be defined in many different ways. One of its meanings in Hebrew is to "bow down in your heart before." So worship

208

essentially means bowing down before God in reverence and submission.

Second, worship of God results in service to God. The seraphim used two wings to fly, signifying their readiness to serve God and do His bidding. But with two wings they hid their face and with two wings they covered their feet in acts of humility, holiness, and worship. This picture portrays that we are to first bow down before the Lord (worship) in order to be strengthened to serve Him and His purposes (see Is. 6:2).

Third, worship is a response to God's holiness. The seraphim called out to one another in praise of God, saying "Holy, holy, holy is the Lord of hosts." Because it is an attitude of the heart and responsive in nature, *true* worship cannot be commanded or coerced. *Forced* worship is *false* worship. Worship relates to holiness, and holiness relates to the fear of the Lord, which is a fragrance that has been missing from the Body of Christ of recent years. The current restoration of worship in the Church is also restoring this fragrance of holy fear. Let this perfume be restored for Jesus' holy name's sake!

These same three elements of worship are displayed in Isaiah's response to the vision. We are not told what his *physical* posture was, but the posture of his *heart* was certainly one of humility and submission: "Woe is me, for I am ruined! Because I am a man of unclean lips, and I live among a people of unclean lips; for my eyes have seen the King, the Lord of hosts" (Is. 6:5). Isaiah's admission of his uncleanness and the uncleanness of his people was in response to the pure, white-hot holiness of God. After his sins are forgiven, a process symbolized by the coal from the altar being placed on his lips, Isaiah responds eagerly to the Lord's call to service: "Then I heard the voice of the Lord, saying, 'Whom shall I send, and who will go for Us?' Then I said, 'Here am I. Send me!' " (Is. 6:8)

True worship—coming face to face with God in all His holiness—ruins us for the ordinary. It changes our perspective forever. Yes, the presence of God ruins us!

With a Thankful Heart

Although worship is an attitude of the heart, thanksgiving is an expression of the gratitude of the heart. A thankful heart leads us to express with our mouths thanks to God for what He *has* done, what He *is* doing, and what He *will* do. Just as worship relates to God's holiness, so thanksgiving relates to God's *goodness*.

Unlike worship, which must be a spontaneous response of the heart, thanksgiving is a direct command of the Lord to His people. Psalm 136:1 exhorts us to "give thanks to the Lord, for He is good; for His lovingkindness is everlasting." The apostle Paul writes, "And whatever you do in word or deed, do all in the name of the Lord Jesus, giving thanks through Him to God the Father" (Col. 3:17); and "Rejoice always; pray without ceasing; in everything give thanks; for this is God's will for you in Christ Jesus" (1 Thess. 5:16-18). So thanksgiving is related to being in God's will. It is the "railroad track" on which to carry the payload of faith.

The Lord commands us to give thanks because it is right and proper to do so as well as because it is the key that unlocks several other important facets of effective prayer. For example, thanksgiving relieves our anxiety and opens the door for the peace of God to fill our spirit. "Be anxious for nothing, but in everything by prayer and supplication with thanksgiving let your requests be made known to God. And the peace of God, which surpasses all comprehension, shall guard your hearts and your minds in Christ Jesus" (Phil. 4:6-7). Thanksgiving also splashes water on our faces to help us stay alert and vigilant in our prayers. "Devote yourselves to prayer, keeping alert in it with an attitude of thanksgiving" (Col. 4:2).

Thanksgiving is a key to releasing God's supernatural power. Before Jesus fed the 5,000 with five loaves and two fish, He gave thanks:

Jesus therefore took the loaves; and having given thanks, He distributed to those who were seated; likewise also of the fish as much as they wanted. And when they were filled, He said to His disciples, "Gather up the leftover fragments that nothing may be lost." And so they gathered them up, and filled twelve baskets with fragments from the five barley loaves, which were left over by those who had eaten (John 6:11-13).

Before Jesus raised Lazarus from the dead, He gave thanks:

And so they removed the stone. And Jesus raised His eyes, and said, "Father, I thank Thee that Thou heardest Me. And I knew that Thou hearest Me always; but because of the people standing around I said it, that they may believe that Thou didst send Me." And when He had said these things, He cried out with a loud voice, "Lazarus, come forth." He who had died came forth, bound hand and foot with wrappings; and his face was wrapped around with a cloth. Jesus said to them, "Unbind him, and let him go" (John 11:41-44).

Thanksgiving also sets a seal on keeping the blessings we have already received. Luke tells the story of ten lepers who cried out to Jesus for healing. After Jesus cleansed them, only one, a Samaritan, came over to thank Him:

And Jesus answered and said, "Were there not ten cleansed? But the nine—where are they? Was no one found who turned back to give glory to God, except this foreigner?" And He said to him, "Rise, and go your way; your faith has made you well" (Luke 17:17-19).

A thankful heart is a balm to our spirits and puts us in direct communion with the heart and mind of God.

High Praises—The Place of God's Dwelling

Praise is an expression of the lips that, like thanksgiving, is a commandment of God for His people. "Praise the Lord! Praise, O servants of the Lord. Praise the name of the Lord" (Ps. 113:1). "Praise the Lord, all nations; laud Him, all peoples! For His lovingkindness is great toward us, and the truth of the Lord is everlasting. Praise the Lord!" (Ps. 117:1-2)

Unlike thanksgiving, however, praise does not depend on the attitude of our hearts. Instead, praise *shapes* the attitude of our hearts. We can *will* ourselves to praise, even when we don't feel like it. Scripture simply commands us to praise. It doesn't matter if we're having a good day or a bad day, if we are sick or well, or whether or not we have all our tax returns ready for April 15. Praise is a choice. The Bible simply says, "Let everything that has breath praise the Lord. Praise the Lord!" (Ps. 150:6) Praise is contagious. Once we begin to praise the Lord with our mouths, it quickly spreads to our minds and our hearts.

Just as thanksgiving expresses gratitude to God for what He does, so praise acknowledges God for who He *is*. If worship relates to God's holiness and thanksgiving to God's goodness, then praise relates to God's *greatness*. "Great is the Lord, and greatly to be praised, in the city of our God, His holy mountain" (Ps. 48:1); "Great is the Lord, and highly to be praised; and His greatness is unsearchable" (Ps. 145:3); "For great is the Lord, and greatly to be praised; He also is to be feared above all gods" (1 Chron. 16:25).

Of course, our praise doesn't make God any bigger than He already is, though He *seems* bigger to us when we praise Him. Somehow praise ignites our faith and expands our vision and understanding of God. Perhaps this is because praise provides a habitation for God.

Have you ever wondered what God's "address" is? It is spelled P-R-A-I-S-E! It's quite simple. He inhabits the praises of His people. God resides in our praise! "But Thou art holy, O Thou that inhabitest the praises of Israel" (Ps. 22:3 KJV). The New American Standard says, "Yet Thou art holy, O Thou who art enthroned upon the praises of Israel" (Ps. 22:3). God is holy and cannot dwell in an unholy place. Praise sanctifies the atmosphere. The Holy One is enthroned on the praises of His people.

Whenever God seems far away, remember that He is really near-by. In fact, we could say that the Lord is as close as the praise on our lips! *Now that's intimacy!*

No matter where we are, no matter how many or how few of us there are, whenever we praise the Lord we build a throne where He can come and sit among us in His manifested presence and speak to us in authority and intimacy. When we enthrone Christ in His glory on our praises He can release His authority and power to us and we can move out in strength and confidence to accomplish His will.

Entrance into the city of God is through the gate of praise (see Ps. 100:4). Speaking prophetically of Jerusalem, Isaiah says, "But you will call your walls salvation, and your gates praise" (Is. 60:18b). Jesus entered His city, the holy city, to the praises of the people. They threw down their garments and cast palm branches across His way as they shouted, "Blessed is He who comes in the name of the Lord!" (See Matthew 21:9.)

It was praise that welcomed and ushered Jesus into the last week of His earthly ministry, and it will be praise that ushers Him into His end-time ministry in the earth through His Body, the Church. Once again praise will pave the way and build a highway for our God. Then the Lord will descend from Heaven with a roar of triumph and usher in His eternal reign.

Bombs of Praise—The Weapon of Deliverance

Since the very presence and power of God are "enthroned" on our praises, it is easy to see how praise is a very potent spiritual weapon. First of all, it is a means of deliverance. "He who sacrifices thank offerings honors Me, and he prepares the way so that I may show him the salvation of God" (Ps. 50:23 NIV). When we praise God in the midst of a terrible situation, salvation and deliverance enter in.

Consider Jonah. From the belly of a great fish in the depths of the sea (how much lower could you get!) Jonah prayed and offered praise to God, and God delivered him onto dry land. Jonah then preached in Nineveh, and his message resulted in the repentance of virtually everyone in the city (see Jon. 2–3). Consider Paul and Silas when they were shackled in the Philippian jail. Their praise, offered to the Lord at midnight, released the power of God to shake the foundations of the prison, open the doors, loose the chains, and bring a pagan jailer and his family to faith and salvation in Christ (see Acts 16:25-33).

Praise is also a weapon that can silence the devil. "From the lips of children and infants You have ordained praise because of Your enemies, to silence the foe and the avenger" (Ps. 8:2 NIV). God has ordained praise that we might silence satan. If we carry the "high praises of God in our mouths" (Ps. 149:6), satan will have no foothold in our lives and no basis from which to accuse us. Satan has no answer, no defense, against praise to God.

I believe that one of the best things the Church could do today in this regard is to go on a prolonged fast of not criticizing any other parts of Christ's Body. It would take enormous power away from the enemy if we would pledge ourselves not to compete, compare, speak against, or slander any other churches or denominations, but speak only blessings, encouragement, and edification. That is in fact what we are commanded to do when Paul says, "Let no unwholesome word proceed from your mouth, but only such a word as is good for edification according to the need of the moment, that it may give grace to those who hear" (Eph. 4:29). This would derail one of satan's primary strategies and stop him dead in his tracks. Just think what would happen if we laid down our legalism, our criticism, our narrow opinions, our "religious" spirit, and our stupid "religious" thinking and focused only on the mind of Christ and those things that edify! It would revolutionize the Church and transform the world!

As a spiritual weapon, praise is the way to release Christ's victory. Let us praise the Lord by any and all means available to us. The "high praises of God in our mouths" releases His power to the maximum in our lives and our churches. There is something irreplaceable about learning to praise God for ourselves. Praise is one of the highest expressions of spiritual warfare. It can place demonic principalities in chains (see Ps. 149:6-9). In praise, we simply declare that which is already written in the Word of God: "It is finished." The outcome of the great war between Christ and satan, between good and evil, has already been decided at the cross. By the death and resurrection of Jesus Christ, God disarmed all the satanic forces. With our praise we enforce and extend the victory Christ has already won at Calvary. This is an honor given to all His holy ones! *Because victory is His, victory is now ours! Praise the Lord!*

The Passions of Worship[1]

Prayer and worship have a synergistic relationship with each other. It's a lot like breathing. Worship is the inhale as we take in the presence and beauty of God, and prayer is the exhale as we receive revelation and work it out in intercession. Worship creates the environment of intimacy with the Lord, an environment in which the seeds of revelation are received and then birthed through intercession. As we worship the Lord we cultivate communion and intimacy with God. Like carefully turned and tended soil, our hearts become fertile for the seed of revelation. As we receive revelation from God, we pray it out in intercession and watch God birth what He wants to birth. From this perspective, I honestly don't believe that we can be effective watchmen without also being ardent worshipers.

We need to be passionate in our worship. Worship needs to really *mean* something to us. We can't be "ho hum" about it. So how do we discover the passion for worship? Let's look at three things.

First of all, *our passion to worship God rises when we realize that, when we worship, we are being like God—in whose image we were created!* Worship has its origin in the very character of God. In one sense, we worship because worship has been going on in the Godhead for all eternity.

In the broadest understanding of the word, *worship* is the expression of pure and complete love and adoration. In that sense, worship characterizes the activity of the Godhead. The Father loves the Son; the Son adores the Father. Together They send Their best gift, the Holy Spirit, as an act of love. God worships—radiates pure love and adoration—because it is in His eternal character and nature. We worship because we were created in God's image. As worship is in God's nature, so it is in ours. Although it is true that we worship God because He is worthy of worship and because He has commanded us to do so, those reasons are secondary. Ultimately we worship because, as creatures made in God's image, it is our nature to do so.

So then, if we know that when we worship we are being like our "Abba" (Daddy) Father, how can we stand to worship *passively*? Knowing that worship is part of our nature as children of God should infuse passion into our worship.

Secondly, *our passion to worship God rises when we realize that, in our worship, we are joining in the angelic procession in Heaven, bringing glory and honor to God.* Paul tells us that "[God] raised us up with Him, and seated us with Him in the heavenly places, in Christ Jesus" (Eph. 2:6). This is more than just "God's up there and I'm down here." We can't begin to understand Heaven if we think in purely directional terms: up, down, left, right. Heaven has to be understood in dimensional terms, as another dimension coexisting with our own. The Bible depicts Heaven as the realm where God is seated on His throne and surrounded by an innumerable amount of angelic hosts who praise and worship Him continually. If we could open our spiritual eyes and look across into that dimension at the great procession of praise and adoration that we have joined, how could we worship passively? Understanding the truth that we are bi-dimensional beings on the threshold of Heaven and earth, living on the heavenly plane with Christ and expressing that reality in the earthly plane, should infuse passion into our worship.

Thirdly, *our passion to worship God rises when we understand that worship is a significant key to knowing God.* The corporate life of the Body of Christ is very visual and participatory. Church life is not a spectator activity. When we come together, what do we do? The Bible says that we are to worship!

If someone came into our church service during baptism and made light of what was going on, we would be upset. If one of our members displayed a flippant attitude toward the Lord's Supper, we would think that was absolutely terrible. Yet how often do we come into "worship" with our minds a million miles away, thinking about anything except God, and simply go through the motions? We have to come to the place where worship is something holy, something to be treasured. When we understand that worship brings us into the presence of God, draws us nearer to Jesus, and releases the power of the Holy Spirit in us, how can we worship passively? The realization that worship is not done in a vacuum, but that it is a reenactment of the resurrection and that every time we worship we show forth the power of Christ's resurrection, should infuse passion into our worship.

Worship and Warfare

Personally, I am convinced that worship *is* a form of spiritual warfare. There is a definite, direct relationship between these two activities. Whenever we worship God, something happens in the demonic realm: the ground rumbles, the pillars shake, and the plaster begins to crack and fall off the walls (so to speak)!

How does worship relate to spiritual warfare? First of all, *praise and worship make room for the Kingdom of God.* The authority of Almighty God is released in the context of His people's praise. So wherever we praise and worship Him, there His Kingdom comes to bear. Our adoration of the Lord in worship prepares us to yield to His authority.

Worship is the most appropriate way to engender a spiritual worldview. There's something about worship that tunes us in to the reality of the spirit world and how that world relates to the "real" world—the realm in which we live out our physical lives. A spiritual worldview birthed through worship teaches us to see all things from God's perspective, which is the only perspective from which we can engage in successful spiritual warfare.

Praise and worship often create the context for the firstfruits in warfare and evangelism. In Acts chapter 2 Luke describes what happened to the 120 believers in the upper room after they were baptized with the power of the Holy Spirit. They couldn't stay put. Flooding out of that upper room they fanned through the streets of Jerusalem and made their way to Solomon's portico, where Peter preached his first sermon. What were these believers doing? They were praising and worshiping the Lord, declaring the greatness of God.

There's no doubt that under the power of the Spirit Peter preached a great sermon; 3,000 people came to the Lord. However, I believe that they came to Christ not just because of Peter's sermon, but because of the praise and worship that were being offered up by all the believers, which released the convicting presence of God. This first harvest had everything to do with the power of God and virtually nothing to do with the ability of man. God wants us to recognize that the firstfruits in warfare, evangelism, or taking back the land are due to His power, not our ability. This places our dependence squarely on God.

Worship maintains our center of balance in the exercise of spiritual warfare. Jack Hayford once said, "Worship is the most important key to maintaining a balanced life. I've never seen a worshiper become unbalanced." A proper understanding of the role of worship will help keep us balanced in our expression of spiritual warfare.

The Balance Beam

The best place to look for a picture of balance for warfare is the cross. The cross was the ultimate battle. In triumph Christ thundered out, "It is finished!" and forever sealed the devil's fate. Yes, our agreeing, worshiping, praising, and thanking the Father for the work of the cross of Christ is a balance beam that we must walk upon.

Consider Jesus' words from the cross as tactics of warfare. Jesus said, "Father, forgive them; for they do not know what they are doing" (Lk. 23:34). How about *forgiveness* as a tactic against the enemy? "Mother, behold your son; son, behold your mother" (see Jn. 19:26-27). Maintaining our relationships is as important a tactic in warfare as pleading the blood of Jesus.

So when it comes to maintaining our equilibrium in spiritual warfare, the plumb has to fall where the greatest battle has been fought and won, and that's the cross. What keeps us with our face pointed toward the cross? *Worship.*

In closing this chapter on worship warfare, I want to quote for you the intercessory song my friend, author, and composer Steve Fry wrote for the Million Man March on Washington D.C. that was sponsored by the Promise Keepers. Imagine the sound of hundreds of thousands of desperate men singing this song, "Breathe on Us Again," to the Lord as an act of humble, intercessory worship before the Judge of all in the Capitol of our nation. As you read the words to this song, you will grasp that it too is an act of identificational repentance.

"Breathe on Us Again"

Oh Lord, hear; Oh Lord, forgive us.
We have lost the awe of You;
Have mercy, have mercy
Oh Lord, cleanse our hearts which are divided;
Stir the faith that we once knew;
We're thirsty, we're thirsty.
Oh Lord, restore the Church that bears Your name,
Oh Spirit, send a revival to this nation.
Breathe on us again, breathe on us again.[2]

We have sinned! Father, forgive us! Forgive us for our halfhearted worship and our ungrateful hearts! Forgive us for our failure to praise You and to lift up Your glory and honor before the world! Renew our hearts; cause us to be thankful once again! Restore the passion in our worship, the power in our praise, and the victory in our walk! Breathe on us again. O Lord, hear! O Lord, forgive! O Lord, act!

Reflection Questions

1. What are some of the biblical benefits of offering up the high praises of God?

2. Why does the devil hate the ministry of praise so much?

3. Does it take a special gift of God to praise the Lord? Who can enter into worship warfare?

Recommended Reading

Worship: The Pattern of Things in Heaven by Joseph Garlington (Destiny Image, 1997)

The Tabernacle of David by Kevin J. Conner (Bible Temple Publishing, 1998)

A God Who Heals the Heart by Steve Fry (Deep Fryed Books, 1997)

Endnotes

1. For the material in the remainder of this chapter, I am indebted to my good friend Steve Fry of Brentwood, Tennessee. These items come from a class session he led on the subject of "Worship and Warfare."

2. Steve Fry, "Breathe on Us Again" (Maranatha Praise, Inc., 1997). Used by permission.

Chapter 13

The Greatest Act in History

istory is full of turning points. A critical victory here, a crucial decision there may affect the lives of millions of people for generations to come. Wellington's defeat of Napoleon at Waterloo in 1815 influenced the course of European history for the next century. Hitler's ill-fated and ill-timed invasion of the Soviet Union in the summer of 1941 and subsequent defeat at Stalingrad in February 1943 was the turning point in the war against Nazi Germany.

Not every major turning point is so dramatic or obvious, though. Oftentimes actions or circumstances that seem inconsequential at the time later prove to be critical junctures that determine the future course of events. Small incidents can set in motion a sequence of events that escalates to monumental consequences. This is the idea behind the proverb that says, "For want of a nail the shoe is lost, for want of a shoe the horse is lost, for want of a horse the rider is lost."[1]

The greatest event in history began in the humblest of circumstances, completely insignificant in the eyes of men. A baby boy was born to a simple peasant girl, perhaps no more than 14 or

15 years old, who had taken shelter with her carpenter husband in a cave used for keeping and feeding livestock. The child grew up in obscurity and at the age of 30 embarked on a brief three-year career as an itinerant preacher and teacher. During His entire life He never traveled farther than 200 miles from His birthplace. He attracted a small group of followers, taught about the Kingdom of God, and even healed some people and cast out some demons.

His unorthodox style quickly ran afoul of the religious authorities, however, and eventually He was betrayed by one of His own followers. Branded a heretic and a blasphemer, He died a humiliating and excruciatingly painful death at the hands of the occupation government, being nailed to a rude and rough cross as an enemy of the state. After His death, He was buried in a borrowed tomb and His small band of followers scattered in fear and grief. It was over. So ended the brief and seemingly tragically failed life of Jesus, the carpenter from Nazareth, now consigned to the dustbin of history. He left no statues or monuments to His memory; no written record of His life, deeds, or teachings to live on after Him; and no children to carry on His name. Or so it seemed.

By the worldly standards of man, Jesus' life was an utter failure. God has a different standard, however, and from His point of view the picture is completely different. " 'For My thoughts are not your thoughts, neither are your ways My ways,' declares the Lord. 'For as the heavens are higher than the earth, so are My ways higher than your ways, and My thoughts than your thoughts' " (Is. 55:8-9).

From God's perspective, the life of Jesus was perfectly fulfilled and gloriously victorious. His monuments are the cross and the empty tomb. The record of His life, deeds, and teachings is the New Testament, written under the inspiration of the Holy Spirit both by those who knew and walked with Jesus personally and by others who were very close to those who did. His children are all His followers through the ages, numbered in the millions—children born of His Spirit into the family of God with Jesus as their elder Brother.

From the Heart and Hand of the Father

The death and resurrection of Jesus Christ was the greatest event in history. Nothing else has so affected the destiny and future of mankind. According to John 1:18, Jesus is "the only begotten God, who is in the bosom of the Father." This means that Jesus represents the very heart of God Himself. There was a moment in history where the Father in eternity placed His hand into His bosom and flung His Son forth into the world of time and space, declaring, "Here is the very best I can give: the love of My own heart."

That love, the very Word of the Father, the perfect embodiment of the nature and fullness of God, was crucified between two thieves. There it pleased God to throw upon His Son all the sin, wickedness, and corruption of every generation, race, and nation of mankind—past, present, and future. Jesus Christ was "the Lamb of God who takes away the sin of the world" (Jn. 1:29b). "[God] made Him who knew no sin to be sin on our behalf, that we might become the righteousness of God in Him" (2 Cor. 5:21). The sinless One became sin for us, and the penalty of our judgment fell upon Him. His blood washed away our sin, and His righteousness was imputed to us. The barrier of sin separating us from God was removed through the most demonstrative act of love in all history.

At the darkest moment of all, when it seemed as though all was lost, Jesus cried out in triumph, "It is finished!" (Jn. 19:30) When Jesus died, sin and death died with Him. When He rose from the dead three days later, sin and death stayed in the grave, conquered forever. Jesus' resurrection sealed the victory won at the cross.

The greatest act in history is also the grandest promise in Scripture: "For God so loved the world, that He gave His only begotten Son, that whoever believes in Him should not perish, but have eternal life" (Jn. 3:16).

The Sprinkling of the Blood

It is the shed blood of Jesus that makes atonement for our sins. Why is the blood so important? Blood represents the life force of all flesh. It is essential for life. According to Scripture, life is in the blood: "For the life of the flesh is in the blood, and I have given it to you on the altar to make atonement for your souls; for it is the blood by reason of the life that makes atonement" (Lev. 17:11).

Blood is also essential for the forgiveness of sin. "And according to the Law, one may almost say, all things are cleansed with blood, and without shedding of blood there is no forgiveness" (Heb. 9:22). The penalty for sin is death. Atonement, or the forgiveness of sin, requires the blood of an innocent whose death is accepted in place of the guilty. This is what was symbolized in the nation of Israel by the lamb sacrifices that were performed daily. These sacrifices pointed to the ultimate sacrifice of the Lamb of God, Jesus Christ.

The Jewish priests ministered the sacrifices daily in the outer tabernacle. Only once a year, on the Day of Atonement, did the high priest—and he alone—enter the Holy of Holies to make atonement for himself and the people. He never entered the Holy of Holies, the Most Holy Place, without the blood of the sacrifice. To do otherwise would mean his death. The Holy of Holies represented the very presence of God Himself. There was no access to the Presence without the shedding of sacrificial blood.

According to the law, after the high priest had ministered at the altar of incense on this day, he would go beyond the veil into the Most Holy Place. There he would take first the blood of the bull and then the blood of the goat and sprinkle it with his finger on the mercy seat and in front of the mercy seat, seven times each. Then, going back outside the veil, he sprinkled blood on the horns of the altar, again seven times (see Lev. 16:11-19).

Why seven times? A closer look at these verses in Leviticus reveals some very interesting things. The blood was sprinkled in three distinct locations seven times each. Some Bible scholars have indicated that the number three represents the Trinity, or the Godhead, and that the number seven is the number of completion and perfection. The sprinkling of the blood seven times in three places is then a picture of what was to come in Jesus Christ. When Jesus, our High Priest, shed His blood, He did a complete work! It was finished. The work of atonement was accomplished perfectly through the blood of this one man—the second Adam, the Lamb of God, Jesus Christ the Lord!

Seven Ways Christ's Blood Was Shed

There is another way that the blood of Jesus parallels the sprinkling of the blood seven times by the high priest. We can identify in the Scriptures seven specific ways that Jesus' blood was shed.

1. *"And being in agony He was praying very fervently; and His sweat became like drops of blood, falling down upon the ground"* (Lk. 22:44).

   Jesus was praying in Gethsemane the night before He died. In the intensity of the moment and from the anguish of His soul as He chose His Father's cup and not His own, as He willed Himself to identify with the sins of the world, blood began to flow from His pores along with His sweat. At that moment Jesus was in the place of mighty wrestling and travail of soul.

   Sometimes the hardest thing of all to do is to decide to go God's way. The cross in our lives is the place where God's will and our will crosses. Actually following God is often easier than making the decision to follow in the first place. This is where Jesus struggled; He knew what lay ahead. By yielding Himself to His Father here, Jesus won the battle in advance. He left Gethsemane and faced the cross with calmness, confidence, and peace. The blood was "sprinkled"—once.

2. *"Then they spat in His face and beat Him with their fists; and others slapped Him, and said, 'Prophesy to us, You Christ; who is the one who hit You?' "* (Mt. 26:67-68)

Jesus was standing before the high priest and the Sanhedrin, the Jewish high council. In response to the high priest's direct question, Jesus acknowledged that He was the Son of God. Enraged at this "blasphemy," the priests and council members vented their hatred for God's Holy One with their fists. The prophet Micah records a comparable passage: "With a rod they will smite the judge of Israel on the cheek" (Mic. 5:1b). Blood from this beating began to flow down the face of Jesus. The blood was "sprinkled"—twice.

3. *"I gave My back to those who strike Me, and My cheeks to those who pluck out the beard; I did not cover My face from humiliation and spitting"* (Is. 50:6).

Although the plucking out of the beard is not specifically recorded in the Gospel accounts of Jesus' suffering, it is a part of Isaiah's prophetic description of the Messiah's travail. Try to imagine for a moment the torturous pain of having the hair literally ripped off your face! As I write this book, I personally sport a short beard. As a man, I cannot begin to imagine the agony and pain of someone forcefully pulling out my beard! No doubt when this was done to Jesus patches of flesh were torn off as well. Now there was more than blood oozing from His pores and trickling from the bruises and gashes on His face; it flowed freely from open wounds of raw flesh. The blood was "sprinkled"—three times.

4. *"Then he released Barabbas for them; but after having Jesus scourged, he delivered Him to be crucified"* (Mt. 27:26).

    Even though he knew Jesus was innocent of any wrongdoing, Pilate bowed to the pressure of the Jewish leaders and ordered Jesus scourged. Psalm 129:3 gives a good description of what it was like: "The plowers plowed upon my back; they lengthened their furrows." The Roman scourge was a whip with multiple leather strips, each fitted with metal balls and sharp pieces of bone designed to rip flesh from the body with every lash. Like a plow opens furrows in a field, the scourging laid open Jesus' back, probably down to the raw bone in places. The blood was "sprinkled"—four times.

5. *"And after weaving a crown of thorns, they put it on His head, and a reed in His right hand; and they kneeled down before Him and mocked Him, saying, 'Hail, King of the Jews!' "* (Mt. 27:29)

    These were not merely short, small thorns such as those on a prickly rosebush. They were probably several inches long and were jammed down on Jesus' head with substantial force. Some scholars believe that the word *crown* here may refer in fact to a "cap" of sorts. If this is true, then the thorns covered Jesus' head, and every one of them drew blood. The blood was "sprinkled"—five times.

6. *"And when they had crucified Him, they divided up His garments among themselves, casting lots"* (Mt. 27:35).

    Nails were driven through Jesus' hands and feet into the rough wooden cross. He hung with His arms at such angle that it cut off His breathing and nearly dislocated His shoulders. The only way He could breathe was to push Himself upright against the nails. Blood poured from His nail wounds. The blood was "sprinkled"—six times.

227

7. *"One of the soldiers pierced His side with a spear, and immediately there came out blood and water"* (Jn. 19:34).

    Jesus had already been crucified and now was completely dead. In a final indignity, a Roman soldier stabbed his spear into Jesus' side, and blood and water poured forth. The blood had now been "sprinkled"—the seventh and final time.

Seven Ways Christ's Blood Avails for Us

One of the ways we overcome as believers is by testifying to what the blood of Jesus has done for us. "And they [believers] overcame him [the accuser of the brethren] because of the blood of the Lamb and because of the word of their testimony, and they did not love their life even to death" (Rev. 12:11). What exactly *has* the blood of Jesus done for us? What good have we received from Jesus' sacrifice? How has His blood availed for us? Scripture reveals at least seven benefits that the shed blood of Christ gives to us.

I briefly addressed this important issue in the book my wife and I co-authored, *Encounters With a Supernatural God*. Let me give you these seven great bullets for your spiritual warfare gun.[2]

1. You have been forgiven through the *blood of Jesus* (see Heb. 9:22).

2. The *blood of Jesus* has cleansed you from *all* sin (see 1 Jn. 1:7).

3. You have been redeemed by the *blood of the Lamb* (see Eph. 1:7).

4. By *His blood*, you are justified ["just as if"] you have never sinned (see Rom. 5:9).

5. You have been sanctified [set apart] through *Jesus' blood* for a holy calling (see Heb. 13:12).

6. Peace has been made for you *through the blood of the cross* (see Col. 1:20).

7. You now have confidence to enter the Most Holy Place by the *blood of Jesus* (see Heb. 10:19).

The blood of Christ intercedes for us! Christ Himself is ever before the Father as our Mediator. "Christ Jesus is He who died, yes, rather who was raised, who is at the right hand of God, who also intercedes for us" (Rom. 8:34). The highest and greatest intercession of all is the blood of Jesus that speaks before the Father's throne!

Yes, Christ's blood has given us life! "For *the life of the flesh is in the blood*, and I have given it to you on the altar to make atonement for your souls; for *it is the blood* by reason of the life *that makes atonement*" (Lev. 17:11). Through Christ's blood we receive eternal life—life that not even death can conquer. Eternal life is not simply biological life; it is *God-life*. The breath of life that God breathed into the first Adam has been restored to Adam's fallen children through the blood of the second Adam, Jesus Christ (see 1 Cor. 15:45). We now have God's breath, God's life, in our lungs. Breathe it in—and breathe it back out on others!

Pleading the Blood

Praise God! We who are born-again believers in the Lord Jesus Christ have been covered by the blood of the Lamb! To some of you that may sound like a bunch of religious jargon, but it's not. We have been purchased by the precious blood of Jesus, the Messiah, the Son of God, our Lord. Joyfully we can proclaim with the hosts in Heaven, "Worthy art Thou...for Thou wast slain, and didst purchase for God with Thy blood men from every tribe and tongue and people and nation" (Rev. 5:9).

He who bought us with His blood now owns us and has complete rights to us. He also has promised to protect and care for us. Just as the lamb's blood on the lintels and doorposts of the Hebrews in Egypt protected them from the scourge of the death angel, so the blood of Jesus protects us. But how do we apply the blood today so that judgment, wrath, pestilence, and disease will pass over us? We do it by pleading the blood.

There is no greater plea, no more prevailing argument to bring before God, than the suffering and atoning death of His Son. In his powerful book *Mighty Prevailing Prayer*, author Wesley Duewel wrote:

> "Plead the blood. Pray till you have the assurance of God's will. Pray till you have been given by the Spirit a vision of what God longs to do, needs to do, waits to do. Pray till you are gripped by the authority of the name of Jesus. Then plead the blood of Jesus. The name of Jesus and the blood of Jesus—glory in them, stake your all on them, and use them to the glory of God and the routing of Satan.
>
> "Bring before the Father the wounds of Jesus; remind the Father of the agony of Gethsemane; recall to the Father the strong cries of the Son of God as He prevailed for our world and for our salvation. Remind the Father of earth's darkest hour on Calvary, as the Son triumphed alone for you and me. Shout to heaven again Christ's triumphant call, 'It is finished!' Plead the cross. Plead the blood. Plead them over and over again."[3]

That's how to prevail in intercession!

The great nineteenth-century English preacher Charles Spurgeon wrote that the blood of Jesus "unlocks the treasury of heaven. Many keys fit many locks, but the master key is the blood and the name of Him that died and rose again, and ever lives in heaven to save unto the uttermost."[4]

One Drop of the Blood of Jesus

When my friend Mahesh Chavda ministered in the African nation of Zaire, he found himself standing in front of more than 100,000 people. The Holy Spirit told him to hold a mass deliverance service the next day. Mahesh said to God, "Lord, I am here alone. Where are my helpers?" To that the Lord responded, "I am

230

your helper. Remember, one drop of the blood of My Son, Jesus, is more powerful than all the kingdom of darkness!"[5]

If we want to see generational curses lifted and sins forgiven; if we want to see true revival come to the land; if we want to prevail in intercession and see God's glory fill the earth, then we need to plead the blood. We must testify to what the blood of Jesus has accomplished for us. Plead the blood of our glorious Lord and King who died and rose again! Plead, proclaim, recite, meditate upon, and put your trust in the work of His spilled blood. There is nothing like the blood of Jesus! The old gospel hymn says it so well:

"There Is Power in the Blood"

Would you be free
From your burden of sin?
There's power in the blood,
Power in the blood;
Would you o'er evil a victory win?
There's wonderful power in the blood.

Would you be free
From your passion and pride?
There's power in the blood,
Power in the blood;
Come for a cleansing
To Calvary's tide;
There's wonderful power in the blood.

Would you be whiter,
Much whiter than snow?
There's power in the blood,
Power in the blood;
Sin stains are lost
In its lifegiving flow;
There's wonderful power in the blood.

Would you do service
For Jesus your king?
There's power in the blood,
Power in the blood;
Would you live daily
His praises to sing?
There's wonderful power in the blood.

There is power, power,
Wonder working power,
In the blood of the Lamb;
There is power, power,
Wonder working power,
In the precious blood of the Lamb.[6]

A Prayer for Cleansing

Since we have been talking about pleading and applying the blood of Jesus, I want to close with a prayer that is beautifully appropriate. The author is unknown; whoever it was obviously had an intercessor's heart and understood what I presented before you in this chapter.

"Father, we cleanse our hands with the blood of Jesus. We apply the blood of Jesus to our eyes, Lord, so that we might see into the spirit realm clearly and with clarity. We apply the blood of Jesus to our ears, to cleanse our ears of any defilement, wickedness, garbage, gossip or slander that have been poured into our ears, so that we might hear clearly what You are speaking to us. We apply the blood of Jesus to our lips and to our tongue, so that You would be able to cleanse us of all those things that we have spoken that really haven't been of You at all. Father, we apply the blood of Jesus to our heart and our minds. So Father, we ask You to put the blood of Jesus on our hearts, our thoughts, and our emotions and to cleanse our minds from the dead works so that we might serve the living God.

"Father, we apply the blood of Jesus to our feet. Cleanse us from the corruption in this world and from the dust of the world. Father, cleanse us of those places that we've walked in that really haven't been ordered of You. Lord, we receive the words of the Bible that say, 'The steps of a righteous man are ordered by the Lord.' We will have holy steps, walking on that highway of holiness. Praise You, Lord! And we ask that You cleanse us from the top of our head to the souls of our feet. Thank You, Lord!"[7]

What is the cure of all evils? What has the power to break generational sin? Where does the power to break demonic darkness come from? Oh, from the greatest act in history—from the completed work of the cross of Christ Jesus our Lord!

Now let's go forth testifying (see Rev. 12:11) what the blood of Jesus has accomplished for us! It is the cure of all evil!

Reflection Questions

1. What is the greatest act in all of history? Describe it, please.

2. How was the blood of Jesus shed? How many times?

3. What are the biblical benefits of the shed blood of Jesus? What does this mean for you?

Recommended Reading

The Blood of the Cross by Andrew Murray (Whitaker House, 1981)

Power in the Blood by Charles Spurgeon (Whitaker House, 1996)

The Cross of Christ by Andrew Murray (Marshal Pickering, 1989)

Endnotes

1. George Herbert, *Jacula Prudentum*, as quoted in John Bartlett, *Bartlett's Familiar Quotations*, 16th ed., Justin Kaplan, ed. (New York: Little, Brown and Company, 1992), 244:28.

2. Jim and Michal Ann Goll, *Encounters With a Supernatural God* (Shippensburg, Pennsylvania: Destiny Image, 1998), 98.

3. Wesley Duewel, *Mighty Prevailing Power* (Grand Rapids, Michigan: Zondervan Publishing House, 1990), 308.

4. Charles Spurgeon, *Twelve Sermons on Prayer*, as quoted in Duewel, *Mighty Prevailing Prayer*, 308.

5. This quote comes from a personal testimony I have heard through my relationship with healing evangelist Mahesh Chavda, now residing in Charlotte, North Carolina, concerning a ministry trip of his into Zaire, Africa.

6. Lewis E. Jones, "There Is Power in the Blood." Public domain.

7. Author unknown.

Chapter 14

The Father's Heart of Mercy

By this time many of you who have stayed with me so far may be asking, "Okay, Jim, what's next? What are you saving for the final course?" Perhaps the Spirit of God has stirred up in you through these pages an awareness of the crying need for corporate confession and repentance and the lifting of generational sins and curses from our land and the nations. Your spirit may be burdened with a heavy weight of conviction over the magnitude of our collective guilt and responsibility. The ache in your heart may be pressing you so hard that you feel like you can't hold it in any longer and have to cry out in desperation, *"We have sinned! Father, forgive us!"*

If that is the case, don't despair; pain is a necessary part of healing. We have confronted many painful truths in this book—truths about ourselves, our nation, and our heritage. Now is the time to come together as priestly intercessors and bring these matters before God's throne of grace. Something amazing and wonderful happens when believers come together in agreement and lift a corporate cry of desperation before the Lord. It is the *desperate* prayer that moves the heart of God; it is the persistent cry that sways His hand.

James 4:2 says that we have not because we ask not. One of the reasons we ask not is because we desire not; we're simply not hungry. God wants to make us hungry. He wants to put in us such a craving for Him that we can no longer stand to live without revival. He wants us to hunger for the bread of His presence even more than we do for natural food. "Give us this day our daily bread" then becomes a corporate plea for the glorious presence of God to come on our homes, our churches, our neighborhoods, our cities, and our nation in a great wave of healing and restoration.

So even though we have faced many sobering and convicting truths in these pages, do not despair. Take heart, for there is hope. *Our Father has a great heart of mercy!*

Established in Mercy

Mercy is one of the foundation stones of the Kingdom of Heaven. How could it be otherwise when mercy is so much a part of the nature and character of God? Isaiah spoke of the prominent place of mercy in God's design:

> *Then in mercy and loving-kindness shall a throne be established, and One shall sit upon it in truth and faithfulness in the tent of David, judging and seeking justice and being swift to do righteousness* (Isaiah 16:5 AMP).

The throne of God signifies His sovereignty and rule over His Kingdom. Being sovereign, God is absolutely supreme in power and position, answerable and accountable to no one except Himself. Yet He has established His throne in mercy. The word *establish* means to fix immovably and implies permanence. Mercy is an eternal characteristic of the Kingdom of God. The character of a king is revealed in the decrees that issue forth from his throne. God's nature is revealed to us in the same way. From His throne issue mercy, truth, faithfulness, justice, and righteousness. Who wouldn't want to live under the rule of such a sovereign?

In God's Kingdom, mercy is inseparably linked with grace. "Let us therefore draw near with confidence to the throne of grace, that we may receive mercy and may find grace to help in time of need" (Heb. 4:16). Grace means getting what we don't deserve (God's unmerited favor), whereas mercy means not getting what we do deserve (judgment and condemnation). Do you see the connection? As sinners we cannot receive God's favor without receiving His mercy. Without mercy there is no grace. Mercy lays aside judgment and the sin that separates, while grace smiles at us and says, "*Come to Me.*" This is possible because our judgment and sin were laid on another, Jesus Christ the Righteous, the Lamb of God, who redeemed us with His blood.

This relationship is critical for understanding our priestly position as intercessors. Because God's throne is established in mercy, we can run to Him and climb right up in His lap. God loves us, takes pity on us, and pours His compassion over us like honey. He wants us to win! His heart is for us, not against us. Paul expressed this so well when he wrote to the Romans,

> *What then shall we say to these things? If God is for us, who is against us? He who did not spare His own Son, but delivered Him up for us all, how will He not also with Him freely give us all things?...Who shall separate us from the love of Christ?...For I am convinced that neither death, nor life, nor angels, nor principalities, nor things present, nor things to come, nor powers, nor height, nor depth, nor any other created thing, shall be able to separate us from the love of God, which is in Christ Jesus our Lord* (Romans 8:31-32,35a,38-39).

God's pulsating heart beats with love and compassion not only for us but for all people. He yearns for all who do not know Him to come to His throne of grace and mercy. Christ opened the way to the mercy seat. God's longing is for a people who will come together in agreement regarding His passion for the world. He is looking for earthen vessels that are willing to be filled with the treasure of His love and then be broken and poured out through intercession so that His grace, mercy, and compassion can cover the earth.

A Psalm of Mercy

If you want to draw near and learn the heart of God, let me suggest that you spend time basking in the warmth of Psalm 103. This entire psalm, penned by David, is simply awesome. David was a man after God's own heart, so he knew what he was talking about. Let's look at some highlights.

Bless the Lord, O my soul; and all that is within me, bless His holy name. Bless the Lord, O my soul, and forget none of His benefits; who pardons all your iniquities; who heals all your diseases; who redeems your life from the pit; who crowns you with lovingkindness and compassion (Psalm 103:1-4).

Look at everything the Lord does for us: He pardons us, heals us, redeems us, and crowns us. That's a nutshell biography of every believer's journey from sinner to saint to ruler with Christ in the heavenly realm. God does these things out of His loving-kindness (mercy) and compassion.

The Lord performs righteous deeds, and judgments for all who are oppressed (Psalm 103:6).

I believe that we need to renew our minds concerning this word *judgment*, because we usually think of it only in a negative light. In reality, even God's judgments are ultimately acts of His redemption and kindness. His judgments are for the purpose of turning those who are judged to repentance so that He can cover them with grace, mercy, and compassion.

The Lord is compassionate and gracious, slow to anger and abounding in lovingkindness. He will not always strive with us; nor will He keep His anger forever. He has not dealt with us according to our sins, nor rewarded us according to our iniquities (Psalm 103:8-10).

It's unfortunate that the image of God that many people hold is one of an angry, wrathful deity ready to fling lightning bolts at us for the least infraction. These verses reveal what God is really like. Certainly God judges and condemns sin, but He has only a heart of love and compassion for the sinner. Slow to anger, God does not have a quick trigger finger, ready to shoot us down in an instant. He would much rather show mercy. He doesn't give us what we deserve. Aren't you glad? I know I am!

> *For as high as the heavens are above the earth, so great is His lovingkindness toward those who fear Him. As far as the east is from the west, so far has He removed our transgressions from us. Just as a father has compassion on his children, so the Lord has compassion on those who fear Him* (Psalm 103:11-13).

How high are the heavens above the earth? Astronomers tell us that the universe stretches to infinity. God's love and mercy toward us are limitless. Isn't that awesome? It is truly beyond our comprehension. He has removed our transgressions from us, and we are now moving in the exact opposite direction from them. Just as a loving earthly father would, God disciplines us in love to shape us into the children He wants us to be. Just as a proud earthly father would, God sits in the grandstands cheering us on and encouraging us to run a good race.

> *But the lovingkindness of the Lord is from everlasting to everlasting on those who fear Him, and His righteousness to children's children* (Psalm 103:17).

Do you get the picture? Our Father's nature is one of love, grace, and mercy. Yes, mercy! Mercy, mercy, mercy! Our God's heart is poised with grace and mercy toward us and all people. Before we can *extend* God's heart of compassion, however, we must first *experience* God's heart of compassion.

God's Heart of Compassion

Like grace and mercy, compassion is part of God's nature. Even a brief examination of Scripture leaves no doubt about that.

"*But Thou, O Lord, art a God full of **compassion**, and gracious, longsuffering, and plenteous in mercy and truth*" (Ps. 86:15 KJV). The Hebrew word here is *rahum*, an adjective meaning compassionate or merciful.[1]

"*The Lord is good to all; He has **compassion** on all He has made*" (Ps. 145:9 NIV). Here the Hebrew word is *rahamim*, which means bowels, mercies, or compassion.[2]

"*This I recall to my mind, therefore have I hope. It is of the Lord's mercies that we are not consumed, because His **compassions** fail not. They are new every morning: great is Thy faithfulness*" (Lam. 3:21-23 KJV). *Raham*, the Hebrew word used here, is the most basic Old Testament word for compassion. It also means to be merciful and to have pity.[3] Specifically, this word refers to the tender, sympathetic feeling aroused by seeing someone else's troubles.

"*And seeing the multitudes, He felt **compassion** for them, because they were distressed and downcast like sheep without a shepherd*" (Mt. 9:36). The Greek verb used here, *splanchnizomai*, means "to be moved as to one's inwards, to be moved with compassion, to yearn with compassion."[4]

"*Shouldest not thou also have had **compassion** on thy fellow-servant, even as I had pity on thee?*" (Mt. 18:33 KJV) In this case, the Greek verb is *eleeo*, which means "to have mercy, to show kindness, by beneficence, or assistance."[5] This is the parable of the ungrateful servant whose master forgives his debt, only to reinstate it when the servant shows a lack of compassion toward a fellow servant. The point is that God the Father, represented by the master in the parable, has this kind of compassion.

"*For He says to Moses, 'I will have mercy on whom I have mercy, and I will have **compassion** on whom I have compassion'* " (Rom. 9:15 NIV). In this instance Paul used the verb *oikteiro* to refer to God's compassion. The word means "to have pity, a feeling of distress through the ills of others."[6]

"*For we do not have a high priest who cannot **sympathize** with our weaknesses, but One who has been tempted in all things as we are, yet without sin*" (Heb. 4:15). Here the Greek verb *sumpatheo* (English, *sympathy*) means "to suffer with another, to be affected similarly, to have compassion upon."[7]

240

*"I urge you therefore, brethren, by the **mercies** of God, to present your bodies a living and holy sacrifice, acceptable to God, which is your spiritual service of worship"* (Rom. 12:1). *Oiktirmos* is a Greek noun meaning " 'the viscera, the inward parts,' as the seat of emotion."[8]

The compassion of God is deep, abundant, and full. He stands ever ready to exercise it on behalf of those who seek Him.

A Revelation of Mercy

Sometimes we relate better to an experience of life than to a textbook definition. God raises up champions who are given a revelation of a portion of God's heart and nature. One of these champions whom I personally grew to love and respect was John Wimber, the late leader of Vineyard Ministries International. He shared in his book, *Power Healing*, a vision that he received regarding the mercy and compassion of God.

> "Suddenly in my mind's eye there appeared to be a cloud bank superimposed across the sky. But I had never seen a cloud bank like this one, so I pulled my car over to the side of the road to take a closer look. Then I realized it was not a cloud bank; it was a honeycomb with honey dripping out onto people below. The people were in a variety of postures. Some were reverent; they were weeping and holding their hands out to catch the honey and taste it, even inviting others to take some of their honey. Others acted irritated, wiping the honey off themselves, complaining about the mess. I was awestruck. Not knowing what to think, I prayed, 'Lord, what is it?'

> "He said, 'It's my mercy, John. For some people it's a blessing, but for others it's a hindrance. There's plenty for everyone. Don't ever beg me for healing again. The problem isn't on my end, John. It's down there.' "[9]

Which type of person are you—the one who wipes the honey off in disgust or the one who receives it joyfully and shares it with others? When we receive God's compassion into our lives, we in turn become extensions of His heart and IIis hands to share His compassion with a dying world.

Cultivating the Compassionate Heart of God

I'm not who I was and, thank God, I am not yet who I am going to be. "What do you mean, Jim? What are you trying to tell us?" (I think I hear some of you saying that right now.) Let me try to explain.

I am on a journey, just like you are. I have not always understood God's grace toward me and the necessity of God's mercy working in and through me to others. This is more than getting accurate head knowledge on some Hebrew and Greek words. It is a major issue of the heart. Through the school of hard knocks, the Holy Spirit has been pounding on my heart to tenderize it—to help me cultivate a heart of compassion.

To be effective intercessors, particularly in the realm of identificational intercession and generational and corporate confession, we need to be in touch with the compassionate heart of God. We need to learn how to see what He sees, feel what He feels, cry as He cries, and love as He loves. This requires that we move from mere prayer to the presence of God. Although it is not always easy to do, it is critical. As I wrote in *The Lost Art of Intercession*,

> "How do you go from prayer to His presence? It's a heart issue. I'm not going to give you five steps. I can't because I don't know them (although I thought I used to). All I can say is: Lay down your life and learn mercy, and God will meet you to commune with you there.
>
> "...God communes with us at the seat of mercy. It doesn't go away; it is the very atmosphere and environment of God's presence.
>
> "This gets to the core of what we call religion. Man's religion is judgment pending criticism, legalism, and debate. God does not want us operating out of judgment. He wants us operating out of the seat of mercy.

"Even though we store up the Word, ask for the cross of brokenness, walk in the reality that God is good and that we are bound together by His extravagance, His richness, and His fatness, and clothe ourselves in the gift of righteousness, made available to us through the blood of Jesus—there is something more. When we take this freshly mixed incense, offer it on the fires of fervent prayer, and take it beyond the veil, *there is still one more necessary thing*. We need to have *mercy* built into our lives."[10]

One way we can soften ourselves to receive God's compassionate heart is simply to open our eyes. Let's take a look at the pain and the suffering, the sorrow and sighing, the blindness and deafness, the injustice and hatred. They're all around us, not as abstract concepts, but in real-life, hurting people. In Jesus' parable of the prodigal son in Luke 15, the father saw his returning wayward son while he was still a great distance away. Compassion exploded from his heart and, casting aside any cloak of dignity, he ran as fast as he could to embrace his son. That's the way God feels about the people of this world. He wants to take them in His arms as they turn to Him.

Jesus told also of a Samaritan who, when he saw lying beside the road a man who had been attacked, robbed, and severely beaten by thieves, felt compassion for the victim. Compassion compelled him to give of his time, his energy, and his means to bind the injured man's wounds and to take care of him.

That's the way we are to feel and act toward the people of our world. Every person is our neighbor. John Wesley had the right idea when he said, "The world is my parish." Just as the priests under the old covenant identified with the weaknesses of others because they were weak themselves, so we are called to identify with our generation.

Do You Know Who You Are?

Finally, we can nurture the compassion of God in our hearts by being clear on who we are. When we know who we are, we will know what to do.

- *"But you will be called the priests of the Lord; you will be spoken of as ministers of our God"* (Is. 61:6a).

  This is who we *are*: priests and ministers to the Lord.

- *"The Spirit of the Lord God is upon me, because the Lord has anointed me to bring good news to the afflicted; He has sent me to bind up the brokenhearted, to proclaim liberty to captives, and freedom to prisoners; to proclaim the favorable year of the Lord, and the day of vengeance of our God; to comfort all who mourn, to grant those who mourn in Zion, giving them a garland instead of ashes, the oil of gladness instead of mourning, the mantle of praise instead of a spirit of fainting. So they will be called oaks of righteousness, the planting of the Lord, that He may be glorified"* (Is. 61:1-3).

  This is what we *do*: bring good news to the afflicted. Notice that Jesus read these same verses in the synagogue in Nazareth when He defined His mission on earth (see Lk. 4:16-21).

- *"Then they will rebuild the ancient ruins, they will raise up the former devastations, and they will repair the ruined cities, the desolations of many generations"* (Is. 61:4).

  This will be the *result*: restoration and redemption.

When we begin to be sensitive to the needs of others and to minister to them in this way, the ruins of the Body of Christ will be rebuilt and repaired and that which has been desolate for many generations will be restored. This type of ministry takes a real laying down of our lives, our desires, and our convenience in order to help and minister to someone else. This is the heart quality necessary to move into authentic identificational acts of confession and repentance, healing, and change.

A Heart for Revival

Why is it that some people respond readily to every move of the Spirit while others seem to be unaffected no matter what God is doing around them? The answer probably lies in the heart condition of the individual. Proud hearts are cold and hard, all but impervious to the gentle knocks and nudges of the Spirit. Humble hearts have been broken before the Lord and are soft and pliable for His molding. These are the people God can use. In his great psalm of confession, David spoke from personal experience: "The sacrifices of God are a broken spirit; a broken and a contrite heart, O God, Thou wilt not despise" (Ps. 51:17).

What are the characteristics of "broken" people and of the heart that God revives? Jesus gives a good description in the opening verses of the Sermon on the Mount.[11]

- *"Blessed are the poor in spirit, for theirs is the kingdom of heaven"* (Mt. 5:3).

  The poor in spirit recognize the depth of their own spiritual need. Aware of their unworthiness, they know they have nothing to offer God except their own broken lives, and they are thrilled that God would use them at all.

- *"Blessed are those who mourn, for they shall be comforted"* (Mt. 5:4).

  The mournful are quick to admit their mistakes and seek forgiveness. They are deeply grieved over the sin in their lives and practice *specific* confession, rather than general. They demonstrate the sincerity of their repentance by forsaking those sins.

- *"Blessed are the gentle, for they shall inherit the earth"* (Mt. 5:5).

  The gentle esteem others as better than themselves and, in fact, have no concern for self at all. They are quick to accept personal responsibility and receive criticism with humility and openness.

- *"Blessed are those who hunger and thirst for righteousness, for they shall be satisfied"* (Mt. 5:6).

These are the ones who strive daily to walk in the light and who are always seeking fresh and deeper intimacy with God.

- *"Blessed are the merciful, for they shall receive mercy"* (Mt. 5:7).

  Full of compassion, the merciful forgive easily because they recognize how much they have been forgiven. Because of this, they have a strong motivation to serve others.

- *"Blessed are the pure in heart, for they shall see God"* (Mt. 5:8).

  The pure in heart have learned to deny self daily. More concerned with what God thinks than with what man thinks, they are willing to die to their own reputations. They are open and transparent before God and, as He directs, before others.

- *"Blessed are the peacemakers, for they shall be called sons of God"* (Mt. 5:9).

  Peacemakers are willing to yield their right to be right. Quick to reconcile, they seize the initiative to restore broken relationships, even if the other person is in the wrong.

The heart that God revives is the heart that yearns to reflect God's heart. The heart that God revives is the heart that desires to be conformed to the image of Christ. The heart that God revives is the heart that craves the anointing of the Spirit in order to minister to others in the power of the Spirit. The heart that God revives is the heart that continually seeks intimate communion with Him. What's the condition of your heart?

Needed: An Upper Room Experience

I am firmly convinced that desperate prayer is a major key to revival. That sounds simple, but the most profound of truths usually do. Yet prayer is one of the most neglected, misused, and misunderstood practices among modern Christians. It is no wonder that so many churches today evidence a lack of spiritual power. They have no power because they do not pray. They have not because they ask not. If revival returns to America it will be because American churches have returned to prayer. I'm talking about corporate prayer: down-home, nitty-gritty, nuts-and-bolts, brass-tacks, heart-wrenching, Spirit-empowered prayer meetings!

Just before He ascended to Heaven, Jesus gathered His followers together and "commanded them not to leave Jerusalem, but to wait for what the Father had promised" (Acts 1:4b). "Wait" in this context refers to prayer. Jesus *commanded* them to abide in prayer until they received power from on high. They obeyed and the result was Pentecost. We desperately need to recapture the concept of corporate prayer as a mandate from our Lord.

The Rev. Armin R. Gesswein, with wise insights into the link between prayer and revival, wrote,

> "Our trouble today is that we have not seen the Upper Room prayer meeting as a command of Jesus. We seem to have little authority when it comes to getting our churches into prayer meetings and all that God wants to do there....This is a great part of our problem and weakness—getting corporate prayer and Revival back into our churches....
>
> "The Spirit of Prayer is the Spirit of Revival. The first revival in any genuine Revival is a revival of prayer. The Revival spirit leaves churches when true prayer meetings depart; and Revival returns with the return of abiding prayer and prayer meetings. It's that simple! And there is no other way."[12]

At the Crossroads

So here we sit at the crossroads passing into a new millennium. What happens now? Where do we go from here? I believe that the choice is ours. We can either leave things as they are or we can answer God's call and rise to His challenge to stand in the gap before Him for our nation and for the world. We can displace the powers of darkness through bold acts of confession of our generational sins and of lifting a cry to the Father of mercies to move.

God is looking for willing, compassionate hearts who will enter into the travail of generational confession and identificational intercession to forgive our sins as a people and to lift the curses from the land. The need is great and the stains are deep—but our Father has a big heart of mercy!

The prophet Micah wrote, "He has told you, O man, what is good; and what does the Lord require of you but to do justice, to love kindness, and to walk humbly with your God?" (Mic. 6:8) My Christian friends, those are our marching orders! The Father is waiting to hear our cry for justice, for mercy, for forgiveness, for restoration, and for healing.

May our hearts ache and our spirits cry out for our people and nation, echoing the words of our forerunner Daniel:

So now, our God, listen to the prayer of Thy servant and to his supplications, and for Thy sake, O Lord, let Thy face shine on Thy desolate sanctuary. O my God, incline Thine ear and hear! Open Thine eyes and see our desolations and the city which is called by Thy name; for we are not presenting our supplications before Thee on account of any merits of our own, but on account of Thy great compassion. O Lord, hear! O Lord, forgive! O Lord, listen and take action! For Thine own sake, O my God, do not delay, because Thy city and Thy people are called by Thy name (Daniel 9:17-19).

If We Will, He Will

If we will do what God has told us to do—pray—then He will do what He said He would do—cleanse and heal us.

If My people, which are called by My name, shall humble themselves, and pray, and seek My face, and turn from their wicked ways; then will I hear from heaven, and will forgive their sin, and will heal their land (2 Chronicles 7:14 KJV).

May it ever be so!

I am willing to go on this journey to hold back darkness and call forth the light of our Father's mercy. Are you? But wait—I have a promise for you. Do you know what promise follows the prayer, "Father, forgive us!"? It is, "Lead us not into temptation, but deliver us from evil" (Mt. 6:13a). Guess what?

Deliverance follows confession!

Resurrection from the dead will occur!

Life will spring forth!

If we will, He will! Our greatest destiny in the Church and this nation could be right in front of our eyes. For when we cry, "Father, forgive us!" He comes running to our aid. So don't be in dismay—just cry out to the Lord!

We have sinned! Father, forgive us! Come, Lord, we wait for You! Come, Lord, forgive our sin! Come, Lord, revive our hearts! Come, Lord, heal our land! Come, Lord, reveal Your great mercy! Father, forgive us, in Jesus' mighty name! Amen. Let it be so!

Reflection Questions

1. God's throne is established in mercy. What does this statement mean to you?

2. Give a definition of mercy.

3. Have you experienced the mercy heart of the Father toward you? How? Give an example.

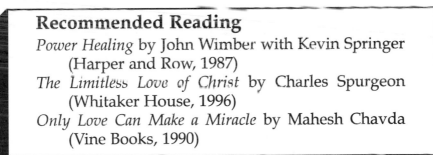

Recommended Reading

Power Healing by John Wimber with Kevin Springer (Harper and Row, 1987)

The Limitless Love of Christ by Charles Spurgeon (Whitaker House, 1996)

Only Love Can Make a Miracle by Mahesh Chavda (Vine Books, 1990)

Endnotes

1. W.E. Vine, Merrill F. Unger, and William White, Jr., *Vine's Complete Expository Dictionary of Old and New Testament Words* (Nashville, Tennessee: Thomas Nelson Publishers, 1985), Old Test. dict., 44.

2. Vine, Unger, and White, *Vine's Complete Expository Dictionary*, Old Test. dict., 43.

3. Vine, Unger, and White, *Vine's Complete Expository Dictionary*, Old Test. dict., 43.

4. Vine, Unger, and White, *Vine's Complete Expository Dictionary*, New Test. dict., 116.

5. Vine, Unger, and White, *Vine's Complete Expository Dictionary*, New Test. dict., 117.

6. Vine, Unger, and White, *Vine's Complete Expository Dictionary*, New Test. dict., 116.

7. Vine, Unger, and White, *Vine's Complete Expository Dictionary*, New Test. dict., 116-117.

8. Vine, Unger, and White, *Vine's Complete Expository Dictionary*, New Test. dict., 117.

9. John Wimber, *Power Healing* (San Francisco, California: Harper and Row, 1987).

10. Jim W. Goll, *The Lost Art of Intercession* (Shippensburg, Pennsylvania: Revival Press, 1997), 85-86.

11. The characteristics listed with each beatitude are adapted from "The Heart God Revives," an outline presented by Nancy DeMoss during the November Fasting and Prayer '95 convocation in Los Angeles. The outline was distributed by Intercessors for America.

12. Armin R. Gesswein, "The Upper Room: God's Revival Model," Intercessor for America newsletter (Spring, 1999).

Appendix

THE PROTECTORATE

Now let's add just a little more to our understanding by taking a peek, once again, at some crucial material penned by Dr. Peter Wagner. Then at the closing of this Appendix, I will add some comments from a revelatory experience I encountered concerning these issues.

A. *Finding the Balance* (by C. Peter Wagner)[1]

As we begin to learn how to move out in spiritual warfare on all levels as did the early Christians, it is essential that we maintain the delicate balance between the upward and the outward.

How does this model function? It is simple. We must never move outward faster than we move upward. The upward is an indispensable prerequisite for the outward, since nothing we do is derived from our own strength, but rather from the strength provided by God through us.

What happens if we are out of balance?

The danger of going upward without going outward is ineffectiveness in ministry. This is serious enough.

But the danger of going outward without going upward is much more serious. It is truly like being a sheep among wolves, but this time a sheep without the protection of the Great Shepherd. The enemy can and will eat us for breakfast.

I like to conceptualize it in a diagram such as the following:

**Positions in Spiritual Warfare:
The Upward and the Outward**

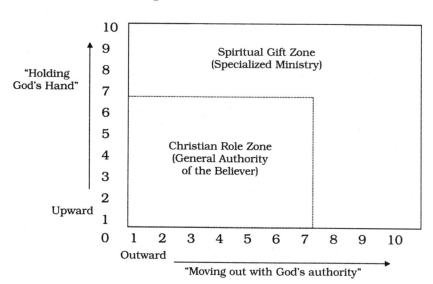

How far out should we go? Those who have read my book *Your Spiritual Gifts Can Help Your Church Group* may recall the helpful distinction between spiritual gifts and Christian roles. It is a Christian role for every believer to engage in ministries such as evangelism, giving, hospitality, healing, teaching and any number of others as needs and opportunities arise.

But this is not to deny that God has also given to a certain number of members of the Body of Christ spiritual gifts known, for example, as the gift of evangelist or the gift of healing or the gift of teaching, in which case the ministry of those individuals will be done on a much broader, more systematic and more effective scale than that of the average Christian.

This applies to spiritual warfare. I know of no 'gift of spiritual warfare' in the New Testament, but I do believe that some Christians have been given a gift mix through which God expects them to move outward more than others. I have arbitrarily numbered the vertical and horizontal scales of the model from 0 to 10 and drawn internal boundaries with the dotted line at 7 on the upward scale and 7 on the outward scale. It simply indicates that there is probably some limit to the level of spiritual warfare which the ordinary Christian without a special gift mix or ministry or calling should reasonably undertake. Past that, especially when it involves dealing with territorial spirits such as are described in this book, only those so gifted and called would be advised to attempt it. Few would be expected to be doing level 8 spiritual warfare, and fewer still level 9. The only human being who would legitimately be a 10-10 on the scale would be Jesus Christ, and His face-to-face encounter with satan in the wilderness might well be regarded as a unique experience which will not be duplicated.

Since it is advisable to be further up than out at any given time, I like to go one step further and super-impose over the diagram a *'danger zone'* in which we should avoid ministering at all costs. In other words, never allow yourself to be found ministering in a position within the shaded zone.

Keep in mind that these lines are arbitrary and illustrative only. Perhaps as time goes by and we experiment more with spiritual warfare we will be able to draw some more objective conclusions.

Positions in Spiritual Warfare:
The Upward and the Outward

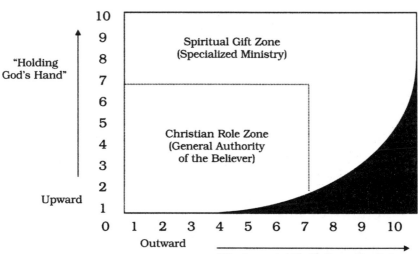

As we strive to hear from God and to know the level and intensity on which He might be calling each of us to engage in spiritual warfare, we can be sure that as we move upward God will draw near to us and as we appropriately move outward satan will flee from us. The scriptures promise us that. And as the power of the enemy is pushed back and the glory of God shines through, we will see the harvest increasingly reaped and multitudes of unbelievers turning 'from darkness to light, and from the power of satan to God' (Acts 26:18).

B. *The Guardian of Intercession* (by Jim W. Goll)

Now, let me add some thoughts from a powerful visionary experience the Holy Spirit gave me.[2]

Early one Sunday morning in January, 1992, I saw an open vision which appeared on the wall in my hotel room. It was a picture of the diagram printed on the preceeding page. In this vision, I saw a "tote umbrella" emerge up through the diagram and then "pop open." It was called "The Protectorate" or "The Guardian of Intercession." It was noted that the "tote umbrella" is especially necessary for pioneers.

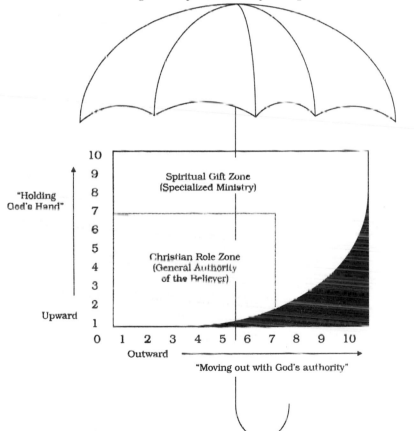

We must join in with our pioneer missionary plow-men and open up an umbrella of protection in their behalf. This prayer shield is even more necessary, immediately after the "engagement" as it is during.

CLOSING

A. *Examples of Common Ground Issues to Avoid*

   1. Grumbling—Miriam and Aaron. Numbers 12:1 —*Then Miriam and Aaron spoke against Moses because of the Cushite woman whom he had married (for he had married a Cushite woman)...*

   2. Thievery and deception

      a. Achan. Josh. 7:1—*But the sons of Israel acted unfaithfully in regard to the things under the ban, for Achan, the son of Carmi, the son of Zabdi, the son of Zerah, from the tribe of Judah, took some of the things under the ban, therefore the anger of the Lord burned against the sons of Israel.*

      b. Judas.

         i. Jn. 6:70-71—*Jesus answered them, "Did I Myself not choose you, the twelve, and yet one of you is a devil?" Now He meant Judas the son of Simon Iscariot, for he, one of the twelve, was going to betray Him.*

         ii. Jn. 12:4-6—*But Judas Iscariot, one of His disciples, who was intending to betray Him, said, "Why was this perfume not sold for three hundred denarii, and given to poor people?" Now he said this, not because he was concerned about the poor, but because he was a thief, and as he had the money box, he used to pilfer what was put into it.*

3. Fornication—Samson. Judg. 16:1,3-4—*Now Samson went to Gaza and saw a harlot there, and went into her...Now Samson lay until midnight, and at midnight he arose and took hold of the doors of the city gate and the two posts and pulled them up along with the bars; then he put them on his shoulders and carried them up to the top of the mountain which is opposite Hebron. After this it came about that he loved a woman in the valley of Sorek, whose name was Delilah.*

B. *Our Response to Truths Concerning Ourselves and the Law of Purification—OR—What to Do in the Wilderness.*

1. Truly thank the Lord for showing you the things in your heart.

2. Repent, asking God to forgive any sin or wrong motives. You may also need to ask others to forgive you.

3. Seek God's help to overcome and create new habits and attitudes.

4. Resist the enemy in his attempts in your life.

5. Never deny that you are going through a wilderness experience.

6. Never feel condemned for that which has surfaced during your wilderness experience.

7. Simply say, "Thank you, God, for showing me what was in my heart. Now I'll do something about it."

C. *Concluding Thoughts*

Satan's condemnation paralyzes because it's general and vague.

But the conviction of the Holy Spirit is specific and can be dealt with immediately. The conviction of the Spirit leads to freedom if we repent and ask forgiveness.

Let us cooperate with the finger of God in our lives, the ministry of the Holy Spirit, so that we will gain continuous on going victory over our internal enemies.

As we cooperate with God's sanctifying fires in our personal lives and seek to hold His hand which by grace reaches down to us, we can be supernaturally enabled to then reach out with the authority that Christ Jesus grants.

Endnotes

1. Taken from *Engaging the Enemy* by C. Peter Wagner. Copyright 1995. Regal Books, Ventura, California 93003. Used by permission.
2. The following material is reproduced from my Study Guide, *Strategies of Intercession* (self-published, 1998).

Other
exciting titles
by Jim W. & Michal Ann Goll

THE LOST ART OF INTERCESSION
by Jim W. Goll.
Finally there is something that really explains what is happening to so many folk in the Body of Christ. What does it mean to carry the burden of the Lord? Where is it in Scripture and in history? Why do I feel as though God is groaning within me? No, you are not crazy; God is restoring genuine intercessory prayer in the hearts of those who are open to respond to His burden and His passion.
ISBN 1-56043-697-2

ENCOUNTERS WITH A SUPERNATURAL GOD
by Jim W. and Michal Ann Goll.
The Golls know that angels are real. They have firsthand experience with supernatural angelic encounters. In this book you'll read and learn about angels and supernatural manifestations of God's Presence—and the real encounters that both Jim and Michal Ann have had! As the founders of Ministry to the Nations and speakers and teachers, they share that God wants to be intimate friends with His people. Go on an adventure with the Golls and find out if God has a supernatural encounter for you!
ISBN 1-56043-199-7

WOMEN ON THE FRONT LINES
by Michal Ann Goll.
History is filled with ordinary women who have changed the course of their generation. Here Michal Ann Goll, co-founder of Ministry to the Nations with her husband, Jim, shares how her own life was transformed and highlights nine women whose lives will impact yours! Every generation faces the same choices and issues; learn how you, too, can heed the call to courage and impact a generation.
ISBN 0-7684-2020-2

Available at your local Christian bookstore.
Internet: http://www.reapernet.com

Other
Destiny Image titles
you will enjoy reading

THE GOD CHASERS (Best-selling **Destiny Image** book)
by Tommy Tenney.
There are those so hungry, so desperate for His presence, that they become consumed with finding Him. Their longing for Him moves them to do what they would otherwise never do: Chase God. But what does it really mean to chase God? Can He be "caught"? Is there an end to the thirsting of man's soul for Him? Meet Tommy Tenney—God chaser. Join him in his search for God. Follow him as he ignores the maze of religious tradition and finds himself, not chasing God, but to his utter amazement, caught by the One he had chased.
ISBN 0-7684-2016-4

GOD CHASERS DAILY MEDITATION & PERSONAL JOURNAL
by Tommy Tenney.
ISBN 0-7684-2040-7

GOD'S FAVORITE HOUSE
by Tommy Tenney.
The burning desire of your heart can be fulfilled. God is looking for people just like you. He is a Lover in search of a people who will love Him in return. He is far more interested in you than He is interested in a building. He would hush all of Heaven's hosts to listen to your voice raised in heartfelt love songs to Him. This book will show you how to build a house of worship within, fulfilling your heart's desire and His!
ISBN 0-7684-2043-1

Available at your local Christian bookstore.
Internet: http://www.reapernet.com

When your heart is yearning for more of Jesus, these books by Don Nori will help!

NO MORE SOUR GRAPES

Who among us wants our children to be free from the struggles we have had to bear? Who among us wants the lives of our children to be full of victory and love for their Lord? Who among us wants the hard-earned lessons from our lives given freely to our children? All these are not only possible, they are also God's will. You can be one of those who share the excitement and joy of seeing your children step into the destiny God has for them. If you answered "yes" to these questions, the pages of this book are full of hope and help for you and others just like you.

ISBN 0-7684-2037-7

THE POWER OF BROKENNESS

Accepting Brokenness is a must for becoming a true vessel of the Lord, and is a stepping-stone to revival in our hearts, our homes, and our churches. Brokenness alone brings us to the wonderful revelation of how deep and great our Lord's mercy really is. Join this companion who leads us through the darkest of nights. Discover the *Power of Brokenness*.

ISBN 1-56043-178-4

THE ANGEL AND THE JUDGMENT

Few understand the power of our judgments—or the aftermath of the words we speak in thoughtless, emotional pain. In this powerful story about a preacher and an angel, you'll see how the heavens respond and how the earth is changed by the words we utter in secret.

ISBN 1-56043-154-7

HIS MANIFEST PRESENCE

This is a passionate look at God's desire for a people with whom He can have intimate fellowship. Not simply a book on worship, it faces our triumphs as well as our sorrows in relation to God's plan for a dwelling place that is splendid in holiness and love.

ISBN 0-914903-48-9

Also available in Spanish.

ISBN 1-56043-079-6

SECRETS OF THE MOST HOLY PLACE

Here is a prophetic parable you will read again and again. The winds of God are blowing, drawing you to His Life within the Veil of the Most Holy Place. There you begin to see as you experience a depth of relationship your heart has yearned for. This book is a living, dynamic experience with God!

ISBN 1-56043-076-1

HOW TO FIND GOD'S LOVE

Here is a heartwarming story about three people who tell their stories of tragedy, fear, and disease, and how God showed them His love in a real way.

ISBN 0-914903-28-4

Also available in Spanish.

ISBN 1-56043-024-9

Available at your local Christian bookstore.

Internet: http://www.reapernet.com